A Stranger's Wish

**Center Point
Large Print**

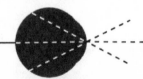

**This Large Print Book carries the
Seal of Approval of N.A.V.H.**

A Stranger's Wish

GAYLE ROPER

CENTER POINT LARGE PRINT
THORNDIKE, MAINE

Published in 2010 by arrangement with
Harvest House Publishers

The text of this Large Print edition is unabridged.
In other aspects, this book may vary
from the original edition.
Printed in the United States of America.
Set in 16-point Times New Roman type.

ISBN: 978-1-60285-849-7

Library of Congress Cataloging-in-Publication Data

Roper, Gayle G.
 [Key]
 A stranger's wish / Gayle Roper.
     p. cm.
 ISBN 978-1-60285-849-7 (library binding : alk. paper)
 1. Art teachers—Pennsylvania—Lancaster County—Fiction. 2. Lancaster County
(Pa.)—Fiction. 3. Large type books. I. Title.
 PS3568.O68K48 2010b
 813'.54—dc22
                                                              2010015749

In loving memory of
SHIRLEY A. EABY
sister in the Lord
writing buddy
special friend

Acknowledgments

Many thanks to watercolor artist and sister-in-love Pamela Pike Gordinier, of Stonington, Connecticut, for her guidance in painting Kristie's pictures. Pam, your instructions were wonderful, and if I had any artistic abilities or sensibilities whatsoever, I wouldn't have to say, "Any mistakes are mine." But I don't, and so they are.

Thanks too to Amish artist Susie Riehl and her business partner and friend Shirley Wenger for sharing a delightful lunch with me. Susie, you're an amazing lady, and Shirley, you're an enabler of the very best kind. Thanks for sharing with me and letting me use your names.

1

By the time Jon Clarke What's-his-name drove me to the hospital, my terrible inner trembling had stopped. My hands were still cold, and the towel pressed to my cheek was still sopping up blood, but I was almost in control again. If I could only stop shaking, I'd be fine.

I'd been so sure I'd lost my face. My stomach still curdled at the memory. All I'd done was bend down to pet Hawk, the sable-and-tan German shepherd sleeping contentedly in the mid-August sun. How was I to know he had a nasty cut hiding under that sleek hot fur?

I was horrified when he lashed out, startled by the pain I had inadvertently caused him. He got me in the cheek with a fang, but despite the blood, the wound was mostly superficial. The thought of what would have happened if he'd closed his mouth made me break out in a fine sweat.

How dumb to touch a sleeping dog. Dumb, dumb, dumb. I knew better. Everyone knew better.

As we entered the emergency room, I rearranged my towel to find an area not stained with blood. I went to the desk and signed in with a woman whose jet black hair stuck out in spikes to rival a hedgehog. When she had my life's history, she patted my paperwork with a proprietary air that made me wonder if she was willing to share the information with the people I'd come to see.

"Have a seat." She gave me a warm smile. "They'll be with you shortly."

Hoping shortly really meant shortly, I took my seat.

"You don't have to wait," I told Jon Clarke as he took the bright orange plastic chair beside me in the otherwise empty emergency room. He smiled slightly and stretched his long legs out before him, the picture of long-suffering and quiet accommodation. His posture said it didn't matter how long things took. He was prepared to be gallant and wait it out.

"Really," I said. "I'll be all right. You can go."

I was embarrassed to have inflicted myself upon this man I didn't know, this man whose last name I couldn't even remember. He'd pulled into the drive at the Zooks' Amish farm just as I bent over Hawk. While Mary Zook plied me with towels and bemoaned my possible disfigurement when she wasn't yelling at the innocent Hawk, John Clarke Whoever climbed out of his car, took me by the elbow, put me in his passenger seat, and drove me here.

What would I have done if he hadn't come along at just the right moment? Gone to the

8

hospital in a buggy? Certainly that wouldn't have worked if I'd had a life-threatening injury. I guess if that were the case, someone would run to the phone down on the road and dial 911 or run to a neighbor with a car. Hmm. Peace and serenity of the Amish variety had a definite downside.

Jon Clarke smiled at me now, looking comfortable in his very uncomfortable chair. "Of course I'll wait for you. I'd never run out on a lady in distress. Besides, you need a way home."

"I could call a cab."

"Bird-in-Hand is too far from Lancaster for that. It would cost a fortune." He smiled at me again, politely patient.

"It's only fifteen minutes max."

"That's a lot when the fare indicator goes *ca-ching, ca-ching*. It's better if I just wait."

I gritted my teeth. Just what I needed, a shining knight when I was in no condition to play the lady. I smiled ungraciously and winced.

"Hurt much?"

Of course it hurt. What did he think? "The strange thing is that my tongue can push into the wound from the inside of my mouth. Only a thin piece of skin on my inner cheek keeps the puncture from going all the way through." I pushed against my cheek with my tongue. It was a creepy sensation to feel the hole, but I couldn't resist the need to fiddle.

He looked suitably impressed and apparently decided to keep talking to distract me from my pain and injury. I must say he shouldered the burden with stoic determination and great charm.

"Have you lived in the Lancaster area long?" he asked, and I could have sworn he actually cared.

"Three years. I love it here."

"Were you at the Zooks' to visit Jake too?"

Too. So he had come to see Jake. I shook my head. "I live there."

That stopped him. "Really? On the farm?" He raised an eyebrow at me, an improbably dark eyebrow considering the light brown of his hair. "Have you been living there long?"

I glanced at the clock on the wall. "About four hours."

The eyebrow rose once again. "You're kidding."

"Nope. Great beginning, isn't it? Todd spent the morning and early afternoon helping me move, and he'd just left. I was on my way into the house when I stopped to pet Hawk." I sighed. "They'll probably decide I'm too much trouble to have around."

I pulled the towel from my cheek and studied the bloody patterns on the white terry cloth. They looked like abstract art. I was an artist myself, but I never painted compositions like these. I liked more realism—which meant my work would probably never hang in important galleries.

Uptight and unimaginative, according to certain professors and fellow students from my college days. "Flex," they said. "Soar! Paint where your spirit leads."

I flexed and soared with the best of them, but the finished work still looked like what it was.

I refolded the towel, burying the modern art, reapplied a clean area, and pressed.

"Who's Todd?" Jon Clarke asked.

I shrugged. Good question. "Todd Reasoner. A friend."

"Ah."

Would that Todd were as easily explained as the conclusion Jon Clarke had apparently leaped to.

"Don't do that," Jon Clarke said.

I blinked. "Do what?"

"Don't push against your cheek like that."

I hadn't even realized I was doing it.

"What if that thin piece of skin ruptures? Scarring. Infection. MRSA. Who knows?"

I frowned. Talk about Worst Case Scenario Man. I wanted to tell him I'd play with the inside of my cheek if I felt like it, but he was probably right about all the dire possibilities. I didn't want to rupture that thin membrane so delicately protecting the inside of my mouth. And I certainly didn't want to do anything to encourage the possibility of scarring. I looked in the mirror enough to know my face didn't need that kind of help.

"Not many people get to stay on an Amish farm." He paused. "Because of their closed society," he added as if I wouldn't understand his point. "You're very fortunate to get the opportunity."

"I know. I consider this chance a gift straight from God. One day my principal mentioned that he had Amish friends who were willing to take in a boarder. I got the Zooks' name and contacted them immediately."

I didn't tell him that when I first went to the farm, I wore one of my conservative suits, a gift from my parents when they were still hoping to quell my tendency toward bright colors and what they considered the instability of the art community, not that they actually knew any artists but me.

"If you're too artsy, Kristina," they said almost daily, as if being "artsy" was the equivalent of having a single digit IQ, "people won't take you seriously."

What they meant was that *their* people, all high-powered corporate lawyers who earned high six figures or even seven annually, wouldn't take me seriously. They were a group that had no time for business casual, let alone colorful artsy.

On that first visit to the Zooks, I hadn't been certain what cultural landmines I'd have to navigate, so I determined to at least defuse the

12

clothing issue, the one I knew about and could somewhat mitigate. I'd straightened my navy lapels and smoothed my cream silk blouse before I got out of the car, another cultural difference that I wasn't willing to yield on, not if I wanted to get to work.

To my delight, I found Mary and John Zook gracious, respectful, and kind. Mary sat there in her pinned-together dress and dark stockings, her organdy *kapp* crisp in spite of the humidity. John wore a white shirt and black broadfall trousers. His beard was full with only a hint of gray, and his straw hat hung on a peg by the door. They might demand the simple life of themselves and their family, but it was immediately obvious they would not demand the same of me.

Wouldn't it be amazing if I had more freedom to be myself here in the midst of this highly structured society than in my own parents' home?

"Your principal?" Jon Clarke asked from his seat beside me. "You teach?"

I nodded. "Elementary art."

"When I first pulled into the drive, I thought you must be Jake's visiting nurse."

"Not me. I'd be a terrible nurse."

"But a good teacher."

"Adequate, anyway. And I get the summers off to study and paint. How do you know the Zooks?"

"I've known them forever. My aunt and uncle

13

live down the road from them. But I haven't seen them in several years. In fact, I haven't been in Lancaster for a long time."

So I'd bled all over his first visit in years. Great. "Was it a job that kept you away?"

"Yes and no. Yes, when I was a youth pastor at a church in Michigan. No, when I went to seminary and graduate school. I just finished my doctorate in counseling."

"Really?" I was impressed.

"No. I confess. I'm lying. I just thought it sounded like a wonderful way to astonish and amaze a pretty girl."

I blinked at him, and he smiled impudently back. "Really?" he said in a dead-on imitation of me.

Flustered, I looked away from his laughing eyes. "I was just trying to make decent conversation."

His smile deepened. It was, I couldn't help noticing, a most wonderful smile, crinkling his eyes almost shut and inviting me to smile along, which I was careful not to do because of my cheek.

"Kristina Matthews?" called the woman at the desk. Her nameplate said she was Harriet. She scanned the empty room as though there might be several Kristinas lurking about, and I resisted the urge to look over my shoulder to see who might have sneaked in while I wasn't looking.

When I stood, Harriet smiled brightly. "There you are. Right through here, please."

As I entered the treatment area, I passed a teenage boy staggering out on crutches and a lady in a bathing suit with her arm in a bright pink cast. The walking wounded. I wondered what my battle scars would be.

Ten minutes later I looked away as a nurse stabbed me efficiently with a needle.

"This tetanus shot may cause your arm to swell or stiffen," she said, her voice filled with sorrow over my possible plight. I couldn't decide whether she was sorry I might swell or sorry I mightn't. "If it swells or stiffens, don't worry. Take aspirin or Tylenol and call your personal physician if the pain persists." She turned away with a great sigh and began cleaning up the treatment area.

I slid off the examination table and looked at my wobbly reflection in the glass doors of the supply cabinet. The flesh-colored butterfly bandage stuck in the middle of my left cheek distorted my face slightly, but I didn't mind. There had been no need for stitches.

"Any scarring will be minimal," the doctor said absentmindedly as he wrote something on the forms Harriet had passed to him. He was a good match for the nurse. I doubted he even noticed her melancholia. "Just keep the wound dry and check with your regular doctor next week to have it redressed." He ripped off the top copy of the paperwork and handed it to me. "It tells you here. And you're certain the dog had his shots?"

I nodded, took the paper, and hurried to the waiting room. At least Jon Clarke hadn't had to wait long once I was seen.

But the waiting room was empty. My angel of mercy had flown the coop. I was standing there wondering what to do next when Harriet at the desk called to me.

"Don't worry, honey. He'll be right back. He said he had to run a quick errand."

I nodded with disproportionate relief.

"Men," she said sympathetically. "You never know what they're going to do, do you? Sometimes they take off, and you never see them again." The edge that had crept into her voice made me think she was speaking from experience. She gave herself a little shake. "But yours looked nice enough to me. I think you can trust him, don't you?"

Her guess was as good as mine. We'd both known him for about the same length of time.

She got up from her desk. "Listen. I've got to go to the ladies' room. I'm talking emergency here, believe me. Stay by the desk and watch things for me, will you?"

Yikes. "What if someone comes in?"

"Tell them I'll be back in a minute. But don't worry," she called over her shoulder as she disappeared through a door. "Nothing big ever happens on Saturday afternoon."

Taking no comfort from those words, I looked at the quiet waiting room.

No one, Lord, okay? Not till she gets back, okay?

The prayer was barely formed when the waiting room door slid open and an older man in khaki work clothes entered. His face, damp with perspiration, matched the color of the white envelopes sticking out of his shirt pocket, and he was rubbing his left arm. He stopped beside me at the desk.

"I think I'm having a heart attack," he said as he might say he was going to sneeze.

I felt my own heart stop beating and my mouth go dry.

He staggered, and I reached out instinctively, taking his arm and lowering him into Harriet's chair.

"I'm sorry," he whispered.

"Don't apologize!" Now my heart was beating so loudly I could scarcely hear myself talk. "Don't worry. Someone will be here to help you in a moment."

Suddenly he stopped kneading his arm and pressed his hand against his chest. His face contorted and I froze. He was going to die right here while Harriet was in the ladies' room!

After a minute he relaxed, and I began to

breathe again. I ran to the door of the treatment area. "Help, somebody! Help!"

The sad-faced nurse leaned out of a cubicle. "Is anyone bleeding?" She was so intent on what was going on behind that curtain that she didn't even look at me.

"No, but—"

"Then we'll be there as soon as we can." And she disappeared.

I could see several pairs of feet below the curtain and hear several voices, including that of my doctor, who was barking orders with impressive authority. Through a door down the hall I could see an ambulance with its back doors still open.

"But he needs you now," I called desperately. "He really does! It's his—"

"We'll be there in a minute," she yelled as a great cascade of blood flowed onto the floor.

Pushing down panic and not knowing what else to do, I went back to the man.

"They'll be here in a minute," I told him with all the confidence I could muster.

"Had one before," he whispered to me. "Don't worry. It'll be all right. I'm not ready to die yet. I've got stuff to do."

I tried to smile to encourage him, but between my punctured cheek and my fear, I think it was more of a grimace. The man seemed to appreciate my effort anyway.

Dear God, I screamed in silent prayer, *where's Harriet? Send her out here fast, Lord! Please!*

The man rested his head against the wall. "What's your name? Are you Harriet?"

"I'm Kristie Matthews. Should you be talking?"

"I drove myself here. You don't think talking's any worse than that, do you?"

"You drove yourself here? With a heart attack?"

He smiled faintly. "I had to get here somehow. And I didn't think you were Harriet. You don't look like a Harriet."

I didn't look like this Harriet. Plain old straight brown hair cut to bend at my chin instead of too-black spikes and the electrified look. Five seven and slim instead of short and a fan of Dunkin' Donuts, if Harriet's figure and the box in the trash receptacle were any indication. A hole in my cheek instead of an abundance of blusher.

Suddenly he raised his head and looked at me with an intensity that made me blink. "Will you do me a favor, Kristie Matthews?"

I leaned close to hear his weak voice. "Of course."

"Keep this for me." He fumbled in his shirt pocket, reaching behind the envelopes. "But tell no one—no one—that you have it." He slipped a key into my cold hand and folded my fingers over it.

I heard a gasp from behind me. Harriet was finally back.

"Heart attack," I said, but Harriet was three steps ahead of me.

Her voice boomed over the PA. "Dr. Michaels, Dr, Michaels, stat. Dr. Michaels, code!" Harriet disappeared back into the treatment area yelling, "Marie! Charles! Where are you? Get yourselves out here fast!"

An arthritic finger tapped my closed fist. "Remember, tell no one," the old man managed to whisper. "Promise?"

"I promise." What else could I say?

He stared at my face as if searching my soul. He must have been satisfied with what he saw because his hand relaxed on mine and his eyes closed. "Don't forget. I'm counting on you." He gave a deep sigh, and I froze. Was that his last breath? "I'm counting on you."

The room came alive with people. Medical personnel converged on the sick man, and I stepped back with relief.

"Don't you ever go to the bathroom again," I hissed at Harriet, who probably never would if she valued her job.

When the doors to the treatment area slid shut and I could no longer see the man, I collapsed in one of the orange chairs, struggling with tears.

This is ridiculous. Why am I crying? I don't even know the man.

I gave myself a shake and stared at the small piece of metal in my hand. Why had he given his precious key to me, a total stranger? Why hadn't he let the hospital personnel keep it for him? Or asked them to hold it for a family member?

What could it possibly open that no one—no one—must know of it?

And what in the world should I do with it?

It was a relief when Jon Clarke finally returned.

"I'm sorry," he said with that winning smile. "I got held up in traffic. I hope you didn't think I'd deserted you."

"Of course not," I said as I slipped the key into my pocket. I hastened to correct my lie. "At least, not after Harriet told me you'd be back."

He cocked that dark, heavy brow at me again, saying as clearly as if I'd spoken aloud that he knew all too well what I'd thought.

I flushed and began talking to cover my embarrassment. "This old man came in and had a heart attack. He scared me to death! I was the only one in the room—Harriet had gone to the ladies' room. I had to be with him until help came. He gave me—"

I stopped abruptly. *"No one,"* he'd said, he'd insisted. *"Promise."* And I had.

Did I owe him my silence? I didn't even know him.

But I didn't know this sandy-haired, dark-browed man standing beside me, either. I only met him an hour or so ago. I couldn't bleed all over him anymore.

"He gave me quite a scare," I said, decision made. I gave a short laugh. "I'm not used to anything more serious than the common cold or one of my students throwing up."

But what would I do if he died?

2

When we pulled into the Zooks' drive, Mary hurried down the walk, her face lined with concern.

"I'm fine," I assured her as I climbed from the car, bloody towel neatly folded in my hand. "Really, I am. No stitches. Just this." I touched my cheek lightly. "And a tetanus shot."

She stared at my butterfly bandage, unconvinced. "When I think of what would have happened if Hawk had closed his mouth." She shivered.

"But he didn't. And I will have only the tiniest of scars, if that." I glanced over my shoulder at Jon Clarke, who was climbing out of the car on his side. "Tell her."

Mary looked at Jon Clarke and he nodded. "She's all right."

"It wasn't Hawk's fault anyway," I said. "I should never have touched him like that."

Suddenly Mary's eyebrows drew together, and she began to blink rapidly. "Well, let's get you inside." She turned and walked to the house with quick strides. The large white structure sat sideways to the road, facing the barn. The *grossdawdy haus* had been added with its front door toward the road.

I heard a loud sniff and a clearing of her throat as I followed Mary, and my shoulders slumped as I thought of the anxiety I'd caused. If I was stupid enough to get myself bitten within my first couple of hours, what else might I do? Burn the barn down? Scare the chickens so they wouldn't lay? Blight the crops?

When I'd indulged my daydreams of living on an Amish farm, they were always haloed in gold and washed in a soft warm glow. I anticipated I would feel the peace and tranquility we *Englishers* so often attribute to these nonviolent people. It's as though we think they never face problems such as illness or poor finances or bad crops or rebellious kids or any of the things that plague the general population.

I'd come to the farm today with my rosy expectations firmly intact. Less than five minutes on my own and boom! Reality. No more golden dreams.

"Well, let me give you a glass of cold root beer before you go to your rooms," Mary said as we entered the house. Her momentary emotional turmoil appeared to have passed. "On a hot day like today you need something cool after all you've been through. Going to the hospital's always scary, ain't? You too, Jon Clarke."

"Root beer sounds marvelous," I said, even though I'm a Coke person and all I really wanted was to go lie down.

"It does," agreed Jon Clarke. "I haven't had your root beer in ages. Why don't I get Jake?"

"I expect that's who you came to see in the first place," Mary said. "He's in his apartment."

Jon Clarke nodded and started for the front door, but Mary called, "No, you don't have to go around to his front door. You can get to him through there." She pointed to a door on the inside wall of the room. "We put that in for him so he doesn't have to go outside so much. Just knock. He's waiting, hoping you'd be back."

Jon Clarke disappeared through the door as Mary led me to a straight-backed chair at one end of what was obviously the relaxing section of the large room that filled the downstairs of the main house. A large hand-hooked rug in a lovely mix of blues and greens covered the tan linoleum at my feet. I wondered if Mary had hooked it. If so, she had a wonderful eye for color.

Nearby, coal oil lamps sat on an end table and

a bookcase. I glanced curiously at the titles in the bookcase and saw mostly Bible study books, many in German, though there were a few lighter volumes. Issues of *Amish Life* were stacked on one shelf. I was particularly surprised to see the brilliant crimson-and-gold cover of *It's Up to You* by Clarke Griffin. It was the very book I was reading.

At least we'll have something to talk about at meals, I thought in relief. When I wasn't wrapped in my golden daydream of life on the farm, I spent a lot of time worrying about whether the Zooks and I would find enough in common to sustain conversation. It appeared we might.

The other end of the big room was the working area and kitchen. Counters and a sink ran under the windows in the left wall, and a great wood-burning stove sat against the far wall by the back door. A large wooden table topped with a blue oilcloth that matched one shade of blue in the rug filled the middle of the kitchen area, a Coleman lantern and a canning jar filled with flowers sitting in its center. A treadle sewing machine was tucked under a window on the right wall beside the propane-powered refrigerator from which Mary was taking mismatched bottles of dark liquid.

For all its Spartan style, the room was welcoming, bright, and airy with windows running on three sides. There were no curtains because curtains are worldly, but well-tended spider plants and wandering Jews graced the windowsills, and green shades hung from the frames.

A doorway at the far end beside the stove led to a one-story addition that housed the propane-fired water heater, the indoor plumbing and bathroom, and the pantry.

The front door burst open, and a young man exploded into the room, followed by a slight girl.

"See, Ruth?" the young man said. "I was right. I knew Mom'd be serving my root beer. Company's all the excuse she needs."

"And my pretzels." Ruth pointed to the plastic tub in Mary's arms.

"Hush, you two." Mary smiled as she pulled the lid off the pretzel tub. "Come meet Kristie."

It was obvious that the pair were brother and sister and Mary's children. All three had the same gray eyes and broad cheekbones.

"These are our two youngest, Ruth and Elam. Elam works here on the farm with John, and Ruth works in a pretzel factory. That's why she calls these her pretzels."

Mary turned to her daughter. "You're home early."

Ruth nodded. "Deacon Dan gave us the afternoon off."

Elam busied himself pouring root beer into a collection of mismatched glasses. He was a lean, compact man filled with nervous energy, the kind of individual who couldn't sit still, who probably relaxed by repairing things.

"Here, Mom, let me," Ruth said. I smiled as she stopped shyly in front of me, offering the pretzels. What a wonderful painting she would make.

Despite her best efforts, little wisps of hair had worked themselves loose about her face and curled softly at her temples. Her brown dress, styled like her mother's, was covered with a much-worn, much-darned tan apron. Her legs were bare, and, incongruously, she wore pink flip-flops with large plastic daisies over her toes. She looked all of ten years old, though I knew she was eighteen.

I took one of the fat, hard pretzels and bit gently so it wouldn't break a tooth. I was pleased when Ruth sat beside me.

"What do you do at the pretzel factory?" I asked.

"Make the pretzels."

"Really?" What did that mean? "Do you work a machine that pushes out the dough, or do you actually roll the dough and bend it into shape?" I'd watched the kids behind the counters at the Auntie Anne's concessions cut off strips of dough, roll them, and twist them into shape, but their sales gimmick was fresh-made, soft pretzels. Watching them get made was part of the excuse for the prices.

"I roll and bend the dough," Ruth said. "There are five of us who do it. Then Deacon Dan puts the raw pretzels in huge ovens to bake. It was the ovens that made it too hot to keep working today. It was so bad Rhoda Beiler almost fainted."

"No air-conditioning?" I asked without thinking.

"No," Ruth said quietly. "He's a deacon."

Of course. That explained the rolling and bending too. Machines that would require electricity from the utility companies wouldn't be acceptable. "Do you like your work?" I knew I'd find pretzel-shaping old in no time. It wasn't as if you could be creative about their shape or anything. They couldn't be lightning bolts or flowers or clouds. Pretzel lovers were very traditional.

Ruth nodded. "I like it a lot. The girls there are all nice, and we can visit while we work."

Elam handed me a glass filled with a chilled, dark, slightly carbonated beverage, and I took a cautious sip.

"This is good!" I hoped my surprise wasn't too obvious. "I've never had homemade root beer before."

"I'm glad you like it," Elam said shyly.

"He's glad because he made it," Ruth said, taking her own glass from her brother.

"You, Elam?" Jon Clarke said as he returned to

the room. "I thought your mother was the root beer person."

"She was, once upon a time. Now it's me." Elam smiled and held out his hand. "It's good to see you again, Jon Clarke."

"It's good to be back, believe me," he said, taking Elam's hand. "And you." He grinned at Ruth and shook his head. "No more teasing the baby of the family. You've grown up very nicely."

Ruth turned a delicate shade of pink and hid her face in her glass. Such compliments were part of the English world, not the Amish.

I drank some more as I watched Jon Clarke smile ruefully and shake his head at himself. In his time away, he'd forgotten that singling out a person with compliments, however sincere, was a subtle breach of the self-denial ethic so central to Amish life.

I held out my glass and asked Elam, "How do you make this?" I'd heard my grandfather talk about the time when he was a kid and his family made root beer. It fermented too long and blew up all over the attic, but I didn't know that people still brewed it. It's too convenient to buy it at the supermarket.

Elam waved his hand vaguely. "You just mix root beer flavoring with sugar and yeast. The sugar and yeast work together, and you get carbonation."

"Not fermentation?" Jon Clarke teased.

"We don't worry about that around here." Elam turned a mock-stern face to his mother. "Mom never lets it sit long enough to ferment. In fact, she barely gives it time to carbonate."

Mary laughed at her son, obviously used to his gentle joshing.

"I'll take a glass," said a voice from behind me.

"Jake!" Mary started to rise and go to her son, and then she forced herself to sit and wait for him to come to her.

I looked with interest at the young man who propelled himself across the room in his wheelchair, noticing his strong shoulders and sad, lean face. I glanced at Mary and saw her force her face to calmness. I couldn't imagine what it was like for a mother to watch her disabled son and know she could do nothing to make it better.

When I'd originally come to the farm to talk about my rooms, which were on the second floor directly over Jake's, he'd been back at the rehabilitation center for a checkup. Ever since I'd been both curious and apprehensive about meeting him. My experience with people in wheelchairs was almost nonexistent, and I wasn't sure what was expected of me or what I should offer.

Jake rolled up to me. "So you're Kristie. I hear Hawk wasn't very welcoming." His voice seemed to contain a slight challenge, though I wasn't certain why.

I touched my bandage. "It's not that bad, and it was my fault anyway." I smiled with apology. "I shouldn't have touched him."

Jake nodded, as though I'd said the right thing, but strangely there wasn't the slightest glimmer of a return smile.

It's not you, Kristie, it's him. It's his life circumstances that make him grim.

Elam and Ruth stared at me curiously.

"What happened?" Ruth asked.

"Hawk bit her." Jake rolled to rest beside Jon Clarke.

"Hawk *bit* you?" Ruth looked horrified.

"He's never done anything like that before." Elam was equally distressed.

"Please don't feel bad. It was my fault," I said again. "And I'm fine. I really am. No stitches or anything." Compared to Jake's troubles, my dog bite was nothing.

"Elam, get Jake some root beer," Mary said, turning the attention from me. I smiled at her in gratitude.

Elam quickly got a drink for his brother and topped off everyone's glasses.

"So, Jon Clarke, are you home permanently or just for a visit?" Mary asked.

"Permanently. I'm going to open an office and establish a practice in Lancaster."

"To teach people what the Bible says?"

"To teach people how to apply what the Bible

31

says, Mrs. Zook. To counsel people with problems and teach others how to counsel."

Mary shook her head. "I don't understand why people can't just read the Bible and figure out what to do all by themselves."

I glanced at the bookshelves and the volumes there. I knew that for every Amish person who read the Bible, there were those who didn't, leaving their spiritual training solely in the hands of their bishops and preachers. Just as there were cultural Christians sitting in the pews of every church, so there were cultural Amishmen and women, those who lived the life rather than practiced the faith. Apparently Mary took the issues of faith seriously.

Her brow was furrowed as she talked to Jon Clarke. "When it says we shouldn't think more highly of ourselves than we should, it means we should put others first. When it says love the Lord with all your heart, it means you should love the Lord, not the world. Why do they need someone to tell them what it says when it's so obvious?" She looked genuinely mystified. "And why did you have to go to school all those years to learn what's written there in black and white?"

To Mary, living in a culture that ended its formal schooling at eighth grade, Jon Clarke's years of education must indeed seem useless at best and vain at worst.

"Not everyone's as smart as you, Mom," Jake said with the faintest of smiles. "Some people need help figuring it all out." It was obviously an old argument and aroused no one's real ire.

"Because they've already made a mess of things by not following it in the first place," Jon Clarke said. "My job is to help them untangle their messes."

As the conversation swirled about me, I drank my root beer and munched my crunchy pretzel. In spite of my butterfly bandage, I couldn't stop smiling. Here I was, sitting in the living room of a real Pennsylvania Dutch home, my hosts and landlords genuine Amish.

The only potential fly in the ointment of my delight was the little matter of telling my parents that I'd left my apartment with its modern conveniences and huge walk-in closet for two rooms on the second floor and a shared bathroom off the kitchen.

I could hear my horrified father. "An Amish farm, Kristina? No electricity? Bed at dusk and breakfast at dawn? Surely you jest."

Or my appalled and bewildered mother. "You've done *what?* Kristina, I'll never understand you."

Or my sister, Patty the Perfect, who had passed her bar exam on the first try and was busy earning her legal stripes at the same law firm our parents were partners in. "Give me a break,

Kristie! When are you going to grow up and get a real life?"

It was difficult living with the burden of being a blight on our family tree, a little ginkgo branch on a stately oak. Generations of Matthewses had been lawyers and judges, even legislators of both state and national consequence. Matthewses understood that life was to be seized with determination and a Juris Doctor after your name. Matthewses accepted responsibility with utter confidence, legal eagles flying high. They could and would fix the wrongs of humanity, at least the part they could get their hands on, and best of all, every moment they seized their appropriate place in the scheme of things was billable.

To deviate from this path was considered a sign of weakness and lack of ability. It meant nothing that I could paint a watercolor that delighted people and touched their emotions while Mom, Dad, and Patty couldn't draw a straight line without a ruler. The only value to be found in the creation of art was that it might turn out to be a good investment if you picked your artist carefully. Although the idea that I might turn into one of those whose work appreciated as the years passed was yet to be determined, such a possibility never even crossed my family's minds.

In short, though they all loved me in their own unintentionally condescending way, they didn't understand me. Nor did they try. After all, in their opinion what I loved to do was of no consequence.

I was a late bloomer in my defiance of generations of Matthews' tradition. All through high school I had been the dutiful daughter with impeccable grades and compliant behavior. I knew I'd go to college, then law school, then join Matthews, Matthews, Broderick, and Jordan. It was what Matthewses did. That I'd never outshine Patty was also understood by all of us. It was as though the family consigned me to life as a law clerk, never graduating to my own clients, my own partnership. Even though they didn't understand what that assessment of me meant, I had come to understand it indicated they knew on some intuitive level that I wasn't cut out for the law even as they ruthlessly steered me toward it.

That I was merely living didn't even occur to me until I went to college and took an art elective just because it sounded like fun. Doing more than doodling in my notebooks or drawing in the privacy of my bedroom gave me a feeling of joy and freedom. It awoke a passion in me I didn't know I could feel. It makes me sound stupid, even to myself, when I think of how I'd been sleepwalking through life without even realizing it.

I was hurrying to art class one day in October when I had my epiphany. I realized I was actually hurrying across campus to get to class early. Hurrying, not because I was late. Early because I couldn't wait to get there. At that moment God reached down with a paintbrush and placed it in my hand. He also gave me an understanding of my purpose in life in my heart.

I was an artist.

This realization had nothing to do with talent, because I still didn't know if I actually had any. It had to do with passion and desire. I felt like that long-ago Olympic champion, Eric Liddell, who said he felt God's pleasure when he ran. I felt His pleasure when I painted.

It took me my whole second semester to whomp up the courage to tell my parents I had dropped a political science class for another art elective, and my ears still rang when I remembered my father's explosion.

"Kristina, what is the meaning of this?" he demanded with an outrage most parents saved for drug abuse or alcoholic excess.

"I don't want to be a lawyer," I managed.

"Of course you do. You will make up this poly sci class over the summer."

"No, Dad. I don't want to. It would be a waste of your money and my time. I'm never going to be a lawyer."

I tried to be polite but firm. Standing up to Dad was a new experience, and I wasn't at all good at it. Not only were there the issues of parental authority and control of the exchequer on his side, he was a litigator with years of arguing before the bench, and he knew how to present his case. I, on the other hand, had let him and my mother lovingly push me around my whole life.

But I'd been praying like crazy all semester. We were Christians in my family, regulars at our church and conservative in our theology and our politics. For me, though, my faith became vibrant when I realized God had given me a gift that brought me joy.

"I don't want to be a lawyer," I repeated to my father. "I want to be an artist."

Dad stared at me as if he'd never seen me. "Kristina, your career path has been set."

"By *you,* Dad. Not by me." I felt both scared and exultant as I tried to explain. "I *love* my art classes. I love drawing, making something where there were only paper and blobs of color. I love imagining a scene or an image and try-ing to make my work match my vision. I want to be a painter. I want to be a watercolorist. I want to have WSA after my name, not JD or Esq."

Temporarily distracted, he asked, "What's WSA?"

"Watercolor Society of America."

"You want to starve to death? Everyone knows that anyone in the arts is a charity case."

"I'll teach school if I have to, but I will teach art."

He sank into his desk chair and stared at the letter before him. It was notification of Patty's unbelievably good scores on her LSATs. The sight of it seemed to brace him, and he looked at me with determination.

I looked back, equally determined. I might not have the Matthews' legal DNA, but I'd gotten my share of the stubbornness gene.

"I have declared as an art major for next year." I managed to keep my voice from shaking like my knees.

"What?" He was on his feet again. "Without consulting me? I'm the one paying your tuition, young lady."

"I've consulted with the Lord." I tried not to sound too self-righteous. "I've prayed and prayed, Dad, and I'm convinced this is His will for me."

What's a Christian parent to say in the face of this argument? Forget God's will? I know better than He what's best for you?

Dad narrowed his eyes, clearly suspecting manipulation.

Help him to hear my heart, Lord!

"Please, Dad. Let me be happy."

He yielded because he saw my desperation, but he never understood. He wouldn't understand my move to the farm, either. Nor would

Mom or Patty. They would try not to be disappointed in their artsy child/sibling who had no common sense.

"She's sweet as can be," I overheard Patty say to one of the guys she brought home for dinner, a young lawyer in the firm. I heard her "but" long before she said it. "But she—" Hesitation as she sought a way to say whatever it was delicately. "She's different."

The confusion in her voice made me shake my head. That day I walked into the living room to a sea of navy pinstripes and smart black shoes, sleek haircuts and bulging briefcases. Mom, Dad, Patty, and her guest all stared at me in my broomstick skirt of many colors, my red scoop-necked ballet top, and white full-sleeved artist's big shirt. It was probably my gladiator sandals that gave them indigestion.

3

I was smiling contentedly when I handed Mary my empty root beer glass and excused myself. I climbed the stairs to my two rooms, my home for the next year at least. I stopped in the doorway and surveyed my quarters with pleasure.

My living room was very attractive, even

though the two overstuffed chairs were obviously much used and the end table had led a full life prior to becoming mine. The truth was that the room could have been as stark and ugly as an army barracks and I still would have loved it. But that uncanny eye for color I'd noted downstairs showed itself again in the blues and green of the chairs and rug with cream decorator pillows resting against an arm of each chair.

Sitting along one wall was a huge, scarred desk of blond wood with a straight-backed chair behind it.

"John found this desk for you at an auction in Intercourse," Mary told me earlier as she ran her hand across its scarred surface. "He said every teacher needs a desk to work on."

What, I wondered, did John and Mary think of a teacher who taught only art, who helped children draw pictures, paint their imagination, and form their clay into shapes that were often totally nonutilitarian? Did Amish schools teach art? Or did they teach only the three R's and Amish culture? I suspected that imagination wasn't a prized commodity because it brought about individualism; community—not individualism— was all important among the People.

I looked at the battered desk and remembered kindergarten and the frightening Miss Stangl who had sat behind just such a piece of blond wood. I should have known art was my true future the day she actually smiled at me. I had drawn my tree with leaves of orange, yellow, and red all swirled together in wild overlaid circles until my fat new Crayola crayons were worn down to the paper wrap.

"My, my, Kristina, you do like color," Miss Stangl said. "You are different from Patty, aren't you?" And she smiled. She never smiled.

I blinked, understanding in an appalling flash that all this wild color I so loved was somehow not good, that if it made me different from Patty, my parents would be disappointed. Even then Patty was perfect. Thereafter all my trees were green leaved and bland, and my crayons were carefully used. The wild glory of sunset and autumn was for God to paint, not me.

I sighed and put a flourishing philodendron on the corner of the desk to make it look user-friendly. My laptop lay in the center and my portfolio leaned against its side. Canvas bags of art supplies sat along the wall, lumpy with the promise of joy. I set my African violets on the broad windowsill where they'd get just the right amount of sun.

My parakeet, Big Bird, sat in his cage in the middle of the room, where I'd left him before Hawk reordered my day.

"You, my loudmouth friend, can go here." I put him beside the chair nearest the window. He squawked his approval.

In my bedroom a patchwork quilt of royal blue, navy, and crimson calico squares covered the great sleigh bed, and a small hand-braided rug in the same shades lay on the floor beside it. The nightstand held a small lamp, and on the dresser by the window sat a vase filled with great magenta and white dahlias Mary grew in the garden off to the side of the front yard. My clothes, at least some of them, hung neatly on the wall pegs to the right of the door.

"Where do I put these?" Todd had asked earlier as he stood in the doorway with an armful of my clothes still on their hangers. He scanned the room for a closet.

"Right here," Mary said with surprise as she pointed to the very obvious pegs along the wall.

"Oh." Todd began putting the hangers on the little wooden dowels. It soon became more than apparent that the pegs weren't installed with the amount of clothes I owned in mind.

Oh, boy. The cultural chasm. Their austerity and my abundance.

"Himmel," Mary said. "I'll get Elam to put up some more pegs. Maybe he can do it after dinner."

"Don't rush him," I said as I laid Todd's second armload over the back of one of the chairs.

"No, no. He'll do it as soon as he can. It's important you be happy here."

She had smiled and I had smiled, and I was

still smiling, warmed by the care Mary had taken with my rooms. They were on the second floor of the *grossdawdy haus*, or granddaddy house. When John Zook's father had given up the main responsibilities for the farm and passed it on to John, a wing had been added to the house with its own separate entrance and privacy for the senior Zooks. John and his family had taken over the main house.

Mr. and Mrs. Zook senior had lived in the addition for several years until they were killed two years ago in a buggy-automobile accident just off Route 340 near Smoketown. Their vacant wing had been the perfect place for Jake to come home to after his accident, though he only used the first floor.

The interior door that had been cut in the wall between the main house and the *grossdawdy haus* provided ready access to both Jake's wing and my stairway to the second floor.

I looked at the suitcases and boxes of things to be unpacked. Their clutter was ruining the perfection of my cozy new home. I eyed the bureau against the wall and wondered if it was big enough to hold everything, or would I have to get a piece of my furniture out of storage?

Get to it, girl, I ordered. *Finish cleaning up this chaotic mess. Then you can lie down.*

Instead I wandered over to the window of my living room and stood looking out over the patchwork countryside. Mary's garden was directly below my window, and on this August Saturday it was filled with cucumbers, celery, squash, tomatoes, peppers, onions, and beans of all kinds—string, lima, and wax. Along the garden's edge grew a profusion of cyclamen petunias whose purpose was to discourage the rabbits by their smell. At one end bloomed an elegant collection of varied dahlias, some with blooms the size of saucers.

In the field beyond the house, two of the mighty farm horses pulled a flatbed wagon beside rows of ripening cattle corn. A man in a dark shirt and black trousers, a full dark beard, and a wide-brimmed straw hat stood balanced on the wagon as he directed his team. I knew it was John Zook, and I itched to grab my digital Nikon and freeze the scene for painting some day.

Later, girl. Right now you need to get to work!

I turned and surveyed the mess. I slid my hands into my pockets as I contemplated what to do first. My hand brushed the key.

As soon as I touched it, I saw the stricken face of the old man as clearly as if he were here with me. My breath caught and my heart lurched. I was flooded with guilt. How had I ever managed to forget him?

Dear God, I pray he's okay. I pray he recovers. Please take good care of him. And please don't let him die!

I carried his key into my bedroom and put it on my dresser. I stared at it, waiting for some brilliant and practical idea to tell me how to deal with it.

All I got was a headache.

I went back to the living room and slumped in my stuffed chair by the window, Big Bird at my side. He fluffed his feathers in his water dish, and I swallowed my nerves and flipped open my cell.

Time to make the phone call.

My mother picked up on the third ring.

"Hi, Mom. It's—"

"Well, Kristina, it's about time. We haven't heard from you in weeks."

Nice to talk with you too, Mom. "It's only been two weeks." And the phone works in both directions. *Sorry, Lord. Bad attitude. Nerves.*

"Hmm. It seems longer, but I guess you're right. We'd just finished Brandon Industries vs. Allied Insurance when we spoke last."

"Right. You'd just won." I swallowed again and pushed on. "I wanted to give you my new address."

"You moved?" Her surprise flowed through the air and zapped me right in my tumbling abdomen. "Why, for heaven's sake? Your apartment was very nice."

Yes, it was. Mom and Dad had helped me pick it out when I first moved to Lancaster. They'd given me the first month's rent and the two months' rent required for escrow and helped me pick out—and pay for—my furniture, now neatly placed in a small storage facility just east of town. I'd appreciated their help because I had no money to speak of at the time, having just spent the summer teaching art at a Christian day camp back home.

They'd stepped back then, telling me that from now on my bills were my bills, and if I couldn't afford something, then I'd better learn to do without. Unspoken was the thought that if I'd been going to law school, they'd still be paying for everything.

Since they'd been involved in getting me the apartment, my giving it up without a very good reason would irk them. I wondered vaguely if they'd want their two months' rent back.

"I decided I wanted a change of scenery," I said brightly. "I can look out my windows at the new place and see rolling farmland. And there's an Amishman working in his field." I didn't say it was John and the field was "mine."

Mom was quiet for a few minutes, and I could almost hear her thoughts as she reminded herself that I was twenty-seven, and if I wanted to move, it was my choice.

"I hope you were careful not to take a place that will strap you financially."

"Not at all," I hastened to tell her. "It's less expensive."

"Huh. Cheap usually means second rate," she said, her voice crisp.

"But not in this case. Here, let me give you my new address." I reeled off the Zooks' house number and street before she could ask any more questions.

When I said Bird-in-Hand, Mom said, "But that's farther from your school than your previous apartment. Why would you want to be farther?"

"It's not that much farther." And it was worth every extra mile to me, no matter how costly gas became. "Now I've got to go settle in. I just wanted to give you that information. Bye, Mom. I love you. Give my love to Dad." And I hung up.

I stared out the window and thought what a coward I was, but I knew how my parents would react to the news that my new place was an Amish farm. They wouldn't understand. Not that I didn't expect them to find out eventually, but later was better than sooner. I didn't want anything to taint my special year or derail my Great Adventure when it had barely begun. I'd met with enough resistance to my plan as it was.

"You're going to do what?" Todd bellowed in disbelief when I told him about the Zooks.

"I'm going to board at an Amish farm for a year. I've already met the family and worked out the details."

Todd stared openmouthed, and I knew he was hurt that I hadn't discussed it with him first.

"Why do you want to do a foolish thing like that?" he asked, genuinely baffled. "You already have a nice apartment."

"So I can paint."

"So you can paint?" Todd was almost at a loss for words, a rare event for a lawyer. "But you can paint here—" he indicated my apartment, "—where it's warm and clean and smells nice. If you must paint."

"Of course I must paint." I was aghast at his misapprehension of what was so important to me. What was it with lawyers? And how had I fallen into an association with one who so resembled my family in his thought patterns? "I'm a watercolorist, Todd. Watercolorists paint. The Country Shop has taken two of my pictures and will take some more when those sell." I shrugged. "It's not much, but it's a start."

I paused, hoping he'd say something reassuring, like, "And I'm sure they'll sell very quickly." But he didn't. He seemed to feel any encouragement would only make me more independent, more determined, and I was bad enough already.

"Paint is more than brushstrokes and color and technique, you know. It's perception and passion. It's feelings and emotion and ambiance."

"Ambiance?" For an intelligent man, he was good at looking blank.

I nodded. "I'm boarding on this farm because I want to get a better feel for Lancaster County so I can paint it more accurately. There's so much to learn."

"You've been learning for four years, ever since you moved here from New Jersey."

"But it's not academic knowledge I'm talking about."

Todd just stared at me, baffled. "Why isn't teaching enough for you?" he asked. "You know you're good at it. You like the kids, and they like you."

At least he wasn't urging me to be a lawyer.

"I like teaching well enough, but I love painting. It's a compulsion." I looked at the kind, somber, slightly stodgy man before me. "Every time I take a clean sheet of paper and begin to block out a scene, I thank God for the indescribable joy it gives me. Don't you feel the same way about practicing law, maybe when you deliver an especially good argument or win a case against the odds?"

He frowned. "No."

"No? You don't like being a lawyer?"

"Oh, I like it okay. I just don't understand all this feeling stuff, this 'indescribable joy' stuff."

Poor man. I took his hand. "Todd, I teach because I have to eat and pay rent, but if I could live off my painting, I'd do it in an instant."

He shook his head. "There's no stability there."

Now there was news. "But some things are worth the risk, aren't they?"

He just looked at me. Risk was something he didn't comprehend. Teaching was an honorable, safe profession, especially for a woman. I should be satisfied with it, and the fact that I wasn't bothered him not a little.

"But painting is so solitary!" he said. "It puts you in your own private world." Which he obviously thought was a bad place to be.

Todd tried every argument he could think of to talk me out of going to the farm. I could feel his frustration that he could argue a case in court and persuade judge and jury with his fluency, but he couldn't budge me.

To him it was another yellow car.

"You can't buy that, for goodness' sake!" he'd said when he saw my just-purchased vehicle. "It looks like a taxicab!"

"Never! I know sunshine and lemon drops when I see them."

"Sunshine and lemon drops?"

And now my foolishness was taking me ten miles from Lancaster to Bird-in-Hand and some backwards farm.

"Why is an Amish family letting someone English board with them?" he asked testily.

I knew he meant "English" in the broad Lancaster County sense of my not being German or Dutch as in Pennsylvania German or Pennsylvania Dutch.

"Why are these people letting you live with them?" he repeated grouchily. "It's uncharacteristic."

"Because they need the money?"

He shook his head. "That doesn't make sense. The Amish are very self-sufficient. If any of them ever need money, their community will give it to them."

"They have a son, Jake, who was paralyzed from the waist down in a motorcycle accident, and his care is costly."

The incongruity of an Amishman in a motorcycle accident bothered neither Todd nor me. We were aware that in their late teens, Amish children, especially sons, often rebelled against the strict ordered life of their parents in a time known as *rumspringa*. Most times the rebellion ran its course, and the children returned to the teachings of the church. Sometimes the children remained "English" or "fancy" or "gay," terms used by the local Amish community to denote people who wore clothes with zippers and printed fabric, people who drove automobiles and SUVs, people who used electricity taken from poles along the road, people who watched TV and listened to iPods. People like Todd and me.

Unfortunately, sometimes events intervened in

a Plain son's wild oat sowing, and rebellion became tragedy.

"But if you live with those folks, you won't have electricity and all the modern conveniences. No TV or telephone. No hot showers!"

"It won't be that bad," I said. "There's a propane hot water heater in the shed off the kitchen, so there's plenty of hot water. And I have my cell phone."

"But what about electricity?"

"When Jake came home from the rehab center, Mr. and Mrs. Zook ran electricity into one wing of the house for him. He has a little apartment on the first floor, and since my rooms are directly over his, I have electricity too. And surely I can survive without a TV if I need to."

Todd snorted, unimpressed. "But it's an election year."

"I do know how to read the newspapers, Todd," I said tartly. Did the man never know when enough was enough? I certainly hoped he harangued juries with more finesse than he used on me. "And I'm every bit as interested in Adam Hurlbert's candidacy for the U.S. Senate as you are."

"So you keep telling me. I know, I know, you even met him at parents' night because his stepson goes to your school. Big deal. And stop trying to change the subject on me."

"Change the subject?" My voice squeaked with

aggravation. "You're the one who brought up politics."

"I don't want to talk about Adam Hurlbert! I want to talk about your dumb farm. How old is this Jake person?"

"What?" For a man who valued orderly thinking, he was being uncharacteristically scattered.

"This Jake guy. How old is he?"

"In his midtwenties, I guess," I said. "About my age. I think the family has made all these liberal concessions like the phone and the electricity because they realize he'll never be Plain again."

"Well, I don't like it." His jaw had a belligerent set to it. "Next thing I know you'll be running around in black stockings, a pinned-together dress, and a *kapp*."

"You're being ridiculous! The last thing I plan to do is become Amish."

"Famous last words." He stared morosely at me.

I shook my head, exasperated. "Listen, Todd. I'm moving to an Amish farm whether you like it or not." I said the last few words slowly and emphatically so he was sure to get the point. We might go out together, but he hadn't the right to call the shots in my life. "And I'd like your support instead of all this flack."

He ran his hand through his hair, something he did only when agitated. His brown curls, now ruffled, escaped the tight control he tried to

53

exert over them and sproinged exuberantly and unprofessionally, at least by his definition, about his head. He hated his hair; I was jealous of it. My straight brown hair fell to my chin with nary a wave in sight.

"I'm not going to the farm to become Amish," I repeated, softened by his obvious distress. "I admire them for their courage to be different, but I don't agree with them. I see nothing sinful about electric stoves or gasoline powered cars or a short curly permanent."

Todd looked at me sadly, and I knew I had failed to be what he wanted me to be, whatever that was.

The story of my life.

4

When I awoke from my post-hospital nap, I felt refreshed and energetic, ready to attack the chore of settling in. The Tylenol had worked, and all I felt was a slight twinge in my cheek. I began unpacking boxes and suitcases, dumping the contents on the bed. Soon the cases were tucked away, and the boxes were piled by the door for disposal. All I needed to do now was to put everything into drawers.

Instead I began to get ready for my date with Todd.

As I rooted through the various piles looking for my makeup, my fancy gladiator sandals with the "jewels" up the central strap, and my flowing dress with the bright splashes of color, my eyes kept going to the key lying on my dresser. I was glad I hadn't discussed it with Jon Clarke, but surely Todd was different. After all, he was a lawyer. He'd know what my obligation to the old man was. He'd know what I should do if the man died or was hospitalized for a long time or was comatose or had a stroke or . . .

I brushed on some rouge, trying not to get my bandage rosy.

But the old man hadn't died or had a stroke or gone into a coma yet. At least, I didn't think so.

"Tell no one. Promise."

Just Todd.

"No one."

I sighed. I probably should just wait and see what happened. Maybe I would never say anything to anyone no matter what happened. Maybe my promise was like the privileged communication between client and lawyer, patient and doctor, or penitent and priest. Maybe I was trapped for the rest of my life with a little silver-colored albatross hanging around my neck.

Maybe I was being melodramatic.

I grabbed my cell phone and hit 411 for the number of the hospital. I could at least find out who the man was so I wouldn't need to drive myself crazy with speculation.

"I'm looking for information about the man who came into emergency with a heart attack earlier today," I told the woman who answered.

"Name?" she asked in a clipped voice.

Feeling rather foolish, I said, "I'm sorry. I don't know his name."

There was a small silence. "Then how can I tell you how he is?" Her logic was as razor edged as her tone of voice.

"Maybe you can find out his name for me?" I suggested hesitantly. The phone lady was as good as Todd at making me feel small.

"I can find out his name?" Her incredulity bubbled down the line. "Ma'am, you made the call."

I cleared my throat and forged on. "I don't think there could have been too many elderly men with heart attacks this afternoon. I was there when he came in, and I talked with him before they took him away. I just want to know if he survived and how he's doing."

A sigh floated to my ear. Obviously I wasn't making her job easy.

"Please," I said with all the plaintive desperation I could muster. I stopped myself before I sniffled pathetically. "It's very important to me."

She put me on hold forever, but she ultimately delivered.

"I think you are referring to Mr. Everett Geohagan. He came in this afternoon and is now in coronary care. He is doing as well as can be expected."

"Which means?"

"I don't know, ma'am," she said. "Probably it means he's still alive."

"How about visitors?"

"Are you family?"

"A close friend," I said, hoping God wouldn't think I was stretching the truth too far.

"Only family," she pronounced with great authority, and I thought she sounded happy to make me sad. But she wasn't as unfeeling as I thought, because she added, "Why don't you call back tomorrow? Call the floor itself." And she gave me the number. "They'll give you a more thorough report, and they'll tell you if you qualify as a visitor."

"Thanks," I said, but she was already gone.

I punched the off button, lay the phone down, and wandered to the window. My stomach growled, and I realized that because of the bustle of moving, lunch had been only a package of peanut butter crackers and a Coke. No wonder I was hungry.

From my window I saw Todd pull into the drive in his silver-gray Lexus. Discreet but powerful, like Todd himself. Why the man chose to date me was a great mystery, as I am neither discreet nor powerful.

I hurried down to meet him and waved to Mary and Ruth, who were working in the kitchen as I went through the great room. I was more than happy to put thoughts of the key and the old man away for a while.

"Had enough yet, Kristie? Ready to leave here?" Todd greeted me as he leaned against his perfectly polished car.

"What?" I looked at him in surprise.

His eyes narrowed. "What happened to your cheek?"

"Nothing much. A dog bite. I'm fine."

"A dog bite? That sounds serious." He studied the bandage as if he could see through it to the damage beneath.

"I'm fine. And it's not really a bite."

"Who did it? That mangy German shepherd?"

"Hawk is not mangy," I said defensively. "And it was my fault."

"Oh, sure. 'Come on, Hawk, bite!' Is that what you said? You could sue, you know."

"Todd! Never!"

He shook his head. "I do not understand you. I don't know why you're so in love with this smelly place and everything about it. I truly don't."

I couldn't help but laugh. His nose was wrinkled in distaste, his nostrils pinched. I had to admit that the barn was a bit ripe in the shimmering heat, but I wasn't about to let him know I thought so. It sat, timeworn but sturdy, across the drive from where Todd was parked. Its large door was open, and out of its recesses tumbled a trio of calico kittens. They chased each other past Hawk, who lay sleeping in the sun once more.

In the fenced area beside the barn, two great farm horses stood sleepily nose to tail, each one's tail swishing flies for the other. One of the beasts shied suddenly and kicked a left rear hoof, sending a red hen squawking in panic.

"You'd think, Todd, that after living all thirty years of your life in Lancaster County, you'd be used to the barn smell by now."

"Not in the summer," he said. "In fact, I consider car air-conditioning the greatest invention since the wheel. I can close everything out."

I took a deep breath. "But everything includes the good things too, like honeysuckle. Besides, manure means growth."

Todd frowned. "When I think of manure—which isn't often if I can help it—I think of many words, and growth isn't one of them. Offensive is, or disease laden, or repugnant. I can't imagine anything worse than dealing with tons of the stuff each year as these farmers do."

"You can't have milk without manure," I said. "Same critter gives both."

"Don't remind me." He shuddered. "I'll have

to start eating my cereal dry if I think about it too much."

I leaned against the car beside him, looking at the farm. "It's all so beautiful."

Todd followed my gaze without comprehension. "I wish you'd listen to me," he said again. "You won't like it here."

Suddenly overcome with the sheer magic of the farm and my future as part of it, I hugged myself and began to sing, "Old MacDonald had a farm, ee-i-ee-i-oh."

"Kristie!"

I stopped abruptly, trying to look contrite but probably failing completely. I didn't look at my vocalizing as the terrible and embarrassing habit Todd did.

"When will you learn that you can't go around bursting into song every time you feel like it?" He looked around self-consciously and then sighed in relief when he saw that we were alone. "People will think you're strange."

I took a deep breath, forgot contrite, and looked him in the eye. "You don't like my yellow car. You don't like my farm. You don't like my painting. And you don't like my singing. Is there anything about me you do like?"

"Come on, Kristie. That's unfair. You know I care for you very much."

I nodded. "So you keep saying. Though how you can like me when you don't like anything about me, I don't understand. Why, I bet you think this outfit is gaudy."

Without answering, Todd pushed himself away from the car and went to the trunk. I made a face at his back, but I had to agree with him; it was gaudy. That's why I liked it.

I remained where I was, staring dreamily at the large two-story farm house. It was painted the traditional white with dark green trim, and an open porch ran across the front. The far end of the porch was hung with the sturdy green-gray leaves of a very healthy wisteria, which must be lovely in June when it bloomed. A neatly mowed lawn shaded by a great maple wrapped itself around the house.

I smiled hopefully at Todd, wanting him to share my pleasure in the beauty of the scene bathed in the golden light of an evening near summer's end.

Instead, as he straightened from inspecting the contents of his trunk, he said, "You know, it still isn't too late to change your mind."

I bent quickly to pet one of the calico kittens and hide my irritation. "Todd, let it go, will you?"

Even after two years we are like two people on opposite sides of a window. We see each other, we admire each other, but somehow we can't touch.

Todd nodded, resigned. "Just remember, when you're ready to leave, I'll be there to help you find another apartment. But since you insist on staying for the moment, I have a gift for you to make things more bearable."

He walked back to me, took me by the arm, and led me around the car so I could see into the trunk. There sat a box with a flat screen TV pictured on it, a big red ribbon tied around it.

"Todd! What in the world?"

"My peace offering," he said. "I've behaved like a boor about your move, and I'm sorry because it's made you unhappy with me. Please accept this with my apologies." He grinned. "Now you'll be able to fill your evenings and keep an eye on our favorite local pol, Hurlbert."

I pointed to the TV, appalled. "You can't do this."

Ignoring me, he bent, picked the box up, and started up the walk to the house. "I'll just take it up to your room."

"Don't, Todd," I said grabbing his arm. "Don't."

But he ignored me, knocking on the door with the TV itself. Mary let him in and watched blank faced as Todd went across the living room and upstairs without so much as a hello. I heard him trip on the last step and waited apprehensively for the crash that by some miracle never came.

How terribly rude he must seem to her, I thought as I waited, embarrassed and uncomfortable. I knew that Todd didn't mean to give offense—he wasn't that kind of man—but that didn't change the fact that he had. He returned smiling happily, unaware of my distress, flicking a little wave at Mary and Ruth.

I got into the car quickly, and when we pulled out of the drive, I said sharply, "Whatever possessed you to bring me a TV?"

Todd looked at me in surprise. "I know you were uncertain about bringing one with you for fear of offending the Zooks, but I saw a TV through Jake's window earlier today, so I figured it was okay. I got you that one on sale. It's little and won't take up much space. It gets a great picture." He grinned at me. "I know because I tried it out this afternoon."

"You can't go buying me TVs!" Aside from the embarrassment, the momentary size of the gift felt uncomfortably binding. I much preferred a bouquet of cut flowers. When the flowers died, so did my need to feel grateful. "Besides, with Jake it's different. Surely you can see that."

Todd turned onto Route 340, heading toward Lancaster. "What's different?" he asked.

"Jake can have a TV because it's a settled issue between him and his parents." My voice was loud, even to my own ears. I tried to calm myself. "I've never even discussed it with them."

"You mean you need their permission to have a TV in your own rooms even though you aren't Amish and even though their son has one and even though you're paying rent?"

I nodded.

"But you have rights here too," he objected.

"It's not a matter of rights. It's a matter of courtesy and respect."

We came on a buggy moving turtle slow in the buggy lane, which was essentially a broad, macadamized shoulder. We zipped past, and I wondered as always what it felt like to have the air currents from powerful cars, trucks, and tourist buses buffet you as you inched along in such a flimsy contraption. You had to be brave or incredibly foolhardy to be on the road in those things.

Most roads in the area didn't have buggy lanes, and cars pulled out to pass whenever there was a break in oncoming traffic. I liked the way the tires sang different tunes as they crossed and recrossed the worn patches down the center of each side of these roads, shallow gullies worn in the macadam by the hooves of numberless horses.

"And it's a matter of grace," I continued as we turned right at the light in Smoketown to avoid Lancaster City and the bypass with its heavy traffic.

"What's a matter of grace?" Todd asked. "I thought we were talking about a TV."

"We are. It's grace that lets John and Mary suffer Jake's TV in their house. It goes against their standards, but their love for him lets them accept it."

"You mean you think they'll let Jake have one and not you?"

"No."

Todd frowned. "You aren't making sense, Kristie."

"I know." I searched for words to adequately describe what I saw as John and Mary's great dilemma. "The Zooks live by a highly codified theological and legal system."

"I know," Todd said stiffly. "As you pointed out, I've lived in Lancaster all my life."

"Then you admit they need a powerful reason to break it or bend it. And Jake's physical condition is that reason."

"So he can have a TV?"

"Right."

"And you can't."

"Not without asking. After all, it's their home. I'm the outsider. I'm certain they won't force their system on me; they've been nothing but kindness itself. But they should be allowed to be gracious to their guest instead of being forced to live with another breach in their code."

"First a trickle, then the world rushes in like a flood," said Todd sarcastically. "One TV, two TVs, then live burlesque on the front porch."

"Todd!"

"Don't worry about their legal system, Kristie. Like any legal system ever devised, it's full of holes."

"Spoken like a lawyer." I sounded as huffy and ill-tempered and sarcastic as he.

"Well, it's true. There are so many inconsistencies. Electricity from public utilities is sinful, but water-generated or battery-generated electricity isn't. Driving a car is sinful, but riding in one isn't. Owning a vacuum cleaner is wrong, but using one for the woman you clean for isn't. Hypocrisy."

"Inconsistency, yes, but not willful hypocrisy." I was furious at Todd's unfeeling generalizations. "You're forgetting that the Zooks are only people trying to accommodate a family tragedy to a very rigid and inflexible way of life."

"Well, if it's such a ridiculous way of life, why are you defending it?" Todd was almost shouting.

"I'm not defending the system! I'm defending the Zooks!"

"Why?" he roared.

"Because I like them!"

Silence reverberated like thunder through the car as we struggled for control.

I glared out the front window. A pair of open buggies came racing down the road toward us, each driven by a young Amishman of about sixteen, each boy wearing a bright blue scarf tied cowboy fashion about his neck. Even as I fumed at Todd, I wondered how they kept their hats on at such a reckless speed and where they had gotten their worldly scarves.

He cleared his throat as a prelude to speaking, and I looked away, out the side window.

"I'm sorry." He cleared his throat again. "I don't really feel that strongly about the Amish. In fact, though I think they're wrong, I actually admire their courage and tenacity. My real worry is you."

"Me?" Startled, I turned to him.

"You're taking this Amish stuff too seriously."

I looked at his profile, strong and sharp against the western light. "I told you I'm fine."

He nodded. "I know. It's just—" He stopped, frowned, and tried again. "I'm afraid of losing you." He looked at me, emotion naked on his face. He reached out to me.

I was moved and automatically extended my hand to take his. "Don't talk nonsense."

A tension within him resolved, and he relaxed. "I promise not to raise my voice again," he said, squeezing my hand. "I'll be good no matter how much I might disagree with you or how silly I think your point of view might be."

"Silly?" I pulled my hand away, and my frail calm fled. "Silly?" A switch flicked on in my head. "That's the trouble with you! I couldn't put my finger on it before, but now I know. You think I'm silly! You condescend to me, just like my parents and sister. Because I sometimes disagree with you, you think my opinions are foolish! Because I like to paint and buy yellow cars and live on a farm, you think I'm an idiot!"

Todd blinked at my attack and shook his head like a punch-drunk fighter. "Don't you think you're overreacting just a bit?" he said. "I never called you an idiot or anything close to it."

"Yes. Yes, you did." I pointed an accusing finger at him. "Oh, not in those words, but you did."

"Come on, Kristie, don't be silly!"

"Aha!" With that final word, I fell silent, and we drove around Lancaster in brooding silence.

Well, we've finally touched.

5

When we arrived at Alexander Bailey's, my favorite restaurant, Todd and I both behaved as if nothing had happened. With no difficulty whatsoever, we slid the glass barrier back between us as we ate a delicious meal of Caesar salad, steak au poivre, and baked Alaska.

Truth to tell, I was appalled about my behavior in the car. I never yelled at people. I considered it undignified and the mark of a thoroughly undisciplined person. I grew up with three people who automatically expressed themselves at full volume, and in reaction I kept my own volume control firmly in the low digits. I might jump to conclusions, the mark of an imaginative, creative person. I might burst into song at the least suggestion, the sign of a culturally literate person. I might like flashy things like yellow cars and beautiful swirls of color, the mark of an *artiste*. But yell in public? No, no, a thousand times no.

My supervisor during my student-teaching days had recommended strongly that I not even consider teaching high school.

"You're too gentle and soft spoken," she said. "Too sweet and kind. They'd eat you alive."

I spent a long time trying to decide if she was really telling me I was wishy-washy and spineless before I decided she just meant I was quiet. Introspective. Deep. At least, I hoped that was what she meant.

All through dinner Todd and I stayed safely on the surface in our conversation. He told me about a case he was working on, a nasty divorce where the parents were using their kids as pawns and both sets of grandparents were also seeking custody.

"All the grandparents agree that the parents are unfit. Their own kids! Of course, that's all they agree on."

I told him about my preparations for the coming school year, rhapsodizing at great length about my new bulletin boards. "I found the most wonderful marbleized paper for the background, and there's lots of room for the kids to display their work."

He told me about his difficulty finding a car mechanic he was happy with. "This guy thought that just because I wore a suit to work, I wouldn't recognize incompetence when I saw it."

I talked about a new art supply store I had discovered. "Brushes of all sizes and of such quality!" I even regaled him with an expurgated version of my afternoon in the emergency ward. "I was so scared I could barely breathe!"

By the time we left the restaurant, I think we were both thoroughly bored. It was not one of our better evenings.

"Can we stop by the hospital so I can check on Mr. Geohagan?" I asked as I snapped my seat belt. I had to do something to redeem the time.

Todd turned to me with the key almost in the ignition. "Now?" He glanced at his watch and frowned. "We'll miss the movie."

"Now. There's just enough time before visiting hours end, and we'll still make the nine thirty show."

"But it's Saturday night."

I blinked. "People aren't allowed to get visits on Saturdays?"

"Okay, okay," he said with a totally uncharacteristic lack of grace. "We'll stop if you're going to be that way. But please don't be long."

I bit back a retort and glanced at my watch.

"Don't worry. They'll kick me out soon."

I stopped at the circular desk in the lobby of the hospital and, smiling as sweetly as I could, asked where Mr. Geohagan's room was.

The receptionist turned to her computer, pressed a few keys, and said, "He's not allowed visitors except family. Are you family?"

"Just a very good friend." *Oh, dear. I've raised my level of relationship again.*

"I'm sorry. No visitors."

"Please," I said, dropping my smile and looking as desperate as I actually felt. "If I can't talk with him, I need to talk with someone who can tell me how he's doing. I'm going crazy not knowing, and I've come all this way because I can't get any satisfaction over the phone."

Just then an announcement came over the loudspeaker. "Visiting hours are now over. Visiting hours are now over."

"I'm sorry," the receptionist said. "Even if they would tell you anything at the nurses' station, it's too late."

I nodded, turned toward the door, and paused. I glanced back over my shoulder and saw that she was already packing up to leave, her head buried in her purse. I spun around and walked as quickly as I could past her and toward the elevators. I kept waiting to hear her yell, "Lady, I told you no!"

But I got around the corner and onto the elevator

without a problem. I hit the button for the coronary care floor and held my breath until the door slid tightly shut without a security person appearing to escort me out of the building. When I reached my floor, I followed the signs to the nurses' station.

A nurse was reading some reports, and I stood and waited until she became aware of me.

"May I help you?" she asked. "Visiting hours are over."

I nodded. "I know. I'm looking for information on Everett Geohagan."

"Family?" she asked.

I shook my head. "Friend. I just want to know how he is and if he can have visitors tomorrow."

She clicked some keys on her computer. "He's doing as well as can be expected."

"Yeah, I know that. But what does that mean?"

She smiled sympathetically. "He had a mild coronary. The next few days are critical, and we will watch him carefully to be certain nothing further happens. If nothing does, he'll be able to leave here soon."

I felt relieved. A mild coronary. That didn't sound too bad.

"If he's still doing well tomorrow, may I see him for a few minutes? I promise not to upset him."

"I'll leave a note asking his doctor. Call tomorrow before you come in." She put the report back. "I'm sorry. That's the best I can do."

I nodded. "Thanks. I appreciate your help."

I found Todd sitting in the car listening to a Phillies game. He was rapping his fingers against the wheel, obviously annoyed at the length of my visit—or was it at the Phillies and their three-point deficit?

"We missed the movie," he announced with the import of a president announcing, "We lost the war."

I shrugged. "So we'll see it next week."

He just looked at me. Todd was a man who didn't shift mental gears easily. If you planned to see a movie, by George, that's what you were supposed to do. "Now what?" he asked.

"How about home?" I said brusquely. I was tired of the responsibility for ruining his life.

We rode the whole way back to the farm in sticky silence. If I put my mind to it, I could be just as stubborn and childish as he could, undoubtedly the mark of a petty person.

As we pulled into the driveway at the farm, our headlights illuminated Ruth and Elam seated in an open buggy, their horse impatiently shaking its head.

Todd pulled up beside them and stopped wheel to wheel with the buggy on my side. I rolled down my window.

"Are you coming or going?" I asked.

"There's a barn dance tonight at Jake Lapp's."

Ruth's voice was bright with anticipation. "Everybody's going to be there."

"Including you two, I assume."

"You've got that right," Elam said.

"Have a good time!" I waved as they pulled onto the road.

"We will," called Elam, flicking the reins across the horse's rump.

They disappeared down the road, the soft jingling of the bridle mingling with the muted rattle of bottles.

"Beer," Todd said critically. "Hear that? He's got a case of beer in the back of the buggy."

"I'm still amazed at Amish dating customs," I said, momentarily forgetting how miffed I was at him. "Unchaperoned dances, drinking, smoking, pairing off in the darkness. Our pastor would have a fit if his young people acted that way, but the Amish elders seem to accept it—or at least put up with it."

Todd shrugged. "*Rumspringa*. This kind of dating encourages early marriage, and the sooner they marry, the less likely they are to leave the group. A single person might risk being shunned, but a married person has many more golden chains binding him to the church and community." He snorted. "Sort of like life insurance, only it's lifestyle insurance."

"That's a pretty snarky tone," I snapped in a pretty snarky voice of my own.

We sat awkwardly as silence enveloped us again. Such tension was so unusual between us that I wasn't certain how to deal with it. Todd appeared as confused as I was.

Finally I said, "At least they're in the buggy, not a car. Or on a motorcycle."

"Meaning?"

"That they're not being too rebellious." Still, I imagined that after the experience with Jake, Mary and John worried about these two.

Todd shrugged and the sounds of the night creatures filled the car.

"Well, good night," I said after a few minutes and climbed out of the car.

"Um," he said eloquently, climbing out and stalking up the walk after me. He bent to kiss me good night, and I turned my head, offering only my cheek.

"What?" he said in that snarky voice. "I'm supposed to kiss it and make it better?"

That's when I realized I'd raised my bandaged cheek to him. "Very funny." I sniffed and let myself into the darkened house without a good-bye of any kind. It was a relief to be alone.

I crossed the main room quietly, taking care not to disturb Mary and John, who were already in bed in their room at the top of the main house stairs. Was Mary like my mother, who never slept until Patty and I got home from wherever we were? Or did acceptance of *rumspringa* allow her to sleep? Or maybe plain old exhaustion from her heavy workload pulled her under. Whatever, the house was silent about me.

When I went through to my stairs in Jake's addition, I could hear his TV faintly in his front room. Did he have a social life, friends he did things with, or did he spend every Saturday night in front of the tube?

I got ready for bed slowly, weighed down not only by the humid August heat but by my thoughts about life and its complications. I hated it when I started thinking before I fell asleep. It guaranteed a restless night and a relentless morning headache. In a stab at getting a good night's rest, I imagined myself picking up my thoughts about Mary and her worries and Jake and his sterile life and putting them in the chair by the window to bother Big Bird throughout the night.

But I couldn't rid my mind of worries about Todd.

Here I was, twenty-seven years old, twenty-eight in November. For two years I'd been dating one man. At my age, that often meant marriage. Mom and Dad certainly hoped so. Todd was, after all, a lawyer.

"Not engaged yet, Kristie? But he's so nice and handsome."

"Not yet, Mom. Be patient."

Unspoken was her thought that Todd would rescue me from the artsy life I was living. In

Mom's mind I was as Bohemian as they came, spending all my time kicking up my heels and accomplishing little. She had no concept of the thought and planning and time that went into a watercolor. She didn't understand that the actual painting itself was only part of the process.

I climbed into bed and plumped the pillows behind me. I took a pencil and a piece of paper. I titled it TODD: GOOD QUALITIES. It didn't take me long to make an impressive list.

1. Fine Christian
2. Good lawyer
3. Good salary
4. Active at church
5. Handsome
6. Intelligent
7. Loves me

I stopped and bit the eraser off the pencil. I spit it out and grabbed another piece of paper.

TODD: BAD QUALITIES
1. Thinks my ideas and preferences are dumb
2. And me too
3. Has no sense of humor

I placed the two lists side by side.
Dear Lord, do seven good qualities mitigate the force of three bad ones?

And what would Todd say if I told him about the key?

"What? You took a key from a man you've never seen before in your life, making a promise with who knows what implications? Who was this man, Kristie? Can you trust him? Was he setting you up for something? Why'd he give you the key and not his family or a friend? What are you supposed to do with it? What if he dies?"

He would run his hand through his hair the way he always did when he got upset. "Kristie, you should have thought!"

It's terrible when you can't even have a mental argument with someone without him pointing out your foolishness.

I snapped off the light and slid down on my pillow. Well, I might not have been thinking when I took the key, but I was thinking now. Too much.

I woke to the rattle of a buggy and the clopping of hooves. I glanced at the luminous dial of my clock radio. Three a.m. Ruth and Elam were home.

Almost immediately I heard a second buggy pull into the drive. Aha! Someone other than Elam was bringing Ruth home. Curious, I went to my window, but I couldn't see anything because of the jutting of the ell.

I hoped Ruth's romance was running more smoothly than mine. Of course, that wouldn't be hard.

I went back to bed and fell into a fitful sleep, only to waken at dawn. I lay there with the predicted headache and listened to the morning farm noises. John and Elam would be in the barn feeding the animals and milking the cows, the extent of their Sunday labors. Mary and Ruth would be fixing a simple breakfast, after which the family would go to church, scheduled today at Uncle Sam Zook's farm over toward Paradise. I smiled. Going to worship in Paradise.

I rolled over and tried to go back to sleep, but after a half hour of tossing and turning and muttering threats at myself, I finally admitted that I was awake for the day whether I liked it or not. I sighed and got up. I went in to the living room and took Big Bird's cover off his cage, and he chirped a good morning. I gave him some fresh food and squirted water into his dish from one bottle of the case I had slid under my bed. With no running water up here, bottled water loomed large in my future.

My future. I got the Todd evaluations I'd written last night and stared at them.

Dear Lord, is it just pride that makes me feel Todd doesn't appreciate me, the real me? After all, he was very nice, and he had many fine qualities. *Maybe after we're married, I can make him realize that he makes me feel stupid.*

"Ha!" I said aloud. "Do you really think you can change a thirty-year-old lawyer who's as set in his ways as anyone you've ever met? Who are you kidding, girl?"

Big Bird chirped at me happily. He loved having conversations.

"What do you think, Bird? I haven't got a chance, have I? It's Todd as he is or not at all."

Nodding his head vigorously, Big Bird sang.

I sighed and reached for *It's Up to You*, the book by Clarke Griffin that both the Zooks and I were reading. I found my place.

The Holy Spirit woos us. He draws us, convicts us, teaches us. But God in his wisdom seems to have left the privilege of final choice to us—and with this privilege comes the responsibility for our choices.

Sometimes we make mundane decisions—to floss or not to floss—and sometimes we make eternally significant ones—to believe or not to believe.

Many times we make wrong choices, and rather than accept accountability, we make excuses limited only by our imaginations.

"My parents always found fault with me. That's why I criticize my wife and kids."

"Everybody cheats on their taxes. Why shouldn't I?"

"Well, Billy started it!"

All these excuses for wrong behavior are just that—excuses, justifications for our falling short. It seems to me that as long as someone else is responsible for our troubles, we have no hope of solving our problems. If someone else consciously or unconsciously makes my choices for me, am I not well and truly trapped? Am I not hopeless?

"Choose for yourselves this day whom you will serve," Joshua said to each individual in Israel. He could not decide for the people even so proper a thing as worshipping God. Each had to choose alone and bear the responsibility for the choice.

The clopping of hooves caught my attention. The Zooks were leaving for church. I glanced at my clock. Seven fifteen.

I watched the buggy disappear out of sight. Did the Amish make fewer choices than I did? Or did they just make different ones? Or the same ones in different garb? Someone brought Ruth home last night. She had to make decisions about him, didn't she?

"And what decisions should I make?" I asked my reflection as I combed my hair.

I heard no answer.

6

I was so happy with the church I had found in Lancaster. The people there loved God, and it showed in their worship and in their concern for each other. They welcomed me from the beginning, and it was there I had met Todd.

Today I found him waiting for me as usual when I came in the front door. I smiled wanly as he followed me down the aisle and sat beside me. Sitting together was a habit we'd fallen into, and in one of those blazing moments of insight I realized it probably meant a lot more to him than it did to me.

Another thing to note in the negative column of my Todd lists.

I turned sideways in my seat to put down my purse and Bible and was surprised to see Jon Clarke sitting behind me.

"Hello," he whispered, and I nodded my head in acknowledgment.

I turned back to the front, frowning. For some reason, I wasn't certain I wanted him sitting behind me. As it turned out, I had difficulty concentrating on the Scripture reading. I stumbled over the words of music I'd sung for years. Instead of worshipping, I wondered whether the back of my hair looked good. Or whether I had any tags showing at my neckline. Or whether Todd looked too possessive. Or whether Jon Clarke noticed I wasn't blood spattered today. When the congregation stood for the benediction and the pastor said amen, I couldn't remember a word he'd said.

I stood frozen in place as the congregation began to move toward the exits, afraid Todd would turn to me, afraid Jon Clarke wouldn't.

Just turn around and smile sweetly. Say something deep and significant like, "Nice service." No need to be as tongue-tied as a junior-high girl. Besides, you can't stand here like a pillar of salt forever.

I slanted my eyes for a quick peek at Todd and was relieved to see him greeting a couple on the other side of the aisle. I took a deep breath and turned self-consciously to pick up my things from the pew. I found Jon Clarke looking directly at me as if he'd been waiting for me to turn.

"How's your cheek today?" His eyes under their improbably dark brows smiled.

My hand went to my bandage. "It's fine. I forget about it most of the time. Except when I smile. Then I feel a tug."

"Then you mustn't smile." And he grinned so disarmingly that I automatically smiled back. I winced.

"Jon Clarke!" a voice called.

Jon Clarke raised his hand in salute to a man several pews in front of us, and then he turned back to me. "Are you free to get dinner with me somewhere?"

"Dinner?" I said intelligently, surprised and pleased.

"Or are you already busy?" He glanced at Todd.

I glanced at Todd too, still talking with his far neighbors. He was probably assuming we were going somewhere to eat because we usually did. But his comments and attitude last night still rankled, and his assumption wasn't good enough. Besides, an invitation in the hand . . .

I turned to Jon Clarke. "No, I'm not busy. Not busy at all. I'd enjoy having dinner with you."

He nodded. "I may be a few minutes," he said as the man who'd hailed him a moment before approached us.

"No problem," I assured him.

As he slowly made his way through the crowd, shaking hands as he went, I slid out of my pew at the end away from Todd. I was almost in the narthex when I felt a tap on my shoulder.

"Where do you think you're going in such a hurry?" Todd asked, but with a smile to show he meant nothing I could interpret as criticism. "I expected you to wait for me."

I shrugged.

"Well, where shall we eat?" he asked. "What are you hungry for?"

"I can't go with you today," I said with surprising ease.

He blinked. "Why not?"

I smiled sweetly, feeling again a slight pull in my cheek.

When it became obvious I wasn't going to tell him, he cleared his throat. "Look, you're not still mad at me about last night, are you?"

"It wasn't one of your finer moments," I said. "Or one of mine, for that matter. And no, I'm not mad."

"Good," he said, relief evident in his face. "Then let's go." He put his hand in the small of my back to guide me to the door.

"I just said I can't, Todd. I wasn't playing games. I really do have other plans."

He stared, obviously startled that I'd made plans that didn't include him. "But, Kristie—"

"If you'll excuse me?" And with that I walked to the ladies' room. I hung around in there for ten minutes, and when I finally peeked out, I was relieved to see that Todd had gone and Jon Clarke was still talking to people. I sat on a bench in the narthex and waited.

Finally Jon Clarke joined me.

"I'm sorry." He took my elbow as we walked. "As I told you yesterday, I've been away for several years, and there are so many people to see."

"So this is your home church?"

"As close to a home church as I've ever had. I've come here off and on since I was a kid. My aunt and uncle brought me along whenever I visited—which included my junior and senior years of high school. I lived with them while my folks were in Brazil on an engineering job."

"You were away from your parents for two whole years?"

"Yeah." He shrugged. "We all survived. I didn't want to finish my high school career in Brazil, so I stayed here with Uncle Bud and Aunt Betty Lou. Nobody forced me or anything. My choice."

"Funny. I was just reading about choices this morning."

"It was one of the best choices I ever made, at least spiritually. Since Mom and Dad sort of ignore God, the years here grounded me in Him."

I thought about my parents, who were committed to God almost as much as they were committed to the law. What would it be like to grow up in an unbelieving home and never go to Sunday school and church?

"I also attended regularly when I went to Lancaster Bible College," he continued. "I worked with the youth pastor here for a couple of years before I took my own pastoring job in Michigan."

"Well, no wonder everyone knows you. Where's your real home—where your family's from, I mean?"

"San Francisco—at least for most of my growing up. That's why Mom and Dad always sent me to Lancaster County for the summer. Country air and all that."

"I left my heart," I sang, before I realized what I was doing.

Jon Clarke looked at me and laughed.

I flushed and realized Todd was right. It was a stupid habit.

We stopped beside Jon Clarke's car.

"What about my car?" I asked. "Shall I follow you wherever we're going?"

"Let's just leave it," he said. "We can come back and get it later."

I looked at my car, and he turned to look too.

"Does it really look like a taxicab?" I asked.

"Only if you're very conventional and yellow means cabs, not sunshine, bananas, and butter-cups."

I smiled happily. What an insightful man.

Because many of the finest restaurants in the Lancaster area are owned by Mennonites, they're closed on Sundays. We decided to try Cracker Barrel just east of town on Business 30. We had to wait a few minutes for a table, so we shopped in the general store, which was loaded with autumn and Halloween items.

"Jon Clarke, look at this." I pointed to a Halloween witch who cackled every time someone walked by her. "She'd get on your nerves very quickly."

He looked slightly pained but not at the witch. "Do me a favor? Call me Clarke. My mother's a displaced Southerner, and she has the Southerner's love for double names. I don't."

"You don't go by Jon?"

"My father's named Jon, and two Jons would be confusing, so I've always used Clarke. But Aunt Betty Lou calls me the whole thing, just like Mom. People around here followed her example."

"What's your mother's name?" I asked, curious.

"Mary Rose."

"Nice."

"She's lucky. I have an aunt named Charlotte Mabel, who's called Lottie Mae, and another named Dolly Belle. Anyway, I sign my name J. Clarke Griffin."

Griffin, I thought as we followed the hostess to our table and placed our orders. "Reverend J. Clarke Griffin."

"Dr. J. Clarke Griffin."

"Right. Graduate school. I forgot. Well, it sounds fine. It also sounds familiar, though I can't imagine why."

"It sounds strange to me. Too new. I imagine I'll get used to it at the college, though."

"You're teaching?"

"Just like you."

"Hardly on the same level."

"Oh, I don't know about that. I can't imagine

what I'd do with a roomful of little kids."

"And I with easily bored college students."

We took turns playing with the triangle peg game resting on our table. He kept ending with three pegs, and I managed to get two about half the time, three the rest. Neither of us managed one. Still, I beat him overall. Great strategy for impressing a first date. Well, not a date exactly. Maybe a first conversation? a first afternoon? a first meal?

If he couldn't take a woman besting him in peg jumping, he wasn't the man I thought he was.

The waitress arrived with our food, and Clarke pushed the peg triangle to the back of the table. "You're good, but I'll get you yet."

I grinned. "Not if I can help it."

As we ate our lunch, we talked about the morning's message (he talked; I mostly listened as I hadn't been able to pay much attention) and after that I shared how much I was enjoying my first weekend at the Zooks'. Then I found myself wanting to know more about what he was doing when not rescuing damsels in distress.

"What are you teaching?" I asked.

"A class in practical Christian living and one in night school on pastoral counseling."

"And the rest of the time?"

"I'm opening a counseling center through the church. I like teaching, and it'll help me until I get established, but my heart's in counseling."

"Like me and painting and teaching."

"You're a painter? I didn't realize that. That's great."

"You sound like you actually mean it."

"Of course I do. Don't most people?"

"No. People tend to view it as a hobby at best, or at worst, a waste of time."

"Are you good?"

I looked at him carefully and saw that he really wanted to know.

"Yes. I think I am. I may never qualify for the American Watercolor Society, but my work is good and constantly getting better. I have some paintings for sale at the Country Shop, and I'm talking with a couple of local galleries about handling some of my work."

Clarke nodded as we rose to leave. "It's too bad it's so hard to make a living from things like writing and painting, but there's no money in either unless you're famous."

Suddenly the nebulous wisp of recognition that had been bothering me took form. I stopped in the middle of the aisle and turned to face him.

"You!" I managed to say before he walked full into me.

The jolt caused me to lose my balance, and he grabbed me around the waist to keep me from falling. For a split-second we leaned against each other. Then he let go, casual, smiling. He seemed much less affected by our collision than I was.

"Have you any pressing plans for this afternoon?" he asked before I could say anything.

"I suppose not."

"Want to go for a train ride?"

"Strasburg Railroad? I've never gone, but our kindergarten class goes there every year . . . are you really Clarke Griffin?"

"It's great fun for adults too." He grinned at me. "Yes."

We got in the car and were quiet as Clarke maneuvered onto the road. Then we both spoke at once.

"They forgot the *J*."

"Do you know my book?"

We smiled at each other.

"You first," he said.

"They forgot the *J* on the cover. It just says Clarke Griffin."

"So you do have my book," he said with satisfaction. He tried to be casual. "Do you like it?"

"Fortunately, I can be completely honest and say yes. Of course, I'm only on page thirty-two."

A little boy's smile when he gets the new red bicycle he wants for his birthday had nothing on Clarke's. I leaned back and looked at him speculatively.

"What?" he said.

"*It's Up to You* is your first book, and it's recently been released. Am I right?"

"How did you know?"

"I recognize the symptoms. You're afraid to let your pride show for fear people will misinterpret it. You can't believe you've actually written something that people will pay money to read. You're afraid people won't like it. And you're concerned about being able to handle both the criticism and the praise."

He looked at me suspiciously. "Don't tell me you write too."

"No. It's just that I react that way whenever someone buys one of my paintings."

We looked at each other with pleased understanding as we pulled into the parking lot at the Strasburg Railroad.

The railroad runs through the Lancaster County countryside from Strasburg to Paradise. We found seats, and while we waited for the ride to begin, we watched a young family in the seat ahead of us. The two small boys wore engineers' hats, undoubtedly from the souvenir shop.

Suddenly the locomotive's whistle blew, and the younger boy grabbed his mother in a panic and collapsed against her in tears. She held him gently, smiling at her husband over the boy's head. Finally the train began to move, and the child's curiosity overcame his fear. He settled back in his mother's arms to enjoy the ride.

"Has your book sold well?" I asked.

"I don't know. It's a recent release. Too soon to tell."

"If it'll help, I'll run right out and buy another copy."

Clarke laughed. "And I'll buy one of your paintings."

"Bit of a financial difference."

He shrugged. "It's only money."

"I've been working on the railroad," I sang. I clapped my hand over my mouth. "Oops. Sorry."

"Do you often burst into song?"

"Regularly. It's one of my worst habits."

"As habits go, it's among the least offensive I've run into in a long time—and in my profession I run into some doozies."

The train puffed to a halt on a siding behind the lumberyard in Paradise.

"The first lap of 'The Road to Paradise,'" Clarke said. "Now they'll move the engine from the front of the train to the back for the ride home."

I leaned out the window and watched with interest as the men worked. The engine was detached from the train and steamed slowly past us on a parallel track.

"How will they turn the engine around?" I asked. "There's no turntable or anything."

"They don't turn it around."

"It goes all the way home backwards?"

"You don't think the engineer knows about reverse?"

"But backwards the whole way?"

"It's not like a car, you know. There's no traffic to deal with, and you don't have to worry that he'll jump the tracks." There was laughter in Clarke's voice, but no mockery or sarcasm.

I looked at him witheringly. "Of course he won't jump the tracks. Casey Jones would never do that."

"Casey Jones, sitting at the lever," sang Clarke in a loud and sound baritone. The little boys in the seat ahead turned to stare.

I laughed. "The secret is in not singing too loudly."

After Clarke dropped me at church, I drove my buttercup car to the hospital.

"Mr. Everett Geohagan?" I asked the woman at the desk in case he'd been moved to a regular room.

"Coronary care, fourth floor, room 410." She looked up from her computer screen. "No visitors."

I went up to the fourth floor anyway, hoping that if I appeared assured enough, they would think I belonged there. The doors to the unit parted just as I arrived, and a weeping woman walked out. I slipped in.

My stomach was queasy as I searched for Mr. Geohagan's room. I expected someone to grab me by the shoulder at any minute, a scary proposition for a rule-keeper like me.

"And just what are you doing here?" this mean person would yell at me. "Don't you understand what Family Only means? Get lost! And don't come back!"

But no one paid any attention to me even when I went into the room where Mr. Geohagan lay with tubes and wires fettering him to several machines. I was comforted by the steady patterns on the screens recording his heartbeat and other functions.

His eyes were closed, his face was pale, there was a slight purplish discoloration about his lips, and he looked what my grandmother would have called "peak-ed."

He must have sensed my presence, because his eyes snapped open.

I smiled. "Hello."

"Kristie Matthews," he said in his whispery voice.

"You remembered!" I was pleased.

"Of course I remember. How could I forget the girl who's been nice enough to call to see how I'm doing?"

"They told you?"

"It's supposed to make me feel good."

"The first time I called, I had an awful time." I took the chair beside his bed.

Mr. Geohagan smiled, and his eyes moved to my cheek. "How's your dog bite?"

"It's going to be fine," I said, automatically

reaching up to the bandage. "It's certainly nothing compared to your problem."

He emitted a burst of air, which I took to be a laugh. "My health is the least of my problems."

I blinked. It seemed to me that not much could be worse than some sort of coronary difficulty. The old ticker stops ticking, and it doesn't matter about any of the other important things.

A nurse came in and started when she saw me. "You can't be here," she said.

"My niece," Mr. Geohagan managed, and I smiled.

She shook her head. "Only immediate family. Parents, spouse, children." She looked at me. "You'll have to go. He's too weak."

"I am not."

But clearly he was.

"Don't worry. I'll be back," I said.

And I did go back three days later, when they moved him to a regular room. He was still weak, but he was appreciative of my visit.

"I don't want to talk about me," he said when I asked how he was doing. "Tell me about you. What do you do?"

"For a living? I'm an elementary school art teacher."

"Those children are lucky to be taught by someone like you," he said kindly. "I know you're very good. You certainly took charge of me last Saturday."

I thought about my near panic and shook my head. "It was all a front."

"Isn't that what teaching sometimes is? Acting like you're the authority when you're not certain you're even marginally qualified?"

"I think it's a lot more than that, but you're right about needing to be the authority. Kids need the structure that a firm but kind authority gives, though there are some kids who challenge you all the time." Kids like Nelson Carmody Hurlbert, stepson of the candidate for U.S. Senate. He seemed to think that his high profile stepparent exempted him from following instructions and obeying rules. I finally managed to disabuse him of that idea, but I suspected that next week, when I saw him, I'd have to go through it all over again.

"Tell me about your students. I imagine you are looking forward to seeing them again."

And so I did, starting with dear Nelson himself. What I had feared would be an awkward visit passed quite easily. In too short a time Mr. Geohagan became visibly weary, and I knew it was time to go.

"I mustn't wear you out," I said, rising.

"No one as delightful as you could do that."

I grinned at the gracious compliment. "By the way, here's your key." I held it out to him.

"Keep it," he wheezed genially. "I'll be here for a while yet. You just hold on to it until I need it again."

"Shouldn't I give it to your wife or someone in your family? Or someone here at the hospital?"

"No," he said quickly. "*You* are its keeper."

I frowned.

"Trust me. I know what I'm doing." He shook a finger in my direction. "I'll tell you when I want it back."

"Okay." But I wasn't happy and I didn't understand.

"By the way, would you be willing to mail a letter for me?" He turned toward his night table.

I saw a couple of business envelopes resting there and recalled seeing them in his pocket Saturday. I reached quickly for the top one to save him the movement. "This one?"

I glanced at it and saw the addressee was Adam Hurlbert. "Hey, he's my favorite candidate too. That Nelson kid I was talking about is his stepson."

"I'm afraid it needs a stamp."

"No problem," I assured him. "I just bought a book of stamps the other day. In fact, they're still in my purse. I'll mail it on my way home. And if there's anything else I can do for you, just ask."

"Thanks." He fell back on his pillows

exhausted, and I left quickly. I dug out a stamp and mailed the letter at the sideways strip mall in Smoketown on my way home.

I spent the evening doing my final preparations for the beginning of school next week.

7

I set my easel by the great sugar maple in the front yard, its massive canopy providing protection from the strong early September sun. My bag with its brushes, paints, pencils, paper towels, and assorted paraphernalia rested against the leg of my collapsible stool.

I took a large sheet of composition board and placed it on my easel. Then I taped a piece of heavy textured paper to it, working flat as watercolorists do. I hummed to myself as I took a plastic bottle from my supply bag and went into the farm house to fill it with water.

Mary was at the sink, looking out the window toward the barn. She moved aside as I filled my bottle.

"You're going to paint?" she asked.

"The barn. And Hawk and the hens."

She looked out the window again, and I realized she wasn't looking at the barn but at my easel. I thought of the color sense I'd been aware of throughout the house.

"You're an artist at heart, aren't you, Mary? I see it in your rugs and quilts. Have you ever done watercolor?"

She got a faraway look in her eye. "Once, when I was about twelve, I found a little tin of water-colors by the road, the kind kids have. It must have fallen out of a car. I opened it, and there were all the primary colors and a paint brush. They had only been used a bit. I took the tin home and hid it."

"Why did you hide it?"

"I didn't think my father would let me keep it."

"Painting is bad?" I knew photographs were frowned on, especially photos of people.

"Hochmut."

I shook my head. "I'm sorry. I don't know that word."

"Pride. Vanity."

"Painting makes you vain?" What an odd thought. Painting brought me joy and satisfaction. Maybe if you became famous and made the big bucks, you could get puffed up with your own importance. Still, if you saw your talent as a gift from the Lord, couldn't vanity be kept in check?

It struck me that the only thing hanging on the walls in this house was a calendar with beautiful nature scenes and Bible verses. "You can't hang pictures?"

Mary began to wipe the oilcloth table cover, already spanking clean. "As a young teen, I painted when my parents were too busy to notice, always in my room when my older sisters were away or working. I painted little things like flowers. Once I painted a meadow with cows grazing and daisies blowing. I took it to school and showed it to my teacher."

"What did she say?" I knew how important a teacher's comments were to a student.

"She thought it was so pretty she told my parents, 'You have an artist here.'" Mary gave a small smile, and I could tell that this compliment was still important to her.

"But you don't paint anymore?"

"*Hochmut.* My father took the paints and forbade me to paint ever again. He said 'We are a community, Mary, a church. We are not individuals to compete, to set ourselves apart as special. Not *hochmut. Demut.* Humility.'" She shrugged. "That's life, or at least my life."

But she yearned to paint. I could see it in her face.

I went out to my easel thinking about the similarities and differences between Mary's experience and mine. Both of us faced opposition from our families as far as our desire to paint went. But I had been taught individuality my whole life, sort of my family's version of the army ad slogan "Be all you can be," and Mary had been taught community and *demut*. I was taught to stand up for myself, which enabled me to finally stand up to my father. Mary was taught to sublimate herself and yield to her father and her church as her authority. The fact that she had been thirteen or fourteen and I nineteen certainly came into play, but Mary was now an adult and had been for many years. She still hadn't stood up for the right to use her God-given talent.

Because she wasn't looking for rights. That good old American concept, so dear to us fancy folk, was foreign to her.

I eyed the barn and checked it against the penciled-in shapes I'd previously drawn, all vague and lacking in detail but setting the composition of the picture. With clear water I wet my paper. Then I applied a wash of cobalt blue, dark to light at what would be the horizon, with a one-inch round brush. Next, I twisted some facial tissues and laid the twist on the paper where I wanted clouds to be. The tissues absorbed the wet paint and the white of the paper showed. I softened the edges of the clouds with more clear water. A touch of gray wash on the undersides of the clouds gave them dimension.

The cornfields with their green stalks and golden tassels came next as I worked background to foreground. I sprinkled sea salt on the still wet fields to create a mottled effect with areas of strong color where the paint diffused under the salt.

I studied the barn carefully, noting where the sun hit and where the shadows slept. So much of painting was about the play of light and shadow. Taking a two-inch wash brush, I lay down a light gray wash that I let dry. Then, using the same ultramarine blue with a touch of burnt sienna, I went over the shadowed areas for a deeper hue. I dropped in some sap green for the roof, letting the roofline blur. I mixed Prussian blue and burnt sienna for the gaping doorway.

Lastly, I took a rigger brush and added details. As always when I painted, I was totally absorbed and completely contented. I lost all track of time.

Finally, I leaned back to survey my work. I was especially pleased with the way the white of the paper was visible in a fine corona around the red hens, making them stand out against the deep gray of the doorway.

"Nice," a voice behind me said.

I started and spun around. On the walk watching me was Jake in his wheelchair.

"Do you always sneak up on people?" I asked, and it came out more brusquely than I intended.

"Sorry," he said. "I thought you were finished."

I looked at my painting again and nodded. "For the time being." I'd need to brush off the salt when everything was completely dry.

I rose and walked across the lawn, carrying my

stool. I sat down by Jake, hoping I'd think of something intelligent to say. I still hadn't grown used to the chair, and it made me nervous. I'd never been around someone with such a raw, recent disability before. My own good health made his situation seem even more stark, and though I knew it was foolish, I felt guilty because of my functioning, albeit skinny, legs.

I glanced at the kitchen window, wondering if Mary was looking out, watching over her son. Or over my painting. What caught my eye was the porch with its four steps.

"You must have a ramp someplace," I blurted. He certainly hadn't come down the stairs.

He nodded. "My entrance has one. Father and Elam built it for me."

I relaxed a little. My spoken-before-I-thought comment hadn't bothered him. "Then you can get around pretty well by yourself."

"Sure. From here to the house and back." His voice dripped bitterness.

"Oh, I didn't mean—" I started, flushing. What didn't I mean? I didn't mean to upset him? I didn't mean to hurt him? Well, I didn't. Still, I was mad at myself for making such a stupid comment and mad at him for making me feel so dumb. "I'm sorry. That wasn't very tactful of me."

Jake sighed, holding up a hand apologetically. "It was no worse than my answer. I'm sorry too."

We smiled ruefully at each other.

I took a deep breath. "Isn't it a beautiful day?" When in doubt, fall back on the weather.

Jake looked without enthusiasm at the sky and then at me. "Beautiful," he said in a flat voice.

"It or me?" I teased.

"What?" He missed the joke entirely. And the idea of trying to explain my cleverness was more than I could handle. No matter what I said, it was bound to sound as if I were looking for a compliment. And so we sat, silent.

I wanted to pick up my stool and go back to my painting, but I didn't see how I could without being even more offensive. I searched my mind for something else to say, something safe, something that would get a nice, general, unemotional conversation started but also keep it going.

"What do you do to pass the time, Jake?" Before I could continue and ask if he watched TV or worked at something with his hands or read mystery novels, he answered. Or rather he reacted.

"What do I do?" He scowled and snorted. "What do you *think* I do? Nothing."

I was doing about as well here as I had back in junior high when boys scared me to death and anything that came out of my mouth when they were around sounded inane. Obviously, talking to Jake was a minefield, and so far I'd detonated more than my share of emotional explosions.

I decided to brazen it out rather than apologize again. I saw that I could easily spend my whole time on the farm saying I was sorry for some accidental comment or inadvertent hurt. Besides, truth to tell, maybe it wasn't my thick tongue but his thin skin that was the real problem.

"How did your accident happen?" I made my voice as matter of fact as I could.

He studied me for a moment, and I thought, *Oh, boy, I've done it again.*

"You sure you want to know?" he finally asked.

"If you want to tell."

He seemed to consider, and I waited.

Apparently he decided to take the risk. "Over on Route 10 south of Honey Brook, there are two steep hills." His hands sketched a deep V.

"I know where you mean," I said, drawing the V too.

"Yeah?" He seemed to like that. "Well, I was speeding down the first hill on my motorcycle last fall. October twentieth, to be exact. It was raining hard, but I was so busy picking up speed for the second hill that I never gave the wet leaves any thought."

I could picture him, crouched forward over the bike, hurtling down the steep incline, preparing for the long pull just ahead.

"As I neared the intersection at the bottom of the hill, a car ran the stop sign right in front of me. I braked and lost control on the leaves. I skidded and flew off and finally came to a stop against a telephone pole. I thought I was going to die. My helmet protected my head and my leathers prevented brushburns and scrapes, but my back was broken when the bike landed on top of me."

His eyes lost focus as he looked into some private middle distance of memories and anguish.

I sat quietly, not daring to breathe, unable to imagine what it must have been like to have your life changed in one irrevocable moment and because of someone else's mistake. Life didn't give do-overs.

Finally, he looked at me. "It took less than a minute, a lot less, to change my life as I knew it. And the car never even slowed up."

"I'm sorry," I said inadequately. "I'm so sorry."

Jake smiled tightly and studied his clenched fists. "Don't let it worry you. If I could stand all those months in the hospital and in rehab, I can survive anything." He turned to glare at me. "Except pity."

I nodded, and we sat quietly again, Jake lost in his memories, I trying to grasp the enormity of his injury and wondering how one showed sorrow without communicating pity. Now there was no awkwardness between us.

He finally broke the silence. "You've been here almost a week. Do you regret it yet?"

I stared at him in surprise. He sounded just

like Todd. "Why would I regret it? I love it here."

"Even with Hawk?"

My hand went to my cheek. The wound was healing nicely. "Hawk was just being a dog."

"You're not going to give in to the English habit of suing, are you?"

I laughed. "Of course not! It's not as though the dog did this with malice aforethought. And besides, I'd never do anything to hurt your parents. They're too nice. After all, I want to stay here, and I think that it will work better if I don't take the family to court."

I looked over at the sleeping dog. "I think Hawk is wonderful." I threw my arms wide. "I think the farm is wonderful."

His eyes traced the barn and the fields visible behind it. "I complain a lot, but I love the farm too. Not farming, you understand, but the farm. The country. The quiet."

I nodded my agreement.

"Though sometimes," he said, sounding lost and small, "it's just too quiet."

Dear God, how do I respond to that?

Since I hadn't any idea and He didn't send a shaft of insight, I changed the subject completely. "My biggest problem on the farm is that my English inner clock just doesn't mesh with your family's German one. I simply can't go to bed at nine or nine thirty and expect to go to sleep. Nor can I wake up at five and expect to think clearly."

"I know what you mean. I finally convinced Mom that I didn't want to get up that early either. It makes the day too long." This time there was no bitterness in his voice. He was merely stating a fact.

"I'm trying to persuade your mother not to stop her work to make me breakfast when I can very well do it myself," I said. "That way I'll be able to sleep as late as I want—at least for the next few days until school starts—and not feel too guilty and lazy."

"Good luck," Jake said.

"Well, I'm a guest, right? And how do you argue with your guests, even—or maybe especially—paying ones?"

"You don't know my mother well, do you?" He waved at my painting, still sitting on the easel under the tree. "Is that kind of thing the reason you wanted to live here?"

I nodded. "I know it probably sounds pure corn to you, but I've fallen in love with Lancaster County. It's beautiful and green and culturally unique."

"It's kind of funny when you think about it," he said, "but I've spent the last ten years, since I was fifteen, trying to escape from this culture thing you want to take on."

Shades of me and my parents. And me and Todd. "But I don't want to take anything on," I said. "I have too many problems with Amish beliefs. I just want to observe and enjoy and paint."

He shrugged, not quite with me. "Well, I guess you'll be all right as long as you keep painting barns."

"But not people?"

Jake shook his head. "Old Order Amish like my parents don't believe in photographs. Or portraits. They see them as graven images. You know, 'Thou shalt not make unto thee any graven image, or any likeness of any thing.'"

"I knew the Amish didn't like having their pictures taken, but I didn't realize there was a religious reason other than the fact that cameras are relatively modern. And, of course, just about anyone would resent the invasion of their privacy by tourists who poke digital cameras in their faces. Since I personally prefer painting landscapes, I shouldn't have any problem. Still, I'd love to do your father's hands."

"His hands?"

"They're marvelous, Jake. Gnarled and strong, a farmer's hands. Do you think he'd let me photograph them sometime so I could paint them at my leisure? Do hands constitute graven images?"

"Who knows? Just don't ask him until he gets to know you. Then he'll realize you're not trying to use him. He's had enough criticism recently because he let me bring in electricity and a phone. He needs a period of rest."

"If people minded the telephone and the electricity, they must not approve of my being here."

Jake shrugged. "Probably not. Some of them are very conservative and very touchy. They're afraid of anything new, anything that might be seen as a breach of community. To them having an English girl living on our farm seems like inviting the world into the living room. But your being here's not as difficult for Father as it might have been because—" he paused for effect—"I'm really your landlord."

"You are?" I was startled, though the information made sense. I'd never quite figured out why John and Mary were willing to open their home to an outsider. I was another complication in a life that already had more than its share.

But Jake as landlord made sense. Some income for him while he tried to decide what to do with the rest of his life. Now I understood why he was afraid I might dislike the farm. He didn't want to lose his tenant.

"The *grossdawdy* wing is mine," Jake said. "Because I don't use the top floor and probably never will, I decided to rent it out. I figured I wouldn't feel like such a charity case if I had some income." He grinned impudently. "I think I'm going to like being a landlord, sitting idle as the money pours in."

I smiled back, but I was moved by how revealing his comments were.

"Anyway," he continued, "everybody knows Father's largely innocent concerning you, though people still gripe to him about me because I'm not Plain and I'm not willing to revert, in spite of the obvious chastisement of the Lord."

I was appalled. "Oh, Jake. Surely people don't believe your situation is God's punishment!"

Jake shrugged. "Some do; some don't. But let me tell you, I wouldn't blame Him if it were true. I was one wild maniac. You wouldn't have liked me. In fact, you'd probably have been afraid of me."

I looked at the man in the chair, his shoulders strong beneath his knit shirt, his hands firm on the wheels. Granted, his face was dark and discontented, but it was hard to imagine him as the man he was describing. "Maybe you're too hard on yourself."

"Maybe," he said. "But I doubt it. I put Mom and Father through all kinds of pain, but they always loved me. They don't seem to agree with those who think I'm being punished, but I do know they wish I were still Amish."

"Sure they do," I said. "I don't find that surprising. But shouldn't they be shunning you?" I had the typical English curiosity about this Amish teaching. "I mean, obviously they aren't, and I'm glad, but why not? You've certainly gone against the Order's teachings."

"You can only be shunned if you're a baptized

member of the church, and that happens when you're around eighteen or twenty or decide to get married. That's when you place yourself under church discipline and rules."

I nodded. "That signals the end of *rumspringa*?"

"Absolutely."

I watched Hawk lope across the lawn and come directly to me. He rested his chin on my lap. I put my hand lightly on his back and stroked. He closed his eyes in pleasure and didn't move.

Jake grinned. "He likes you. And he's sorry he hurt you."

"He probably doesn't even remember," I said. "Please. Tell me more about shunning."

"Everybody has to decide when they want to join church. My two older brothers, Andy and Zeke, decided not to join at all but to go fancy like me. My older sister, Sarah, decided to take the vow. She lives with her farmer husband, Abner, and their three and a half kids over near Honey Brook. Elam and Ruth have obviously chosen Plain too, or will when their *rumspringa* is over."

I thought of the beer rattling in the back of the buggy Saturday night.

"Why do parents allow this wildness? I mean, everything else in Amish life is so structured and ordered. It's hard to understand why everyone looks the other way when their kids go nuts."

"It has to do with joining the church. To make an informed decision to live under the *Ordnung*, you have to know what you're choosing to give up."

Ah, the mysterious *Ordnung*. I thought I knew what it was, but I wasn't certain. "What exactly is the *Ordnung*?"

"The unwritten code of conduct that tells you how many pins a woman can have in her dress and when a man can grow a beard. Stuff like that."

I'd been pretty much right. "You sample the world and all its vices so you can decide to give up those vices for the orderly life of the community and the rules of the *Ordnung*."

"Basically, yeah. Though lots of kids don't sample all the vices by any means. They follow the traditional pattern of sings and frolics and volleyball games and ice skating parties. They may stay out late and experiment with sex like lots of regular kids, but they have limits. Not everyone's a wild man like I was, doing everything. But I never did drugs like some of them. I may be stupid, but I'm not an idiot. Okay, maybe a toke of pot now and then, and alcohol if you consider that a drug. But coke or meth or crack or any of the others—not me. Speed, the fast kind, not the drug kind, was my major addiction."

"Regrets?"

"Basically one. The guy who ran the stop sign."

That was a given. "Would you have become Amish if the accident hadn't happened?"

"When I'm free to pick my own rules, I can function fine. When they are forced on me, I rebel." He shrugged. "Good or bad, I rebel."

I looked at his chair and thought about "forced on." "So because you never joined the church, your family doesn't have to shun you."

"Or Andy or Zeke because they've never been baptized and taken their vows, either."

"But if Elam gets baptized like you think he will, then changes his mind and buys himself a car and starts growing a mustache, he'd be shunned?"

Jake nodded.

"Do you know anyone who's been shunned?" I asked.

"Sure. David Stoltzfus from the farm across the way." Jake pointed across the cornfield. "He wanted to race cars of all things. And my uncle."

"Your uncle?"

"My father's younger brother. He just couldn't accept all the teachings of the *Ordnung*. He said he couldn't find them in the Bible. At twenty-two he broke with the church, saying he believed in salvation by grace, not works."

"And now none of you sees him? Ever?" Such an ostracizing was hard for me to imagine. As frustrating as Mom and Dad and Patty could be, I would never want to face life without them.

"It's not quite that bad," he said, smiling. "I see him. Or at least I did when I could get around. He lives in Lancaster, has a nice wife and a couple of kids. One's even named Amos after Grandfather, but I don't think Grandfather and Grandmother ever saw Uncle Jake again after he was excommunicated. They couldn't understand his difficulty with what they considered the God-ordained way of life."

"Uncle Jake? Are you named for him?"

"Father has never admitted it, but I think so. I know Uncle Jake was his favorite brother."

"And they never see each other, your father and your uncle?"

"Once in a while Uncle Jake comes to visit, but it's hard for everybody. And he never stays for a meal. If he did, he'd have to eat at a separate table. It's too awkward."

"And they never go to him?"

Jake shook his head.

"That's a sad story."

Jake smiled thinly. "In a way, being shunned is like being dead. If you're under the ban, people can't eat or do business or socialize with you. If you're married, your husband or wife can't have normal relations with you. It's a pretty brutal situation, and not many people can handle such total rejection by family and friends and community. But it's one way the Amish church keeps itself pure."

The screen door slammed, and Mary came outside. She waved at Jake and me and went to my easel as if pulled, a metal filing drawn to a magnet. She looked at it, and a finger came out to touch something. She glanced at me, smiled, and went to the garden to pick beans for supper. Hawk deserted me to follow her.

"Take Mom as an example of how the Amish think," Jake said. "She prays for me more and cries over me more because of my non-Amish status than because of my paralysis. She can no more understand me than Grandfather could understand Uncle Jake.

"But she and Father are realists. They didn't want the rift of excommunication in our generation of the family. That's why they didn't force us into the fold. Many of their friends disapproved, especially since Father's a preacher in the district."

I reached over and grabbed a little marmalade kitten as he ran past. I handed him to Jake. The animal spit and slashed the air with tiny claws, then wiggled and squirmed until Jake let him go. Falling over himself in his haste to escape, he raced for the safety of the barn.

Jake watched the kitten until he disappeared from sight. "I guess you could say that Father and Mom have bent tradition some, but they haven't actually broken the *Ordnung*. And our family's still intact."

I was impressed. While I had no difficulty understanding why Mary was more concerned about her son's spiritual welfare than his physical condition, I knew I had only the vaguest comprehension of the magnitude of the accommodations she and John were making to ensure family unity.

Jake laughed. "It's really funny on off-Sundays when there's no church."

"Off-Sundays?" How had I missed that?

He grinned at my surprise. "Every other Sunday there's no service. Then Andy and Sally and their kids and Zeke and Hope and their kids all drive up in their cars, and everybody climbs out in their jeans and Phillies T-shirts. Sally and Hope have the latest hair styles and manicured nails. Sally brings the ham she had in her electric oven while she was at church, and Hope has a store-bought pie still warm from her microwave.

"Then Sarah and Abner pull up in their buggy, Sarah wearing her rimless glasses and carrying cheese and bread she baked Saturday because Sunday baking isn't allowed. Abner and their boys have on black pants and suspenders, and their little girl has her hair pulled back in a knot just like Sally's and Mom's and Ruth's. The contrasts are a riot. It took Abner a while to get used to us."

I could just imagine. "I think it's wonderful

that your parents have managed to keep you all together."

"It is. And you have no idea of the pressure some people put on them. If their Christian character weren't so consistent, I don't know what would happen to our district."

A buggy rattled by on the road, the driver a white-haired gentleman whose beard reached almost to his waist.

"It's Abraham, the patriarch," I said, enchanted. "Though I doubt Abraham wore a straw hat."

"With a brim three and a half inches wide, not a quarter of an inch wider or narrower," Jake said as he waved to the gentleman.

There was a barely perceptible nod in return.

"That's Big Nate Stolzfus from over the way," he said. "He's one of the ones unhappy with my father, especially since he took such a strong stand with his own son Dave, the one who's the race car driver."

I studied the old man with his set face, my imagination gripped by his story. Could a broken heart be hiding under his frosty exterior?

Jake stared at the man too, but with no pity.

"Dave Stoltzfus was one of my best friends, but I haven't heard from him since he left. It's like he wants no part of his past, even those of us who sympathized. Sometimes I read about him in the paper, and once I saw him on *ESPN*."

Jake's voice became hard again. "They wanted

him to confess to the congregation his sin of liking fast cars, but he wouldn't do it. All the terrible grief and pain, and for the life of me, I can't see the difference between Dave's gasoline-powered car and Big Nate's kerosene-powered motor on his well. It's that kind of hairsplitting that drives me wild! Dave says he refuses to be a Christian if he has to be so bound, and I agree with him completely."

I was startled by Jake's vehemence.

"But I'm a Christian," I said, "and I'm not under any of those laws. It's not being Amish or keeping the *Ordnung* that makes a person a Christian. It's believing that Jesus died for your sins."

"You sound just like Jon Clarke." The way Jake said it, it wasn't a compliment. His dark scowl returned, and he said nothing for a few minutes.

Then, "Is that big, grumpy guy who helped you move in a permanent fixture? The one with the curly hair?"

As a change of subject it was a bit heavy handed, but I cooperated. I shrugged. "Todd is a nice guy and all that, but we're . . . I'm . . . not committed."

"The proverbial 'good friend'?"

"And what's wrong with that?"

"Nothing. I've had a few good friends of my own."

"Any special girl now?"

Jake's mouth twisted. "Are you kidding?"

Great. Back to square one. But I no longer had the strength to deal with my indiscretions and Jake's touchiness. Excusing myself, I collected my supplies and painting and prepared to visit Mr. Geohagan. Tomorrow he was having bypass surgery, and I wanted to see him before his ordeal.

"You'll be fine," I told Mr. Geohagan a couple of hours later. "Bypass surgery is a common thing these days."

"Not on me, it's not." His jaw was clenched and his forehead furrowed. "I've got stuff to do. Important stuff. I can't stay sick!"

"Isn't that why you're having this surgery? So you won't stay sick?"

"I'm having it because some doctor wants to earn more money."

"Mr. Geohagan!" I stifled a giggle, knowing he wouldn't appreciate it. "What a terrible thing to say."

He glared at me for a few minutes, but I didn't blink. The corner of his mouth quirked up. "Cathleen."

"Kristie." But I smiled.

He pointed in the direction of his bedside table. "In case I don't make it, I wrote you a long letter about what to do with some of my belongings. The instructions are in the drawer. I need someone I can trust to see that the right things happen, things I've never mentioned to anyone."

"Then you shouldn't mention them to me." I already had the key, and that was more than enough.

He stared at me though narrowed eyes. "Only read it if I die."

"Mr. Geohagan!"

"And don't lose that key."

"A lot of good it'll do me if I don't know what it opens."

"It's written in my letter what you're to do with it if I die. Just don't lose it in the meantime! And mail this letter for me." He reached toward his table.

I felt like saying, "A bit bossy tonight, aren't we?" but I didn't. I knew the grumpiness was pre-operative stress. I took the envelope he indicated and glanced at the address.

"Another letter for Adam Hurlbert. Are you a big contributor or something?"

"Right. I'm a big contributor." He gave that little snort that passed for a laugh.

"Okay, so it's not money. It's a letter of endorsement. It's questions about his platform. It's—"

"None of your business," he cut in, smiling to take away any sting.

I made a face at him, but he was right. I backed off.

"Now promise me you'll come see me as soon as they let you, okay?" he said. "I told them you were like family and they should let you in whenever they decide I'm not going to kick the bucket."

"You're not going to die. You're too ornery."

He liked that and smiled at me.

I smiled warmly back, but my heart was chilled by the thought that he had written all those instructions for me. Me, for heaven's sake. How tragic to have lived sixty-five years and have no one closer than a friend of a few days' acquaintance.

8

Summer still filled the air when school began, but new notebooks, new teachers, and a surfeit of summer boredom made the transition easier for the kids. I was surprised at how glad I was to be back, though I struggled with learning the names of all my students. To cover my ignorance, I smiled a lot. My jaws ached each afternoon when I unglued my fingers and scrubbed paint from under my nails.

Teaching elementary school art might be draining, but it was also fun. The kids didn't yet feel it uncool to enjoy the class, and most of them were willing to try anything I asked. Much as I wished I could make a living from my painting, I enjoyed helping little hands create something original, even if only a mother could call it lovely.

A few students, though, drove me to distraction. Nelson Carmody Hurlbert was one. The boy was enough to make any adult vote against his step-father in protest. If the man couldn't control a child, how would he ever manage the federal government?

But most of us at school excused the would-be senator because he and his lovely wife, Irene, had married when Nelson was eight, and the child's obnoxiousness was already well ingrained. Of course, if Adam won the election, he'd be getting involved with a national govern-ment well over two hundred years old. Talk about ingrained bad habits.

Evenings I collapsed before my TV and watched the occasional news reports of Adam and the ever-smiling Irene, sans Nelson, dashing around the state making well-crafted speeches and shaking hands with everyone in sight. I hated to admit Todd had been right about how much I enjoyed the TV.

The key lay on my bureau day after day. When-ever I looked at it, I prayed for Mr. Geohagan. He was stabilizing nicely after his bypass surgery, and he'd soon be going home. My heart ached for him because he seemed so utterly alone. I never saw anyone else visiting him, and he never mentioned anyone. I stopped in almost every day to give him someone to talk to besides the hospital staff.

But after he was well? Maybe he wouldn't need or want me then.

On the farm harvesting was progressing at a fine rate. The eating corn was in and the cattle corn was almost ready. It was the tomatoes that occupied everyone's efforts now. Ruth was completing a two-week leave from the pretzel factory to harvest the fruit that lay rosy and fragrant in the fields. Even Mary left her kitchen to join her family for the gathering.

"We have to finish today," John said at lunch on Saturday. A scowl hung on his usually taciturn face. "A storm's coming, according to the weatherman." John had a battery-powered forecaster he kept in the barn and used to track the weather. "What we don't get in will be ruint, and we don't want that, eh?"

"Let me help," I said as I sliced a piece of Mary's homemade oatmeal bread. "I don't know much about farms, but I know how to pick tomatoes. Our housekeeper always grew several vines because she liked to make her own tomato juice and spaghetti sauce."

I glanced up to see the family staring at me,

and I wondered what had gotten their attention most: the mention of a housekeeper or my offer to help.

"I mean it. I'll help."

And I did.

I couldn't quite hide my smile at the picture we women made walking down the road to the tomato fields a half hour later. Ruth and Mary were in their caped dresses while I wore my oldest jeans and a T-shirt with a huge sunflower I'd silk-screened way back in some college art class. Their hair was neatly tucked beneath their *kapps*, while mine, made flyaway by the humidity, was tucked behind my ears, from which dangled red, yellow, green, and blue triangles of different sizes. I wore sunglasses with mottled red frames while they both squinted. Ruth had her pink flip-flops on, Mary a pair of much-darned black stockings and black shoes, and I a pair of scruffy canvas sneakers with a hole by the left big toe.

"We used to grow tobacco on this acreage, like many of our neighbors," Ruth said as she fell in step beside me. Mary walked a bit behind but close enough to talk with us if she chose.

"When did you change?" I asked.

"About ten years ago. My older brother Andy kept telling Father that tobacco was a sinful crop —which didn't make Father very happy. Andy said that if we believed our bodies were temples of the Holy Spirit like the Bible says, then we wouldn't be growing a crop that was harmful to the body. I don't think Father cared about being a temple and all, because back then so many raised tobacco that it couldn't be that bad. He hoped that by going along with Andy he could keep him from *fremder Glawwe*."

I shook my head. The phrase wasn't familiar to me.

"Strange belief," Ruth explained. "Andy was starting to go to church with Jon Clarke, and that got him asking all kinds of questions. Father was trying to stop him from turning away. I was only a little kid at the time, but I remember the day Andy told Father he thought you could be sure of your salvation." There was shock in her voice even now.

"You don't agree?"

"Oh, no. You can't know for certain until you die. It's prideful to assume salvation, and sinful."

"I see." Then she'd undoubtedly think me prideful and a terrible sinner. I believed the Bible said you could be certain of your salvation. *My sheep hear My voice*, Jesus said about those who believed in Him. *I know them, and they follow Me. And I give them eternal life, and they shall never perish; neither shall anyone snatch them out of My hand.*

"You probably know our Andy." Mary had moved up to walk with us. "He goes to your church."

"Andy Zook is *your* Andy?" I said in surprise. "I never made the connection; I guess because Zook is such a common name around here. He was my Sunday school teacher last year. He and Sally are wonderful."

Mary nodded, but her smile was sad.

"He looks like John." Now that I knew, the resemblance was obvious. "I don't know how I could have missed it before. And Jake. He looks like a happy Jake."

Mary permitted herself a wry little smile. "You'd never know it now, but he was such a happy little boy, our Jake. Always in trouble but so happy. And Andy was such a good boy. He loved helping John in the barn."

I thought of Andy, who had a large real estate business, and tried to imagine him growing up here on the farm, wearing a Dutch boy bob and a black felt hat. I thought of a little Jake running around in broadfall trousers and suspenders, happy instead of morose.

I wondered which son had hurt Mary more, the one with the strong faith that disagreed with hers or the one with no faith.

Mary looked up and scanned the clear skies, so brilliant that the crystalline blue hurt your eyes. "You'd never think it was going to rain, would you?"

I dutifully looked up at the heavens and the cumulus clouds sailing majestically across the cerulean sea. "You surely wouldn't."

We walked in silence for a few moments. I thought of the way Mary moved up beside Ruth when the conversation turned to issues of belief. Did she see me as a threat to Ruth, the one to lead another child from the community?

Possibly. I didn't mean to cause any problem by living here, but my sunflower T-shirt and dangly earrings and ardent faith apart from the *Ordnung* might seem an attractive alternative to a young woman who felt hedged in—if Ruth felt hedged in, and I saw no sign that she did.

I again marveled at Mary and John. Trying to balance Jake's unique needs and the contact with the outside world those needs forced on them against keeping Ruth and Elam spiritually safe required some fancy footwork. It necessitated great skill in the art of compromise, and I was increasingly struck by the fine line these parents walked.

"See those flatbed wagons?" Ruth pointed with pride. "There's the one we filled yesterday."

The wagons stood at the field's edge, one with dozens of baskets stacked pyramid style on it. Mary, apparently satisfied with the innocuous topic, dropped behind us again.

"Tonight the truck will come from Campbell's Soup and take the tomatoes. They come every day or two during picking season."

"I'm going to be picking tomatoes for

Campbell's Tomato Soup?" I was fascinated by the idea. "The Campbells are coming, hoo-rah, hoo-rah."

Mary and Ruth exchanged a look, and I shut up.

I soon found there was nothing to sing about in picking tomatoes. In a very short time my back ached and my hands were green from the juice of the vine. The acrid odor of the plant was everywhere, and the sun was baking every ounce of moisture from my body. Next thing I knew, I'd be hallucinating an oasis at the edge of the field—date palms, camels, and all.

"If it gets to be too much, Kristie, you can stop anytime," Mary said as she offered me a drink of absolutely delicious water from the picnic thermos she'd brought along. Never had any liquid tasted so sweet and cool. "We appreciate all you've already done."

I stretched painfully, listening to my back creak in fascinating and distressing new ways. My neck felt permanently elongated, like a turtle's, and my nails would give a manicurist a heart attack. I watched Ruth move among the plants, her nimble fingers relentless in their search for the fruit. In the distance Elam was lifting a basket to John, who stood splay legged on the flatbed, the better to swing the basket to its place in the pyramid.

Now I understood why the Amish went to chiropractors so often. I'd have to go along on the family's next visit. If I could wait that long.

I rubbed the small of my back.

"Oh, I'm doing fine, Mary," I lied as I brushed my damp hair off my forehead. "I'll work as long as the rest of you. Todd's not coming til six thirty, so I have plenty of time."

The afternoon was an endless haze of agony, of plant after plant and row after row. It was sweat dripping off the end of my nose and spiders lurking under leaves, ready to pounce. I became resigned to the fact that I was going to walk bent over at a right angle for the rest of my life. I'd develop an obsession with shoes, the only attire I could still appreciate, and I'd paint caterpillars and insects and dirt, the only subjects I could see. One thing was for sure: I was never eating another bowl of tomato soup in my life.

I jumped as a hand touched my shoulder. I straightened slowly, each vertebrae shrieking in protest, to face a smiling Ruth.

"Father says we can stop now. We've gathered most of the tomatoes, and we've run out of baskets."

I tried to smile back. "Great," I mumbled.

We turned to walk back to the house, and there stood Clarke at the side of the road watching us. He looked fresh and energetic and clean in worn jeans and a yellow knit shirt. My slumping shoulders dipped further.

"You look a bit tired," he said as we approached him.

"Perceptive of you," I said tartly.

He grinned that marvelous grin and fell into step with us.

"Staying for dinner, Jon Clarke?" Ruth asked. "Mom went back a while ago to make it."

He nodded. "She already asked me, just as I was hoping she would. In fact, she sent me down to collect you."

Suddenly I saw my plans for the evening as less than inspired.

There was a soft plop and an explosion at our feet. I looked in disbelief at the tomato pulp and juice all over my thoroughly dirty left sneaker, staining it an anemic red-brown. I looked up just in time to see another tomato sail past and splat against a fence post.

"Elam, you've lost your touch," Ruth yelled as she broke into a run. "I'll have to help you." She raced toward her brother and a pile of rotting tomatoes he'd stockpiled.

"That's right. You help him, Ruth," Clarke shouted as he grabbed my hand. "He's going to need all the assistance he can get."

He began running across the field, dragging me behind him.

"I should have known better than to visit today. That shows what a long absence will do. Come on, Kristie. Hurry up."

"What in the world is going on?" I dug in my heels and pulled my hand free.

"Tomato fight. It's a Zook tradition. John always lets the kids have a bang-up battle at the end of each year's harvest as a reward for all their hard work."

Two tomatoes zinged past my head, one falling harmlessly to the ground, the other bouncing off Clarke's chest. As juice and pulp dribbled down his shirt, a delighted Elam punched the air. "Bull's-eye!"

"That does it!" Clarke yelled. "Battle stations, Kristie!" He grabbed two tomatoes and threw.

"You're crazy!" I watched in disbelief as Elam dodged Clarke's tomatoes and threw another of his own. It hit Clarke in the leg.

"For a believer in nonviolence, you're an awfully good shot." Clarke shook his leg free of seeds.

"Two to nothing," Ruth called. Elam was too busy laughing to talk.

"Come on, Kristie. Don't be so inhibited." Clarke threw, missed Elam, but caught Ruth on the skirt. "Can you imagine the chaos when the others were home and Jake was well? It was great!"

"How did you get involved?"

"When I lived with my aunt and uncle, Mr. Zook would hire me to help with the harvest— corn too, but that was never as much fun."

"I guess not. Ears of corn tend to hurt when they hit."

"Here." He put a split tomato in my hand, juice and pulp oozing. "Throw."

I stared at it a minute. Then something went *pop!* inside. I wheeled and threw. I missed my target. In fact the tomato seemed to disintegrate as it traveled, and nothing was left by the time it reached the enemy camp. Still I laughed aloud.

"Good girl." Clarke smiled approval.

"Over hill, over dale," I sang as I bent for more ammunition. A tomato hit me, exploding amidships. I straightened abruptly.

Clarke sputtered with laughter. "Ruth did it."

"Sorry," she called, totally unrepentant.

We pursued each other across the fields in the general direction of the house. Crushed fruit lay all around, offering a bounteous supply of ammunition. Even Hawk rushed madly about, barking happily.

The piercing sound of someone whistling through his fingers got our attention. I whirled, ready for a rear guard attack, to find Jake by the edge of the road. I assessed the wisdom of firing the mushy weapon in my hand, an undoubtedly evil grin on my face. He silently double dared me with the narrowing of his eyes. I laughed and threw my tomato to the ground.

He studied us and shook his head. "Mom says dinner's in fifteen minutes. You might want to clean up just a bit."

I looked at myself and then at the other three.

We were absolute messes. "Even my hair!" I tried to run my fingers through the sticky mess. "Good grief, I'm too old for this."

"You're too old?" Clarke said. "I bet I've got a few years on you, and I haven't had so much fun in years."

I smiled agreement.

We walked slowly down the road past the farm pond with Elam pushing Jake and Hawk loping beside us. The dog gave a sudden bark and detoured to the pond, ducking under the battery-charged electric fence.

"He wants us to wait while he gets a drink," interpreted Ruth.

Hawk began drinking, his tail waving happily. It was a terrible surprise to him when his tail connected with the fence. The shock, mild though it was, jolted him. He let out a yelp as he jumped, landing ignominiously in the middle of the pond. While we dissolved in laughter, Hawk swam with great dignity to the shore, shook himself off, and stalked away, his feelings hurt.

"A car," gasped Elam as he tried to get his breath. "Behind us."

We crowded together on the shoulder to make room for the car to pass. I looked up curiously and found myself staring into Todd's incredulous face.

9

I backed through Mr. Geohagan's door, staring down the hall in wonder at the retreating figure, tall and elegant with his prematurely white hair. An entourage of aides and a bevy of newsmen scurried about him, eager to do his bidding or report his every word.

"Mr. Geohagan, did you see him?" I sank into the chair beside the bed, breathless as a schoolgirl who's seen a rock star. "That was Adam Hurlbert! He looks even better now than he did when he came to school that one time for Nelson. He wasn't a candidate then, and his hair wasn't quite as wonderful. Do you think he puts something on it? I bet he does."

I knew I sounded like an idiot, but Adam Hurlbert! "I wonder what he was doing at the hospital?"

Everett Geohagan, pale and frail, grinned lopsidedly and tried to look modest. "Visiting me."

"Visiting you? You must be a big contributor or something if he came to see you," I said.

He gave the little wheeze that was his laugh. "Big contributions are beyond my pocketbook. I used to work for him. I'm not certain how he found out I was sick, but in he strolled."

"You worked for him? At Hurlbert Construction? You mean I know somebody who knows somebody? That's almost as good as knowing somebody myself."

When he laughed gently at me, I flushed. How naive I sounded. "Still, it must be fun watching someone you know become famous."

Mr. Geohagan shrugged. "Are you going to vote for him?"

"I certainly am. Aren't you?"

"I suspect that all I'll be doing Election Day is reading about the outcome here or in some nursing home."

"There's always an absentee ballot, but you'll be out of here by then and walking into the polling place under your own steam."

"That remains to be seen. Now tell me, why are you going to vote for him?"

I thought for a moment. "Well, he's very assured, very controlled. He makes you think he knows exactly what needs to be done and, by George, he's the one to do it. He's been well conceived and well packaged. If he's a fraction as knowledgeable about politics as he is about public relations and image, he'll be terrific. And he's a political novice. No backroom debts to pay."

"And perhaps no political savvy either?"

"You think not? You think it's all a well-rehearsed act? He doesn't really know anything?"

Mr. Geohagan shrugged. "I do know he's been successful at every other project he's put his mind to, so why not politics? He joined the army right out of high school for the educational benefits. The same week he was discharged, he formed Hurlbert Construction, and in the fall he started college full time at Franklin and Marshall. He finished college in three years and kept the company going the whole time. Granted, it was a small company then, but it was still quite a feat. I was one of his first employees."

Mr. Geohagan shook his head. "One thing I'll say for Adam. He's never lacked ambition or self-confidence. In fact, there are those who accuse him of overweening pride. I think he just decides what he wants, goes after it, and lets nothing stop him. 'We're going to be the biggest construction company Lancaster County has ever seen,' he said." Mr. Geohagan shrugged again. "We are."

"Why do you think he decided to go into politics if he's so successful in business?"

"Power. That and new worlds to conquer. People like him can get bored with things the rest of us would be more than content with. Of course, marrying the governor's widowed daughter was no drawback, either."

Irene Parsons Carmody Hurlbert was fifteen years younger than her new husband, and their whirlwind courtship had been splashed all over the media. I followed every detail of the romance as avidly as everyone else—the meeting at a local party fund-raiser; the immediate spark; the glamorous wooing with candlelight dinners, political galas, and vacations at posh resorts in the Caribbean; the soft-soaping of Adam's nasty divorce five years earlier; the huge wedding with the first lady and the vice president and his wife among the multitude of elegant and well-connected guests. The bid for office was probably inevitable. As was the outcome of his race against a sturdy but thoroughly uncharismatic opponent.

"Irene seems so gracious and charming, to say nothing of beautiful. Is she as wonderful as she appears?"

"I can't say I know her," he said. "She's not the kind who stops at the office like the first Mrs. Hurlbert. Maggie poured her life into the company right beside Adam, ate peanut butter sandwiches when things were tight, raised the kids by herself when he was working all those long hours. Terrible shame when he left her. I liked Maggie. She was real. I'm not so sure about Irene."

"Rats. I want to hear she's wonderful and madly in love with her husband."

Mr. Geohagan smiled his sardonic, lopsided grin. "Did I ever tell you that you remind me of my daughter, Cathleen?"

"Why, thank you," I said, surprised. "What a lovely thing to say. I didn't even know you had a daughter." But I remembered him calling me Cathleen once before.

"I miss her terribly. I think that's why I enjoy you so much."

"Do I look like her?"

"Not particularly. I've always thought of her as absolutely beautiful."

I swallowed hard. Not that people tell me I'm beautiful on a regular basis, but this was the most direct repudiation I'd ever had, even if unintentional, which I thought this was. Mr. Geohagan didn't seem to notice the insult.

"She had red-gold hair that was naturally curly, not straight brown like yours. And she had great dark eyes. Of course you have marvelous dark eyes too," he hastened to add. Maybe he realized what he said after all, or maybe he'd seen something in my face. Or maybe he was just as politically astute as Adam Hurlbert. "You're very pretty in your own way, but you don't look like Cathleen. You've got a square jaw and you're too skinny. She had a wonderful figure, full in all the right places."

I put on my polite face, trying not to become too depressed by his assessment of my assets or lack thereof. After all, a man's daughter should be beautiful to him.

He studied me a minute. "You've got pale,

creamy skin. She had the cutest freckles across her nose, and they drove her crazy. I thought they were adorable."

"Does she live far away?" I hoped this paragon lived in Oregon or Washington or maybe up in Hudson's Bay so that I'd never have to compete face-to-face with her.

"She's dead." The statement was bald and unemotional.

I gasped. It was more an involuntary rush of air than a word. I felt as if I'd been kicked by an Amishman's mule.

"Don't look so upset," he said. "It's not your fault."

"No, but—" I was at a loss for words.

"In case you haven't noticed, life's not always nice," he said with more than a touch of bitterness.

We sat quietly, thinking about life's low blows.

"But," he said after a minute, "you bring me great pleasure with your interest in me and my health. I love your enthusiasm for life. Cathleen was that way, always bubbly, always happy. She lived for fun and parties and going out. She always said that people were the most interesting things on the face of the earth, and she had loads of friends. Everyone loved her because she loved them, and she could talk to anyone about anything. She was our sunshine."

Though she didn't sound much like introverted, intense me, if it made him happy to think of her when he talked with me, that was fine.

He studied the ceiling tiles without really seeing them. "If I'd listened to her, I wouldn't be in such a bad fix now. 'Stop smoking, Dad,' she'd always say. 'It's bad for you. You'll get cancer.' I'd laugh at her earnest young face and keep right on. Three packs a day. Then one day I couldn't go up the steps without puffing, but it wasn't cancer. Emphysema. Now I have to blow into those foolish machines for the nurses. Or try to blow up balloons. Or listen to lectures by respiratory therapists on the evils of tobacco."

He gazed sadly at me. " 'Oh, Dad,' she said when I was diagnosed. 'I'm so sorry.' " He sighed. "She didn't know what sorry meant then. I didn't either, though I sure do now."

I looked at him with concern. "I didn't know you had emphysema."

"There's a lot you don't know about me, young lady." His voice had a bit more life in it. "I've had it for five years now. Or it's had me. I've got about five years left, they say—if something else doesn't get me first. I have a heart condition, a lung condition, and a blood condition."

I knew about the heart and now the lungs, but a blood condition?

"I'm a full-spectrum patient." Frustration colored his voice. "No matter what your medical specialty, I'm your man."

"What blood condition?"

"I have hepatitis. Maybe I got it from the transfusions during surgery, though that's dubious these days. Maybe it was just from germs floating in the air or from some doctor's germ-laden necktie. Who knows? But I've got it, and that's what counts. Didn't you see the sign on the door? I'm contagious."

I got up and walked to the door. I pulled it open and saw a very obvious sign warning me not to touch anything and to wash thoroughly if I did. I must have been too taken with Adam Hurlbert to notice it.

"You're looking at a human pincushion," Mr. Geohagan grumped as I took my seat again, my hands safely in my lap. "Do you know that there's one person whose job it is to go around all day and take blood from people? That's all she does—stab people! What a job, sucking blood from already ill people. A modern day vampire. She only gets away with it because we're too weak and sick to fight her off."

I leaned back in my chair. "Now, you know you're fortunate to have someone like her caring for you. You should be thanking God instead of griping."

"See? That's just the kind of in-your-face, cheer-me-up comment Cathleen would have made. And I need cheering up. Did you know they're going to send me to a nursing home

143

when the hepatitis clears up? With sick, old people! And they'll probably try and make me stay there forever."

"You can't stay there forever," I said, trying to tease him into a better mood. "You've got too much to do. You told me so yourself."

"I do," he agreed. "I've got lots to do, and it needs to be done now. And I can't do it stuck in here!"

My heart went out to him. "What can I do to help? Just tell me."

"See? Cathleen. And actually there are a couple of things you can do. I was just hoping you'd ask." He handed me a piece of paper and a key.

I looked at the key. "Another one? Do I have to keep it for life too?"

"Don't get all worked up. It belongs to my apartment. I'd appreciate it if you'd go over and get some books and things for me. I've written down everything I want, and I've drawn you a map."

I read the list written in a spidery hand and looked at the map with its tremulous streets.

"You live near my school," I said. "I have to go to parents' night tonight. I'll stop for your things on the way and bring them to you tomorrow. Is that soon enough?"

His appreciative smile made the slight inconvenience negligible.

"The apartment isn't much," he said. "Cathleen never lived there. Neither did my wife. We had

144

a wonderful house in the country, but . . ." His voice trailed off.

The three of them? Or just him and Cathleen?

All the way home I thought about Everett Geohagan. Here was a man who hurt both physically and emotionally. His weakened body might or might not recover from its multiple attacks. And he deeply mourned for Cathleen, obviously much loved. How long was it since her death? How old had she been when she died? And what had she died from?

And where was Mrs. Geohagan? For there to be a Cathleen, there had to be such a lady. Was she dead too? Was that why I was the errand runner, the heir apparent? Or were they divorced and she was no longer involved in his life?

Full of unanswered questions and frustration because I couldn't fix any of Mr. Geohagan's real problems, I arrived home just in time to be included in dinner. We gathered around the oilcloth-covered table and bowed our heads for the silent grace. Mary's chicken and stuffing went around the table, as did the fresh beets, beans, and tomatoes.

"Guess who I saw today?" I asked as I spread some apple butter on Mary's delicious potato rusk.

The five Zooks asked who? with their eyebrows.

"Adam Hurlbert!"

Ruth looked at me blankly. "Who?"

"Adam Hurlbert. You know. The man who's running for U.S. senator."

"I'm afraid I don't know him, either," Elam said around a mouthful of chicken.

The cultural gap yawned wide at my feet. I'd forgotten that politics were a foible of the fancy.

"I've seen him on TV," Jake said, coming to my rescue. "Tall, handsome, white hair, too many teeth. Beautiful wife. Hurlbert Construction."

"That's him," I said.

"Hurlbert Construction? I know the company name." Elam stabbed another piece of chicken from the serving platter. "I seen their equipment and projects around."

"They're the ones that built the motel and restaurant on what used to be Fishers' farm, ain't?" asked John. "They put all that rich, black soil under macadam?"

Elam nodded. "That's them."

John looked up from his noodles. "And you saw him today?"

"At the hospital. He was visiting Mr. Geohagan because Mr. Geohagan used to work for him."

"Well, if you see him again, tell him to leave farmland alone." And John returned to his food.

"Okay," I said, though I couldn't imagine doing any such thing. "But he's Mr. Geohagan's friend, not mine."

"And how is your friend coming along?" Mary asked.

"I think he's doing all right, but he has emphysema and hepatitis, and they're complicating his recovery. He's going to have to go to a nursing home, and that scares and angers him."

I washed down a mouthful of fresh beans with sweetened iced tea. "Today he told me I reminded him of his daughter Cathleen, though I'm not as pretty."

"He actually said that? That you weren't pretty?" Ruth asked, aghast. "But you're beautiful."

"Ruth," Mary said in quiet reprimand. Compliments led to pride.

I blushed. I caught Ruth's eye and mouthed thanks. She grinned, and I wondered again what she really thought of me and my dangly earrings and brightly colored clothing and yellow car.

One evening last week she and I had washed the dinner dishes together. She was talking about the new dress she was sewing.

"Would you ever wear a pink or yellow dress?" I asked. I knew red, my favorite color, was out of the question. It was the color for harlots. Prints were also verboten. But soft, plain hues? "God made those colors too. Just look at the flowers."

"Oh, I'd never wear bold things like that," Ruth said, immediately rejecting the idea. "I wouldn't want to wear anything that called attention to me."

I nodded, thinking that if I dressed the way she did, I'd be doing exactly what she wanted to avoid. It all came down to whom you hung around with.

"Cathleen," Jake said from his place across the table from me. "Cathleen Geohagan. Why does that name sound familiar?"

We all looked at him expectantly, but he shook his head. "It'll come. Just give me a few minutes."

I was finishing my last spoonful of corn starch pudding when Jake yelled, "Aha! I have it."

"Tell me," I said eagerly.

"I read about her in the Lancaster paper about six or seven months ago. I remember because she used to date one of the guys I worked with at the trailer plant before she threw him over for some other guy. Broke my friend's heart, but that's another story."

"That was in the paper?" If so, it took the term "slow news day" to a whole new level.

"Very funny." He helped himself to more pudding. "Actually, I read about her death. She killed herself with pills and booze."

10

I was stunned. I remembered Mr. Geohagan lying in his bed, hands resting on his stomach, eyes staring at memories.

"I miss her," he had said. I just bet he did.

"I remember something else about her death," Jake said. "It was her parents who found her, and it was too much for the mother."

"She died too?" I was afraid of the answer.

"No, I don't think so," Jake said. "She just had a stroke or something like that."

Just a stroke. No wonder she never came to visit. As we bowed our heads for the silent post-dinner prayer, all I could think about was poor Mr. Geohagan.

Oh, Lord, he needs You so badly! How can I help him find You?

I left early for parents' night so that I'd have time to detour to Mr. Geohagan's apartment to pick up the things he needed. I wore the conservative navy skirt I'd worn when I came to meet the Zooks for the first time. I even wore the cream silk blouse. Anything to impress the parents with how trustworthy I was. However, I suspect I shot the whole conservative image with my silver-studded denim blazer, the product of another art class. I particularly liked the great appliquéd pumpkin on the back and the artfully arranged fall foliage at its base, so seasonally appropriate.

I followed Mr. Geohagan's directions in a blue funk. I'm good at feeling depressed even when nothing's wrong, and the circumstances of Mr. Geohagan's life provided more than ample fodder for my blues.

"You may have a sensitive artist's nature," my mother used to tell me after my secret was out and during one of my melancholy moods. "But that's no excuse to inflict your pessimism on the rest of us. Rain on your own parade if you must, but not on mine. Now shape up or spend the day somewhere else."

There was something about lawyers that made them unafraid to speak their minds, at least the lawyers I knew.

I've learned to spare the general populace my blue periods as I've matured, but tonight I felt justified in feeling positively morose. Even my sunshine car did nothing to relieve my dark mood.

As I walked down a long, dingy hall of the unimpressive tan brick apartment building, I studied the door numbers, looking for number 10. I was nonplussed when I found two 6's until I realized one was a 9 whose top screw had come out, causing the number to rotate 180 degrees—a great metaphor for the condition of the building.

Everything was a dirty, dreary beige. Even the straw wreath someone had hung on number 5 was shaggy and uninspiring. The brass plate on number 8 was so tarnished and pitted that it looked like wrought iron.

I found number 10 at the end of the hall and turned the key silently in the lock. I felt like a cat burglar, sneaking about where I had no business. I imagined a neighbor calling the police, and I couldn't help wondering whether my principal would see the humor if I were arrested on parents' night. I glanced furtively down the hall, and then I carefully and quickly opened and closed the door behind me.

It was no surprise to find the apartment as depressing as the hallway. There were no smiling family pictures in gilt or silver frames personalizing the rooms. Nothing hung on the walls or sat on the end tables to lighten the dull grayness of the room. It was more than obvious that Cathleen and Mrs. Geohagan had never lived here. No woman could have stood the sterility.

I walked to the single bedroom and stood in the doorway, staring. The double bed was unmade, left just as it had been the day Mr. Geohagan became ill. A pair of gray trousers hung from the closet doorknob, the legs pooling into wrinkles. A plastic hamper held a pair of dirty blue socks and some underwear, and the dresser top was empty except for a sprinkling of small change.

I set my purse on the floor and put the pants on a hanger after hand-pressing them flat. I stuck them in the closet. After that I quickly made the bed. I couldn't help wondering if the pants would ever be worn or if the bed would ever be slept in again. I smoothed the bedspread carefully over the single pillow and sighed. A double bed should never have only one pillow.

Feeling even more deeply melancholy, I gathered the stationery and paperback Westerns I had come for, found the pajamas and underwear, the slippers and robe. I tossed them in the canvas tote bag I'd brought. I stood by the window and looked out at the gathering night, resting my head against the pane. I felt tears very near the surface.

Suddenly, with all the sound and fury of crashing surf, the toilet in the bathroom flushed.

I froze, not even breathing. A bomb detonating beside me couldn't have shocked me more.

Water rushed from the bathroom tap as someone—someone who shouldn't be here—washed his hands.

Are clean thieves nicer than dirty ones? *Help, Lord!*

I heard the bathroom door open, and I grabbed my chest to keep my heart from popping right through my rib cage. Where to hide?

For want of a better place, I rushed to the closet, tote bag thumping against the wall as I ran. I pulled the door quietly closed after me, hoping the muffled thuds hadn't been audible to anyone but me. I held my breath in the small, dark space and pressed my ear to the door.

I heard footfalls as he—I assumed it was a he—came into the bedroom. And stopped. I could almost feel his surprise through the door.

The bed! I had made the bed! If he had been in this room before, he now knew someone else was in the apartment.

And my purse sat on the floor beside the bed. I might as well just yell, "Hey, you've got company!"

He walked from the bedroom, and I strained to hear. Maybe he'd missed the significance of the bed, hadn't seen the purse, and was just going to leave. There obviously wasn't anything in this place worth taking.

Then again, maybe he wasn't leaving. Over the thudding alarms of my heart I could hear him moving from room to room, undoubtedly looking for the newly arrived maid. I was doomed.

I pulled the light cord dangling from the ceiling. I had jumped and bitten back a scream the first time I bumped it when I rushed into the closet. Now I blinked in its weak light as I looked wildly around for some clever place to hide. Hanging from the rod were half a dozen shirts and three pairs of slacks, including the ones I had just put there. No hope of concealment there.

But the top shelf was completely empty. I could hide there.

Yeah, right. Even if I'd been able to scramble up there on thin air, I'd be a bit obvious when the door was wrenched open.

Once, years ago, I saw a cowboy movie on TV in which the hero and his girl hid from the bad guy in a closet. He stashed her on a high shelf, and he lay on the floor. When the villain shot through the door at regular people height, they were safe.

Such a ploy was extremely clever if you knew the bad guy wasn't going to open the door, knew he would only shoot at the middle of the door, and if you had a hero to boost you up.

I stared at the floor, my alternative hiding place, weighing whether being safe from bullets (aimed only at the middle of the door) was worth the risk of being found curled in an extremely vulnerable position if the door were thrown abruptly open.

Suddenly from the other side of the door, the door I was actually leaning on, came the most malevolent chuckle I had ever heard. I leaped away from the wood as if it were aflame.

Lord, help! He's got me!

But he didn't open the door. Instead, I heard sliding noises and a grunt or two, and I realized my villain had made his move. He wasn't going to shoot me; he wasn't even going to open the door. There was no need. He was just going to block me in.

I reached for the doorknob and pushed wildly. The only response was another wicked chuckle from the other side, followed by some more sliding. Then silence.

I drew back into a far corner, feeling defenseless and frightened. Every crime and Gothic flick I'd ever seen flooded my mind. The images did nothing for my nerves, especially since I knew I had no knight in armor, either shining or tarnished, to rush to my rescue.

I crouched in my corner and shivered and prayed and listened. I was unpleasantly aware of the watcher standing on his side of the door, waiting just as I was.

Eventually there was movement in the room. I crept to the door and listened. Whoever was out there must have become tired of waiting to see what I'd do and had begun searching the place. I could hear drawers being pulled open, sometimes falling to the floor as if wrenched off their tracks.

What was the person searching for? Certainly, anyone could see that there was nothing of value in this lonely, godforsaken place. Except my purse.

Lord, help! I really didn't want to go through the process of canceling credit and bank cards and getting new ones, of applying for a new driver's license, and all the other things that had to be done when you were robbed.

But he wasn't interested in me. I hoped my things didn't concern him, either. In fact, he seemed to have forgotten me. He was now in the living room, now the kitchen, taking no care to be quiet with his movements. He knew that the location of the apartment, first floor corner, largely did away with being heard by neighbors. Besides, he was probably hurrying as fast as he could. I might have friends who would show up at any moment.

I got down on my knees and tried to peer under the door. All I could see was more of the rug that covered the closet floor, a very unattractive shade of brown, perfect for a drab place like this.

I slumped in my corner and waited, willing the intruder to leave. Finally, I heard the front door slam. I jumped to my feet and listened. All remained quiet.

I twisted the doorknob and pushed, hoping against hope that whatever was blocking me in would move. It didn't. That would have been too easy.

I turned and leaned my back against the door, pushing, pushing while the slick soles of my new Mary Janes sought traction on the carpeting. Without warning my feet flew from under me, and I grabbed at the nearest thing, an old red-and-blue plaid shirt, to keep from falling. I fell anyway, my spine bouncing hard in spite of the rug. The shirt landed on my head, the collar button holding it on the hanger popped by the pull of my weight. The now-malformed hanger bounced noisily above me.

I got to my feet, rubbing my sore backside. This time I faced the door, placed my palms flat, straightened my arms and shoved as hard as I could. Nothing happened except my shoulders, still tender from the tomato picking and fighting, protested what they obviously felt was more abuse.

I stared at the door, trying to picture what was piled against it out there in the free world. The dresser? The bed? Both?

The hinges! The idea burst like an epiphany, and I was thoroughly impressed with my cleverness. I would take the hinges apart the way the painters did whenever my mother wanted the house painted. They slid the long round things out of the little round circles. I'd do the same, then pull the door loose and climb out.

But the thoughtless builder had put the hinges on the room side of the door, not my side.

All right. I'd just power the door down.

I rammed it with my shoulder a couple of times, astonished at how abruptly I bounced back. Rubbing my soon-to-be-black-and-blue shoulder, I quickly and decisively rejected physical force.

I think I realized then that I wasn't going to escape. I don't know how else to explain my screaming, pounding fit. When my fists were too sore to continue, I stopped my ridiculous behavior. Maybe later on tonight, when I might be more easily heard, I could try again, this time in conscious choice.

I sat cross-legged with my back against the wall. I looked at the Louis L'Amour and Max Brand books that had tumbled from the tote bag. *I need to introduce Mr. Geohagan to Steve Bly and Sigmund Brouwer,* I thought. Get him reading some Christian Westerns.

I picked up one of the paperbacks. I might as well pass the time profitably. If I thought of Mr. Edgars, my principal, storming up and down the halls looking for me, I'd only upset myself more. I glanced at my watch. I was already a half hour late.

Please, God! Let Mr. Edgars sound the alarm.

I glanced at the weak bulb on the ceiling and wondered how damaged my eyes would become reading in this dimness.

The light! No wonder the intruder had known exactly where I was. The glow must have shown around the edges of the door in the almost dark bedroom. Sighing at my stupidity, I began reading.

I understood that I was in the closet for the night when my second and third screaming and pounding fits brought no more response than my first—unless you counted a sore throat and tender, tender hands. My watch said one a.m.

I began to feel sorry for myself big time. Here I was, missing for the night, and no one cared enough to come and get me. Apparently, no one even missed me. I felt the tears rise.

I blinked them back. After all, I was a strong, modern, independent woman. So what that I was trapped, thirsty, hungry, and in need of a bathroom. So what that if I wanted to sleep, I would have to do so on the floor. Who cared that it was getting chillier all the time and that I had no covers and that I couldn't even stretch out all the way because the closet was too small. The pioneers had survived worse situations than this, and so would I. I was tough. I could take it.

Sighing, I turned out the light and lay on my back with a couple of Mr. Geohagan's shirts and his bathrobe over me for warmth and my knees bent so I would fit. I stuck a couple of the paperbacks under my head for a pillow. Every time I moved, I slipped off, thonking my skull on the floor.

"I want Clarke to come and rescue me," I said aloud into the darkness. Then I giggled. Where had *that* come from?

But I couldn't deny that the idea had a certain appeal. He could blast me free with an Uzi, something all Christian counselors keep hidden under their mattresses. Or he could push the offending furniture away and throw the door open while I huddled beguilingly on the top shelf, just waiting to be grasped by the waist and lowered tenderly to the floor.

Or he could loosen the hinges—they were on his side—and manhandle the door open, lifting me from my swoon (from lack of food and water, not fear) and carrying me to safety in his strong arms. Who cared that if he got to the hinges, he wouldn't need to do anything but pull the door open? Rescues demanded marvelous feats performed on behalf of the damsel in distress.

Obviously, being in the dark in small, closed places wasn't good for me.

Lord, I have the distinct feeling that this is one of those situations in which I have to choose. You saved me from potential physical harm earlier this evening, and I thank You most sincerely. But somehow this is the harder part, isn't it? Somehow sleeping in this dumb closet on this hard floor is going to develop me as a Christian —if I choose to let it. I can keep pitying myself, or I can just trust You.

I sighed. *I'll trust.*

I actually slept, my slumber interspersed with abrupt awakenings every time my head slid off the books.

In the morning I read the fourth Louis L'Amour book and prayed most thoroughly for everyone I had ever known when, at about nine o'clock, I heard someone enter the apartment. Then I heard a, "Hello? Is anyone here?"

"In here!" I pounded on the closet door. "I'm in here!"

"Don't worry! I'm coming," yelled a male voice which did not belong to my imagined hero. I had no idea whom it did belong to, but whoever he was, he was my new best friend.

There was much scraping and grunting, but finally the door of my prison opened, and a gray-haired policeman stood there, a middle-aged angel in blue. He was somewhat startled when I threw my arms around his neck and hugged him hard. Then I almost knocked him over in my rush for the bathroom.

"I'm all right. Truly I am," I said to Mr. Geohagan several hours later. I'd collected my purse, left untouched by the bed, given the police my statement, gone home and changed, and made my afternoon classes. Then, as soon as I could leave school, I drove to the hospital. "No scars, bumps, or bruises." He didn't need to know about my sore shoulder and fists.

"But you might have been badly hurt!"

I patted his thin hand as it lay on the covers, telling myself to remember to wash thoroughly before I left. The last thing I needed was hepatitis. "But I wasn't. I'm just sorry it was necessary for you to be informed."

"No one knew where I lived. They had to contact me so they'd know where to find you. I can't believe it took them until today!"

I made a wry face. "Me neither, but I understand how it happened. Last night Mary and Ruth assumed they'd just missed seeing me. John wouldn't have noticed whether I was there or not, and Jake would have been in his own apartment all evening. I think Mr. Edgars was quite angry with me when I didn't show for parents' night, but he assumed I was either sick or for some reason of my own had decided not to come. He planned to talk to me about it this morning when I came to work."

"Is he an understanding man, or should I write a note for you?"

"Dear Mr. Edgars, please excuse Kristie. She got locked in a closet?"

He grinned, and I was happy to see him smiling instead of fretting. "Beats 'The dog ate it.' "

"Anyway," I continued, "this morning Mary was very concerned when I didn't come down to breakfast. She finally checked my bed and, surprise, surprise, it hadn't been slept in. She made Jake call the school, and it became obvious as they talked that I hadn't been seen after I left the house last evening. Jake remembered I was going to your place, and he called the police."

"And they called me. Let me tell you, I thought

I was going to have another coronary. The news that you were okay was such a relief!"

I was touched by his concern.

"And you didn't see the thief?" he asked.

"Not a glimpse. The laughter I heard through the closet door was so deep that I'm certain it was a man, but that's all I know. I'm just sorry your apartment was ransacked. The man did a thorough job of it."

Mr. Geohagan shook his head. "I don't care about the apartment at all. It's only somewhere to sleep. It's not my home, my house. I lost the one when Cathleen died and Doris became sick, and sold the other not long after. I just couldn't stand being there anymore. There's nothing in that apartment I'd miss—except you."

My eyes misted. "That's so sweet." But I was struck again by the emptiness of his life.

Lord, I'm alone too. Don't let me ever have a life that barren. Please! And help me fill some of the holes in his life.

I handed him today's *Intelligencer Journal.*

"You were right," I said, pointing to page one. "Sick calls are indeed good copy, and now you're famous."

He looked at the front page picture of himself and Adam Hurlbert shaking hands. Hurlbert had health and vitality oozing from every pore. Even his toothy smile had vigor. Mr. Geohagan looked worse than ever by contrast. The black-

and-white picture drained what little color he had and left him looking cadaverous.

"How convenient for Adam that I chose this time to become ill," he said cynically.

"But not very convenient for you. You need to get better so you can get back to normal living. You've got all that stuff to do!"

"Nothing's normal about my life anymore," he said, his bitterness and self-pity kicking in with a vengeance. "My daughter's dead, my wife's had a stroke and doesn't even know me, and I'm sick, sick, sick!"

Forcing down my sympathy, I said, "To what do we owe your rousing good spirits? I'm the one who spent the night in the closet, not you."

To my surprise, Mr. Geohagan laughed. "Just like Cathleen. That slight touch of hauteur when upset. You're so good for me, Kristie."

I smiled. "I'm glad."

"You'd have liked her," Mr. Geohagan said. "She was a marvelous girl until—" He stopped abruptly.

"Until?" I prompted automatically, and then I regretted speaking for fear I'd overstepped my bounds. Though I reminded him of his daughter, I didn't have the right to pry into family business. When he finally began to speak, I was relieved.

"Until she became involved with a man. Isn't it always a man?"

I nodded obligingly.

"They had an affair. She moved out of our house and into an apartment of her own to facilitate matters. Then he dumped her, and she couldn't handle it. She began drinking and taking massive doses of relaxants that she got for a 'sore back.' One night she took too much of both." Mr. Geohagan sighed with utter desolation. "And I don't know if it was an accident or not."

My heart lurched. To not know whether your daughter committed suicide must be the only thing worse than knowing she did.

"Her mother and I found her, lying on the floor in the bathroom. Doris had become concerned because we hadn't heard from her for a few days and couldn't get her on the phone."

Mr. Geohagan stared out the window. "She was a fairy child, quick, happy, beautiful, born long after we despaired of having a baby. Even her teen years were joyous. She never had the traumas others had. Everyone loved her and she them—until the affair collapsed."

Mr. Geohagan folded and refolded his sheet, making linen accordion pleats. "Not that we minded the affair—at least not at first," he said, hastening to assure me that even it hadn't caused a rift in his marvelous relationship with his daughter. "The man was a fine man—we thought."

"You really didn't mind?" My father would have had a fit. Other women might live with some man, but not his daughters. Never his daughters.

Mr. Geohagan looked surprised. "Of course I didn't mind. It's not like she was sixteen. She was twenty-one, a woman. A wonderful woman. And I'll never forgive God for letting her die."

I started, not because what he said shocked me, but because he spoke the last sentence with such animosity.

Mr. Geohagan saw my expression. "My feelings toward God shock you, don't they?"

"Sadden me," I said, but he didn't hear.

"I have no use for God." The hard edge in his voice could have cut steel. "Where was He when Cathleen was hurting? When Doris had her stroke? No." He shook his head. "I have no time for a 'loving God' who would allow those things to happen."

He closed his eyes, his bitterness wrapped around him like a cloak about a freezing man. "Why don't you come see me the day after tomorrow?"

11

As the days passed, I found myself much preoccupied with concern for Mr. Geohagan and uncertainty about Todd.

I knew there was little I could do for Mr. Geohagan except pray for him and visit him whenever I could manage it. A few minutes of my time was a small price to pay for the smile he gave me when I entered his room and the gentle teasing I suffered at his hand.

"Why aren't you married?" he asked me one day. "You must have a secret flaw I haven't found yet."

"If I tell you, then it won't be a secret flaw any more," I answered with a cocky smile. "Once flaws leave hiding, they can't be put back, you know."

Nonplussed, he then took aim at my wardrobe. "Didn't you ever hear of good taste? That purple-and-pink thing you're wearing has a crooked front and the colors boggle the mind."

"It's not purple and pink," I protested. "It's mauve, lavender, and lilac. And it's not a thing; it's a sweater. It's also not crooked; it's called an asymmetrical opening. And, I'll have you know, I made it."

"I knew that. Certainly no store would sell it."
And he grinned.

"You are a mean old man."

I began to pray more and more that by my love
and concern I would show him the heart of the
God he was so angry at. I wanted his bitterness
to be lost in the embrace of God's love.

Todd was another story.

"If only he were a jerk," I told Hawk one late
September Friday evening as we sat together on
the front steps. Since the night in the closet, I
hadn't allowed myself to daydream about
Clarke, but the fact that I had once done so
threw my feelings for Todd into a starker light
than ever. "But he's so nice, and I don't want to
hurt him."

Hawk looked at me with his tongue lolling off
to one side. His eyes held sympathy for my
dilemma, though what he'd say if he knew Todd
had once called him mangy, I could only imagine.

"Do you often talk to dogs?"

I started and looked at Jake as he wheeled up
beside me. "Sheesh, guy! Do you always sneak
up on people? That's twice you've gotten me."

He grinned, clearly pleased with himself. "I've
been looking for one positive thing about this
chair. If sneaking is it, I'll take it."

I shook my head in mock indignation. "Yes, I
like talking to dogs. They never sass or complain,

and they always look so interested and intelligent. And they run right up to you, announcing themselves with barks and wiggles, not like some people I know. What more could I ask of a companion?"

Jake reached out to Hawk, and the dog immediately deserted me.

"Of course, faithfulness and loyalty might also be nice," I said.

Jake laughed and ran his hand gently over the dog's head. "Tell me, Hawk, what should I do with my life? What should Kristie do with hers?"

Hawk wagged his tail happily.

"Should I stay forever on this farm?" he asked. "Should she marry that Todd person? Give us your answers, please."

Hawk placed his forepaws on Jake's knees, raised himself, and licked Jake's face in great, moist swipes.

"What *are* you going to do with your life?" I asked as Hawk sank to the ground beside the wheelchair.

Jake shrugged.

"Come on," I encouraged him. "You cut in on my conversation with Hawk. Now you've got to answer. It's the rule."

"Right. One you just made up."

"My conversation. My rules. What do you want to do?"

He studied the field across the road. "My life may not seem very exciting to you, but it's safe and I like that. All I want is for it to stay the same."

"That's it?" I was disappointed. Where was the guy who didn't automatically buy into the way of life he was raised to, who rode motorcycles, and who claimed to have been a wild man? Had his rebellious spirit been broken along with his back?

He gave me a weary look and slapped the side of his chair. "Look where risk and excitement got me."

"And it's enough just to be safe?"

"For now, anyway. At the moment sitting around is all I feel like doing."

"But it's so passive, and you used to be so active."

He was studying the field across the road again. "In other words, I should get a life?"

"What did you do before the accident?"

"I worked in a trailer fabricating plant riveting the shells of travel trailers together. There's no way I can do that now. You have to be completely mobile."

"Okay, what else would you like to do?"

"I don't have any other skills. After all, I left school at fourteen."

"I've always thought the concession by the state that lets Amish kids leave school so young, in spite of the law that says sixteen is the minimum legal dropout age, is a mistake," I said.

"Most Amish kids don't go beyond eighth grade. They're supposed to go to Saturday morning classes for another year to study religion, but no one cares much if it doesn't happen. Of course, Mom and Father made us go. They always do everything the right way."

I knew I was the product of a family that had a lot of respect for education and its power and had instilled that mind-set in me. Still . . . "Eighth grade isn't enough education to manage in today's world."

Using his arms to raise and then lower himself, Jake shifted his weight. "My grandfather and great-grandfather were some of the Amish elders who went to jail in protest over the sixteen-years-old law. They felt the community should be able to set their own educational requirements."

"Interesting, and maybe it wasn't too bad when most everyone was still farming. But now, don't you agree that eighth grade is too little?"

"It didn't seem so when I was able to work at a job that required brawn over brains. Or I should say, over book learning. I worked for Father here on the farm until I was eighteen. Then I went to the plant. Much better money. When I turned twenty-one, I was allowed to keep all my salary for myself. I bought one of the trailers we made and parked it at the edge of some woods."

I listened to this obviously intelligent man and thought about the waste of a good mind. "Have you ever thought about getting a high school equivalency degree? It would allow you to find a better job or maybe even go to college."

"Amishmen don't go to college. Education makes you prideful."

I snorted. "You're about as Amish as I am. And since you can't climb around on the trailer shells anymore, you're going to have to depend on your mind."

"That's what Todd suggested."

I blinked. "Todd?"

"The last time he came out here, he brought me a book and some CDs from the Lancaster library. They're all about GEDs and how to get one. I spent a couple of hours reading and listening." He shrugged again. "It was interesting enough, and I do like learning stuff. Maybe I'll try it someday."

"Oh, I think you should," I said too enthusiastically.

Jake raised an eyebrow and I felt foolish. I sounded as though I were encouraging one of my less academically nimble school kids.

"Well, you should," I said more quietly.

"Maybe someday," he repeated. "I've got a new toy to keep me occupied for the time being." He pointed to the dark green Caravan in the drive. "I finally took my driver's test for hand-controlled driving. Andy and Zeke have been after me to do it for some time. Even Father encouraged me as a way of getting me involved in life again. Then Jon Clarke started on me too, and I finally got tired of fighting everyone. The same thing'll probably happen with the GED."

I stared at the van and wondered if Jake had always been so passive. Did he always need people pushing him, encouraging him, urging him on? Or was it a side effect of becoming disabled? Either way I was willing to be part of his cheering section if it would help him move forward.

But who was I to criticize? In my own way, I was just as passive, just as indecisive. I sighed.

"What's wrong?" Jake asked.

"Todd."

"What about him? He's losing interest? You're losing interest?"

"I don't know."

"Bad sign, Kristie. If he's the one for you, shouldn't you be certain? Shouldn't you *know?* Feel all lovey toward him?"

"I should, to all three."

"But you don't." Jake slanted me a thoughtful look. "He's an okay guy, if you want my opinion. Maybe a bit stuffy and more than a little opinionated, but nice enough in his own way."

That was Todd all right.

"The only thing is," and Jake became very serious, "maybe nice isn't enough to marry on."

All night that thought flowed through my mind. *"Maybe nice isn't enough to marry on."* When I pulled myself from bed at six thirty Saturday morning after a ragged night's sleep, it was the first thing I thought of. *Maybe nice isn't enough to marry on.*

I grabbed my robe and padded downstairs to the bathroom. As I walked through the kitchen, Mary and Ruth, already up for well over an hour, were finishing the breakfast cleanup. They were so cheerful I shuddered.

Maybe nice isn't enough to marry on.

I turned on the shower and let the hot water nudge me awake. I put Todd from my mind and thought again about the Amishman's wonderful ingenuity and expediency. An electric motor in the house to pump the water for the shower would be anti-*Ordnung*, so a water tank on high stilts stood outside the shed. The water was pumped to the tank by a waterwheel on the farm stream. From the tank it fell by gravity to the coal-fired water heater, was pumped by a battery-operated pump to the shower, and was therefore "legal" as it sprayed gently on me.

I quickly toweled myself dry and hurried upstairs to dress. The morning was brisk, forecasting colder days coming. Soon I'd be seeing my breath and longing for the comforts of central heating. I needed to talk to Jake about electric baseboard heat.

The big kitchen stove was still warm when I finally came down, so I scrambled myself an egg and enjoyed it with a cup of tea and some potato rusk Mary had baked yesterday.

By seven thirty Mary and I were in my car, ready to leave for the Bird-in-Hand farmers' market on 340. The back of the car was filled with jar upon jar of Mary's delicious preserved goods—chowchow, tomatoes, tomato juice, salsa, green beans, beets, pickles, pickled melon, and relishes. Two large boxes were filled with bags of homemade potato chips and breads.

Though the Bird-in-Hand farmers' market was neither the biggest nor best known in the area, it was good sized and convenient for Mary. We transferred all her goods from the car to a booth in the market and arranged them for sale. At eight thirty the doors opened, late for a farmers' market but early for the tourists who often visited it.

"Don't bother coming back for me," Mary said as she accepted money from her first customer. "I'll find a ride home."

I walked around the market, enjoying the sights and smells and sounds. The largest crowd stood patiently before the meat counter, waiting to buy fresh beef and pork products.

"I just love the ham loaf they sell. It has pork in it as well as ground ham," said a well-endowed woman with her sunglasses perched on top of her head.

The Mennonite woman standing beside her nodded. "We love the homemade sausage."

A pair of Amish women sat behind a display of handbraided rugs chatting in Pennsylvania Dutch as they waited for customers. When I stopped to admire their handiwork, they immediately switched to English.

"May we help you?"

I smiled and shook my head. As I turned away, the women picked up their Dutch conversation where they had dropped it.

It fascinated me that, though basically what most people (including me) would call undereducated, the Amish were trilingual. At home they spoke their Pennsylvania Dutch dialect, a form of German, *Deutsch* having somewhere through the years become *Dutch*. They spoke English to non-Amish, and used High German for religious and ceremonial occasions.

The Zooks, ever gracious, always spoke English in my presence, though on the occasions I had come home to find a house full of company, they had all been speaking Dutch. As Mary introduced me around, everyone spoke politely in English. However as soon as I moved on, the conversations reverted to Dutch.

I left the market and drove to the nearest Christian bookstore, spending time searching for new teaching ideas for kindergarten church. I was starting a month's teaching on the first Sunday in October, and I felt I hadn't planned my program very well yet in spite of the materials given me. Perfectionist that I was, I didn't like the unprepared feeling. I skimmed several books of ideas and programs and decided on three. Only one month serving but three books of ideas. Overkill as usual.

Just before I left, I went to the section where books on counseling and psychology were displayed. Clarke's book was there, prominently promoted under a sign that read "local author." To keep my promise, I bought one.

"Good book," the woman at the register said. "Nice man. My daughter has him for a class at Lancaster Bible College."

"Yes," I said. "He's a personal friend."

I smiled all the way to my car because the woman and her daughter liked Clarke. Stupid.

But Clarke wasn't my problem. Todd was. I was so glad I'd committed to helping Mary today since her usual ride to the market was away for the weekend. It was a ready excuse when Todd asked me to go with him to his family reunion. I flinched at the idea of being introduced to curious and hopeful relatives as "Todd's girl." In many ways he was my closest friend, but the problem was that he didn't want to be my friend, and I now recognized that I didn't want him to be anything else.

I spent the rest of the morning at Rockvale Outlet Mall just east of Lancaster City, wandering from store to store, buying an item here and there.

"Mom! It's my art teacher!" more than one dumbfounded kid whispered to a harried parent as I passed. There was something about seeing a teacher in the real world that undid kids. One of my most vocal and active six-year-olds stood in line behind me in one store, struck dumb and paralyzed as she held on to her mother's shirt. I smiled at the girl and said, "Hello, Hillary," but she didn't even blink.

"Thank you for being here," her mother said to me. "It's the first time she's been quiet all day."

In the lingerie outlet, I selected a slip with a great froth of lace at the hem. As I waited my turn at the cash register, I stood behind a young Amish girl about Ruth's age, lovely in her caped dress, apron, and head covering. She was buying a slip, panties, and padded bra in a brilliant shade of yellow. I couldn't help wonder whether she'd hang her purchases on the clothesline with the family's somber clothes, or if she'd keep them hidden from the eyes of the general populace, especially her mother and father. I suspected the latter. A little *rumspringa* rebellion, I decided.

On my way back to the farm I stopped at the Bird-in-Hand Bakery, surprised that with the swarm of tourists I actually found a parking place in their tiny lot. Before I went into the bakery, I climbed the stairs to the quilt shop on the second level. I loved looking at the fabric works of art. For many Amish women, quilting satisfied the need to create beautiful things, and quilts, of course, were acceptable because they were so functional.

I thought of Mary and her love of beauty and her artist's eye. I'd seen her yearning as she studied my painting of the barn. It occurred to me that while the creative urge was a broad human instinct, the way we wanted to create was highly individual. Quilting, as intricate and artistic as it could be, wouldn't satisfy me. I needed paint and brush, and I suspected that for her inner urge to be satisfied, Mary did too.

I wandered around, separating the great dowels on which the quilts hung so I could see the different patterns and color combinations more clearly. At one point I turned to see if the quilt I was studying really did match a pillow I'd seen earlier. I almost plowed into a man wearing a baseball cap standing behind me as he looked at quilted table runners.

"Sorry," I muttered as I stepped around him. He didn't acknowledge me; he just turned away to study the quilted hangings on the far wall. Poor man, dragged up here by his wife, probably trying to hold on to his patience. And fearful she'd want one of the big quilts with their big price tags.

I spotted some pretty postcards with paintings of quilts reproduced on them. They probably caught my eye because I was used to pictures of buggies against the sunset or in the morning mist. I studied the cards and then turned them over to read the credit on the back. Susie Riehl. A new name to me. The information said she was an Old Order Amish woman.

I blinked. An Old Order Amish woman who not only painted but had her work reproduced and sold? How fascinating and how very unusual. Did Mary know about this woman? Did she even realize another woman was doing what she so clearly yearned to do? I bought several of the cards to show her.

I went downstairs and bought a whoopie pie in the bakery. I loved those small chocolate cakes with white icing between. I got a diet soda to assuage my guilt over the whoopie pie's calories and sat in the car to eat and drink. The only thing missing was an Auntie Anne's pretzel. Auntie Anne, Anne Beiler, had been raised Amish in Lancaster County, though she'd left the People many years ago. If I was going to ruin my dinner appetite, I might as well do it big time.

I opened today's *Intelligencer Journal* as I

chewed and looked at the handsome, photogenic faces of Adam and Irene Hurlbert at a political gala the previous evening. With them was retiring United States Senator Vernon Poltor, smiling broadly in his support for Adam.

I was pleased. Each day it appeared more and more certain that the Hurlberts would be in Washington in a matter of weeks. One nice sidelight to Adam's election would be the passing from Lancaster of one Nelson Carmody Hurlbert, aged nine. All the more reason to vote in November.

As I drove slowly back to the farm, I saw a sign for a yard sale and a yard full of tables still littered with items. On a whim I pulled over and climbed out. I didn't expect to find anything because it was late enough in the morning that the true salers would have taken everything of genuine value.

But I fell in love the moment I spotted the red high-top Converse sneakers sitting beside an aqua vase with a pink rose twined about its base. The Chucks were barely worn, and they were my size. I shoved the two dollars in the woman's hand and ran before she decided she couldn't part with such a treasure.

I was wearing a pair of red walking shorts with a red-and-yellow knit top. I had on my matching red flip-flops, but I sat in the car and slipped them off. I slid the Chucks on and laced them up.

They were perfect.

"Perfectly ugly," my mother would say, and for the courtroom, she was correct. But for me on the farm, they were just right.

I pulled onto the road, driving around a car whose driver looked a lot like the guy back in the quilt shop. At least his cap did. He was studying some old 75 RPM records. *What a nice, patient husband,* I thought. Maybe if he didn't like the records, he'd like the pair of old baseball cleats beside the nesting mixing bowls so used that their original design was worn off.

I was almost back to the farm when a car backed hastily out of a driveway without checking for oncoming traffic. I stamped on my brakes and squealed to a stop, my front bumper inches from his back one. The young Amish driver, identifiable by his haircut and shirt, screeched off, never even looking my way. A second car followed none too gently, but its young Amish driver, his straw hat pushed back on his head, did remember to look before he roared into the street. He was obviously very unhappy.

With some surprise, I realized I was stopped in front of Aunt Betty Lou and Uncle Bud's house. As I waited for my heart to regain its normal rhythm after the close brush with a collision, I watched Clarke in the driveway talking with yet another Amish boy, who climbed into a third car and drove off after his companions. Clarke followed him down the drive to watch him on his way.

I lowered my window. "Whatever's going on?"

He walked over. "It's the Stoltzfus brothers. They all have cars and keep them hidden in the cornfields most of the time. At least they thought they were hidden." Clarke grinned. "Ammon Stoltzfus is nobody's fool, and he told his boys to get all the cars off the property. Church is at their house tomorrow, and he doesn't want anyone accidentally finding one."

"So they parked here?"

"And forgot to ask permission. I guess they figured that anyone with a long driveway wouldn't mind a few extra cars for a night or two. Unfortunately for them, Aunt Betty Lou happened to be looking out the window as they were parking. The boys seemed to have trouble understanding that she wants her drive free for her own guests this evening."

"Are they related to the Stoltzfus boy who was shunned? Jake's friend?"

"Cousins. Their uncle, Big Nate, would be very upset if he saw those cars. By the way, I've been trying to get hold of you."

I hoped my eyes didn't light up as obviously as I feared they did. "I've been shopping." I indicated my packages.

"So I see." He made believe he was counting

the packages. "And doing a thorough job of it too."

"You wanted to talk to me?" I said to divert his attention from my profligacy.

"Right. Aunt Betty Lou decided this morning that she'd like to have one last cookout as the summer fades into memory. She told me to invite someone, so . . . I know it's very last minute, but can you come to dinner?"

I was inordinately pleased. I hadn't seen Clarke to talk to since the tomato fight and had feared he wasn't interested in me at all, especially since he'd watched me leave for a date with Todd.

"I'd love to come," I said. "What time?" I thought of my new jeans lying in a bag on the backseat. I thought of my red V-neck shirt and the white camisole to go under it. I thought of a hairbrush and toothbrush, rouge and lipstick.

"How about six o'clock?"

"Plenty of time to make myself beautiful—or as close to it as possible."

"You look fine to me."

I looked up at him, astonished. "I didn't realize you had such a severe vision problem."

He grinned. "I'll walk down for you, okay?"

I nodded. When had I last felt a fluttering in my stomach over a date? I wasn't sure I'd ever felt it this badly.

"By the way," he said, "I love your sneakers."

I looked at my feet, resting on the floor of the car, astonished. "Really?"

"They make quite a statement. Be sure you wear them tonight."

I drove the short distance to the Zooks, examining the fact that Clarke liked my footwear. He didn't look askance. He didn't make snide comments about how ridiculous they were. He took them as the over-the-top fashion statement they were, no more, no less.

I could get used to such acceptance very easily.

12

I walked into the house to find that Mary still wasn't home from the farmers' market and Ruth was working with black permanent press fabric at the treadle sewing machine.

"What are you making?" Ever nosy, I walked over to see. I find anyone who makes something from scratch very impressive. The last time I had sewn was in a class in junior high. We had to make blouses, and mine somehow had sleeves of two different lengths and button holes that didn't match the placement of the buttons.

"It's a dress for Mom."

I wondered how they had decided it was time for Mary to have a new dress. The decision wasn't dependent on changing fashions, as many of my purchases were. The caped dresses had been the same forever. Well, slight exaggeration, but for a very, very long time.

Did you automatically make a new one every fall and spring, or did you wait until the old one got holes? Did you make a new one for an occasion like a wedding you were attending, or was that seen as prideful because you wanted to look your best? I decided that given amazing Amish frugality and practicality, holes got my vote.

"Careful you don't get lost in all the fabric," I teased. Ruth was such a tiny girl. Tiny, slim, and petite. I'd noticed that she was wearing her dresses with the hem at the knees, very daring for an Amish girl and a subtle sign of *rumspringa*. Mary's dresses reached well down her calf, almost to her ankles.

"Love your shoes," Ruth said with a smile.

I glanced down at my red Chucks and wiggled my toes. "Me too. I found them at a yard sale."

"I've got a girlfriend who would love them."

"Really?" Intriguing. An Amish girl in Converse high-tops?

"Rhoda Beiler."

"The one who almost fainted at the pretzel factory?"

Ruth nodded, looking around as if she were

checking for anyone listening. She leaned toward me and said softly, "Her running around has gone real wild. She wears jeans and smokes and goes to the hoedowns where they drink and some do drugs. She stays away all weekend with guys and listens to rock music on her iPod all the time. She went to a couple of rock concerts with some of the older kids, and now she wants to be a rock star."

An Amish rock star boggled the mind. "Does she play an instrument or sing?"

Ruth glanced around again. "She's taking guitar lessons. She got a raise at work and didn't tell her father. That way she can keep the extra money for lessons instead of turning it in to him like me."

"You give all your money to your father?" My dad might have tried to manage my life, but he never asked for any money I made, even when I was young. "Tithe some and save some," was all he said.

"I give Father most of it. Everyone does." She glanced toward Jake's doorway and said softly, "Jake's care has cost a fortune. If my little can help, I'm glad to give it."

I pulled a chair from the kitchen table and sat beside Ruth. "Jake didn't have health coverage on his job?"

"Some but not enough." She frowned. "Mom and Father worry about losing the farm. They don't think I know, but I do. Elam does too, and Jake."

"I thought since the Amish don't believe in insurance, they took care of their own." Though Jake wasn't really one of them, come to think of it.

"We do, and people have been very generous with their assistance. But every time we think things are paid off, something new happens or a new bill comes. Father doesn't like being such a burden to the church. He doesn't want to take so much because others need help too."

She picked at a loose piece of thread on the black fabric lying in her lap. "Father and Elam would be so miserable if we had to sell. And Jake would have extra guilt to carry. He knows his injury has changed all our lives, especially Mom's and Father's, and it hurts him. I think his guilt is more painful to him than his paralysis."

She must have seen skepticism on my face because she said, "People think Jake's a wild man with a hard heart, but that's not true. Sure, he was wild and now he's bitter, but he was never mean. He's a good man, Jake is. He worries because he's a financial burden."

I didn't think Mary and John or Jake would be happy with this discussion of the family finances. Apparently the same thought occurred to Ruth because she colored and turned away. "I shouldn't have said so much."

"It's all right."

She clasped her hands and closed her eyes as if she were praying, and maybe she was. "God will supply. He always does."

We sat quietly for a few minutes until she placed the material under the needle and lowered the presser foot. The machine whirred as she worked the treadle.

"So," I said when quiet returned, wanting our conversation to end on an innocuous note, "do you ever want to do something as wild as wearing red high-tops or playing in a rock band?"

Ruth rolled her eyes and shook her head vehemently. "Not me. I'm going to join the church sometime soon. I know it. I never wanted to do anything else. I'm not interested in cruising and boozing like Rhoda and some kids. I know they think I'm uncool because I enjoy the sings and the frolics, but that's okay. I think you should get baptized and join church and obey the *Ordnung*. It's God's way."

"How about Elam?" After all, there was that beer in the buggy the other night.

"He wants to be Amish too. Him and his friends like beer, but that's about as wild as he gets." She laughed. "His friends decided that if he could make root beer, he could make regular beer. He tried and gave me some to taste." She made a terrible face. "I think they dumped it all in the creek."

I had a sudden vision of tipsy cows.

"He wants to join church soon too," she said. "He's going to stay on the farm. It's what he wants. He likes the hard work. Some of his friends think he's crazy when he could go to a factory or do construction and work limited hours and make lots more money, but he loves farming and he loves the dairy herd. You should hear him talk to the cows. I think he's given all of them names, which Father thinks is stupider than beer." Ruth grinned.

I tried to picture Elam in the barn encouraging his girls to give more milk. *Come on, Josie. That's a girl, Maisie. I knew you could do it, Missy.*

"Some people think animals are just for using, not for caring," Ruth said, and I thought of the bad publicity over the Lancaster County puppy mills, many run by Amishmen. "Sure they're for using, but they depend on our care. Elam's a bit extreme, but it's a nice way to be."

I had to agree.

"Anyway," Ruth said, looking at my feet as black fabric cascaded over them, "Rhoda would love your sneakers. She keeps talking about her outfit for being on stage."

I laughed at the doubt I heard in that "on stage" comment. "You don't think she's going to be a star?"

"With six months of lessons? I don't know anything about rock bands, but I bet it takes a lot of learning and a lot of practice. She met some guys who have a band in a garage, and she thinks she's in love with the drummer." Ruth's hands stilled on the pins attaching a sleeve. "I'm afraid she's going to go so wild she won't find her way back."

She glanced out the window. "That would be very sad." She frowned, stood, and walked toward the window. "Someone just drove up to the barn in a big black car."

Todd dropping in for a visit? I made a face. That would complicate tonight. But his car was silver.

I stood, slid my chair back to the table, and went to the window. My blood congealed and I made a little gagging sound as my breath caught in my throat.

"What's wrong?" Ruth asked, all concern.

"It's my parents." I watched them climb from their car, identical looks of disbelief on their faces.

You should have told them, you idiot! You should have told them.

"That's so nice," Ruth said, heading back to the sewing machine. "You haven't seen them in a while, right?"

"Right." I went to the door and then outside to greet them. My stomach was churning acid like a washing machine agitated soapsuds.

"Hey, Mom, Dad." I hoped I sounded cheery and welcoming. "I must have missed the memo. I didn't realize you were coming."

"We wanted to surprise you," Dad said, staring into the black maw of the barn's door. A working dairy barn was quite a revelation to a fastidious man like him. Given the smell alone, he might never again drink milk.

"You surprised me all right." I gave him a hug and he absently hugged me back. He was too busy scowling at the buggy sitting beside the barn.

"Kristina," Mom hissed, all the while watching a pair of hens pecking in the yard as if afraid they were about to peck her eyes out. "Is this an Amish farm?"

I pumped up my smile. "Isn't it great?"

She blinked and turned horrified eyes to my father.

Even on Saturday, wearing chinos and a knit shirt, Dad looked what he was: Mr. Professional.

"You didn't tell us." His tone was accusatory.

I acknowledged that truth with a bob of my head.

"Why not?"

I cleared my throat. "Because I knew how you'd react."

"You knew we'd be appalled?" Mom asked.

"Yeah, something like that."

"And yet you did it?"

"Mom, I'm twenty-seven."

"And twenty-seven-year-olds shut out their parents?" Mixed with her shock and disapproval about my new home was a touch of hurt that they had found out about it in this manner.

Guilt sank its talons. In trying to protect myself from their disapproval, I'd caused them pain. I hadn't meant to. I thought they'd call before they came, and I'd tell them then. That way they'd only have to stew about it during the drive here, and I could hope they would be somewhat accepting of my crazy behavior by the time they arrived. *Best laid plans.*

I put my arms around my mother and kissed her cheek. "Come inside and see where I live. Meet the Zooks. Or at least Ruth. She's the only one home right now." And maybe Jake, but I wasn't going to bother him.

As we went inside, Ruth rose from the sewing machine. She looked adorable and otherworldly in her caped dress, darned apron, and *kapp*, her feet bare.

"Mom, Dad, this is Ruth."

Everyone greeted everyone, and then I said, a touch too brightly, "Ruth's making her mother a dress." I seemed to be in the if-they-see-how-much-I-like-it-here-they-won't-lecture-me mode.

"Do you make all your clothes?" Mom asked, interested in spite of herself. I knew for a fact that sewing a button on one of Dad's shirts stretched her needlework abilities to the hilt. Like mother, like daughter.

"Our dresses. Everyone's jackets and coats. Sometimes Mom makes shirts, but it's easier to buy them ready-made."

Mom looked suitably impressed, but whether by the making of coats or the buying of shirts I wasn't sure.

"I'm going to show Mom and Dad my rooms," I said as I led the way upstairs. I was very conscious of my red Chucks as I climbed, Mom right behind me, Dad bringing up the rear. I wasn't certain which they would consider worse, my living on an Amish farm or my being gauche enough to wear such foolish footwear.

We stepped into my living room with its desk and overstuffed chairs, and I watched my parents as they took it all in. Big Bird gave a little chirp of greeting, as if on cue.

I thought the place looked homey and comfortable with the plants at the windows and the papers and laptop cluttering my desk, but I knew that after their luxurious and spacious home, this looked small and spartan to them.

"Don't they believe in curtains?" Mom whispered, looking back over her shoulder as if she expected to see Ruth coming through the door.

"No, they don't. I could probably get some if I wanted—they don't ask me to conform to their austerity—but I won't."

"But you have a TV," Dad said.

Long story, Dad, I thought, but I decided not to tell it. "I have electricity."

"I thought they didn't believe in electricity." He stooped to look at an outlet as if he expected it to be merely an illusion.

"We're in the *grossdawdy haus*," I said, and then I explained about Jake. "So he's my landlord."

"Why didn't they shun him?" Dad asked. "Don't they shun people who break their rules?"

"He was never baptized and he never joined the church. They don't have to shun him."

"But he was raised Amish."

"He was, but until you join the church as an adult with knowledge of the choice and commitment you're making, you aren't held accountable."

"Sort of like informed consent?"

I nodded. "They know they're counterculture, and they know agreeing to be bound by the *Ordnung* is possible only when you know what you're willingly turning your back on."

Mom picked up the green-and-blue chenille afghan tossed over one of the chairs. "This is lovely, Kristina."

"Mary made it," I said. "She's the mom. She's selling homemade canned goods at the farmers' market."

"She's very talented."

"She is. Come see the rest of the place." I led them into my bedroom and thought again how welcoming it looked. I noted that a fresh dahlia was in my little vase.

"Beautiful quilt."

"I think I'll need it as the weather gets cooler."

"Just crank up the heat." Dad frowned. "Or don't they have central heating?"

I shook my head.

"Bathroom?" Mom said. "Kitchen?"

"Downstairs."

"Communal?" There was that appalled expression again.

I nodded.

They merely looked at me.

"Donald," Mom finally managed. "They gave us the wrong baby at the hospital. I've long suspected this, but now I'm sure. Not that this cuckoo in our nest isn't lovely and sweet, but she *can't* be ours. And as if this weren't bad enough," she indicated my rooms with her hand, "just look at her footwear!"

We all stared at my high-tops.

"They match my shorts," I offered lamely.

Mom, in her sleek navy slacks and her soft rose blouse, discreet gold studs in her ears and a diamond on her third finger faceted to blind people when the sun caught it, merely looked at me and sighed.

We wandered back into my living room, where

they each took a chair and I sat on my desk, Chuck-clad feet dangling.

"I love it here," I ventured. "The Zooks are wonderful, and they have been very gracious to me."

They nodded and seemed to be waiting for more. The only trouble was, I didn't know what more was. Where did I go after *I love it?*

Finally Mom said, "But why? You had such a nice apartment."

"Because I wanted to?"

Dad raised his eyebrow. "That's it? You wanted to?"

I thought that was a very fine reason. "Yeah."

"Not because it's cheaper or because you expected to learn interesting sociological information?"

Mom suddenly looked horrified. She actually gasped. "You aren't becoming Amish?"

I smiled. "I don't think my high-tops would go with a caped dress, Mom."

She sighed with relief.

"Then why?" Dad asked. "Explain it so we can understand, Kristina, because right now it seems like one of your more foolish actions."

Like giving up the law for putting colored water on paper.

I hesitated. After Todd's reaction when I tried to explain my reasons, ones that seemed eminently sound and sensible to me, I was wary. "I wanted to soak up the atmosphere. I wanted to experience the ambiance. I wanted to *paint*."

Dad looked at Mom. "Atmosphere. Ambiance."

She nodded. "Paint."

All at once I was angry. I thought the Amish community was wrong to deny someone like Mary the opportunity to use the talent God had given her, but she chose to put herself under their oversight and accept their ruling. However, I wasn't Amish. I was an independent woman free to make my own choices, and I wasn't going to let my parents make me feel the way the church made Mary feel.

I jumped off the desk and stood facing them, feet planted and hands on hips.

"Enough," I said. "Enough! So you wouldn't choose to live on an Amish farm—"

"You've got that right," my father muttered.

"—but I do. It is neither wrong nor illegal. It's neither immoral nor unethical. It's merely a choice. So you wouldn't live here. Fine. Am I mocking you because you think differently than I? No, I am not. I would appreciate it if you didn't mock me." I felt tears gather in my eyes and blinked furiously. "Just accept I'm your friendly, loving cuckoo and let your dreams and your wishes for me *go*."

Mom started to protest, but I held up my hand to stop her.

"I hate that I was afraid to tell you what I was doing. I knew you'd think me an idiot. I knew you'd roll your eyes and look at each other with that poor-child look. I knew I'd end up feeling sick to my stomach because I'd failed you *again*. And all because I just want to be the me God made me!"

Mom and Dad stared, aghast at my outburst. I was pretty aghast myself. This was so unlike me. I let my hands fall to my sides and took a deep breath. Silence ricocheted about the room, deafening us all.

I walked to the window and stared blindly out while I tried to gather myself. I had no idea what to say, and for once Mom and Dad seemed struck as dumb as I.

I loved my parents. I respected them. They loved me. I didn't doubt that. I did doubt their respect, and I knew there was little understanding. So what should I do? Yell every time I saw them? Fracture our relationship further? I cleared my throat self-consciously and turned.

"Come on. Let's go get some lunch, and then I'll take you to the farmers' market."

"Right, right," Dad said, standing.

"Wonderful," Mom said with a strained smile.

And we all clomped down the stairs, happy to leave my strong words behind.

Our lunch was polite and genial . . . but when they left to go home, nothing was resolved. No surprise there. In their minds I would be forever their little cuckoo.

13

Clarke walked down to pick me up just as he'd said. He looked great in jeans and a long-sleeved deep green T-shirt. I'd traded my walking shorts for jeans, but I had on my Chucks, not just because he'd asked me to wear them, but because they matched my top. Or so I told myself.

We walked up the road, enjoying the golden glow of the October evening. The first subtle signs of autumn were evident in the wild bittersweet berries beginning to pop their golden jackets to reveal their orange undershirts and in the crimson leaves now dressing the dogwood and the fire bushes. We stopped by a patch of jewelweed, the yellow flowers cheery and the seedpods fat and ready to burst. We touched the seedpods with gentle fingers and, laughing, watched them explode, curling on themselves and shooting seeds everywhere.

Somehow, by the time we got to Aunt Betty Lou's, we were holding hands. I found his touch to be unexpectedly intoxicating. It was all I could do not to burst into song.

Dinner was delicious, the company more than pleasant, and Clarke attentive. Not look-at-my-girl-isn't-she-wonderful attentive, but still enough to make the evening a delight.

When we left to walk back to the Zooks', I discovered another not-too-subtle sign of fall. It was chilly, and I had neglected to bring a sweater. When I shivered, Clarke couldn't help but notice.

"Let's get you a jacket," he said and led the way to the garage.

"You've got a jacket in your car?"

He shook his head and pointed. "My apartment's over the garage."

We climbed the outside stairs and he held the door for me. I looked with interest around his living room as he went to get something for me to slip on.

Neat but beige-bland. A man's apartment.

Until I turned and my breath was taken away.

Clarke, coming into the room with a navy fleece jacket in his hands, heard my audible gasp and came up behind me and put his hands on my shoulders.

"I thought that seemed like the best place for it. Do you think it looks okay hanging over the sofa?"

It was my painting, the one bright splash of color in the monochromatic room. In it the Victorian front porch held several fat white planters with geraniums and ivy tumbling from them. A pair of black-and-white cats lay sleeping on a wicker chair and a third, a fat, fluffy gray, sat on the top step grooming himself. A red door with a large brass knocker blazed in the otherwise subtle background.

I couldn't contain my delight. "I can't believe it! You shouldn't have! But I'm so glad you did!"

"We said we'd each help the other along by buying the other's work. I only kept our bargain. After all, you already had my book."

"Well, sure. And I bought another one. But I know how much this picture cost! There's no comparison."

He shrugged. "You can always go buy lots more of the book and even us out. I certainly won't stop you."

I spun around and hugged him. "Thank you so much! You don't know what a wonderful gift you've given me."

"Will you hug me like this every time I give you a present?" he asked as he hugged me back. "Or is this only for paintings?"

Anytime, I wanted to say. Anytime at all, gift or no gift.

Instead I unwrapped my arms and turned back to look at the painting. It was just too comfortable with my cheek against his chest. Too intimate. But he kept his arms around me, and I leaned back against him, liking very much the sturdy feel of him behind me.

"Do you know, I've never seen my work on anyone's wall unless I've given the thing as a gift," I said.

"You will. Just give it time. I'm not an art expert by any means—"

"But you know what you like?" I finished.

He laughed. "Well, I do, but I was going to say that you have a very fine sense of color and composition. People will find your work easy to live with."

I sighed with pleasure, and he kissed the top of my head.

He gave me the navy jacket to slip on for the walk home. It fit somewhat—after we rolled the sleeves up a few times.

"You're a skinny little thing," he said as he pulled on his own jacket.

"Is that good or bad? Not that I can do much about it either way."

His look from under those dark brows made my breath catch in my throat. "I think you're wonderful just the way you are, skinny, colorful, and charming. I can't imagine you being any more lovely."

Wow!

"So," I said, his shoulder bumping mine as we walked, "how did you come to be involved in counseling?"

"It was no great moment of calling, of God's voice in my ear. It was more a matter of getting a sense of what the Word of God can do for a person and wanting others to find the same help there I did. Look." He pointed skyward. "There's the Big Dipper and Orion."

Not to be outdone, I nodded and said, "And there's the Pleiades, the seven sisters, though you can only see six stars. The seventh seems to have disappeared. The seven daughters of Atlas, put there by Zeus."

Clarke stopped and looked at me.

I grinned. "Don't be impressed. I've just blown all my knowledge of things astronomical. I had to do a report once in high school on the constellation Taurus, which the Pleiades are part of."

"Whew," he said as we resumed walking. "You had me worried. I thought you might be an astronomer as well as an artist."

I laughed at the absurdity of the idea of me and anything scientific.

"Tell me more about how you became a counselor," I said. "I want to know what made you find such help in the Bible that it led to your life's calling."

He glanced at the sky again. "I already told you about the two years Mom and Dad spent in South America."

I nodded.

"What I didn't mention was how betrayed I felt when they decided to go. It was my junior and senior years in high school, and I took the move as a personal affront and a deliberate decision to make me miserable. I saw them as ruining my life, and I wasn't the least bit hesitant in telling them." He looked at me. "It's still embarrassing to realize how selfish and petty I was."

I shrugged. "It's the age. So what happened?"

"I refused to go with them, threatening to run away or join the army, both of which would take me away from home if I'd thought about it, which I didn't. I even went by the army recruiting office and collected information, which I left lying around so they could see how serious I was."

I tried to imagine him at sixteen or seventeen, those dark brows in a perpetual frown. At the same age I was Little Miss Compliant, only half living in my desire to please Mom and Dad. Sometimes it was definitely better to meet someone when you and he were older and some of the worst wrinkles had been ironed from sin-crumpled personalities.

"Obviously, my parents wouldn't leave me in Los Angeles alone, though I was convinced I could take care of myself—as long as they gave me a good-sized allowance, of course. Instead they gave me the option of living with Aunt Betty Lou and Uncle Bud, something I hardly saw as an improvement over Brazil. I chose here because at least I knew the language."

I thought of atmosphere, ambience, and

painting, my rationale for choosing here. "Language sounds reasonable to me."

He brushed at a stray mosquito and continued. "At first I was so mad at God I must have been a festering thorn in everyone's side, but my aunt and uncle were gracious. I found myself going to church and youth group regularly because in their house there wasn't a choice. Gradually, God and His love broke through my hurt, and I committed my life to Him. After all, who else cared about me?"

Probably every girl in his class. "You poor boy."

"I know. Like I said, selfish. When I thought about Mom and Dad, it was, 'Well, God, at least *You* love me.' Then one morning I was reading my Bible and found the verse where Paul says he has learned to be content whatever the circumstances. In one of those 'aha' moments I realized I had to choose. I could stay mad at my father, who in my mind put a career move before me, and my mother, who supported that move, or I could learn to be content in quiet, provincial Bird-in-Hand, hardly the exciting place Los Angeles had been." He grinned at me. "I decided to stop fighting things and try to learn to be content. It didn't happen right away, but by my senior year, I was happy here in Bird-in-Hand."

"And that change happened from reading the Bible?"

"It's full of practical advice that, when taken seriously, makes a huge difference. That's what I want to show people."

We climbed the front stairs at the Zooks' and turned to face each other.

"So you're more like an engineer, big on application, than a scientist, who's big on theory," I said as I slipped out of his jacket and handed it to him.

He laughed. "I never heard anyone put it that way before, but that's about it. A theological engineer."

Then he cupped the side of my face. "Good night, Kristie. I couldn't have asked for a better evening."

I floated upstairs.

It wasn't until the next morning that I realized Clarke hadn't said anything about a repeat date. *Well, rats.* That brought me down to earth fast enough and filled me with regret. And the two weeks that passed without a call or a visit tempered my disappointment with a needed dash of reality. One evening did not a deathless romance make.

Well, if I wasn't seeing the man, I could at least read his book. Somehow that made me feel closer to him, especially when I read things that sounded like a continuation of our conversation.

Learning contentment is often coming to the realization that some circumstances are changeable and some aren't. Contentment is partially found in learning to tell the difference.

I laughed as I read his account of his parents going to Brazil and his anger and eventual learning of contentment.

Part of what allowed me to be happy was realizing that I had two choices. I could go to Brazil or I could stay in Bird-in-Hand. No matter how much I wanted to, I couldn't stay in Los Angeles. I was not given that option. Of course, I could have run away or joined the army, but that's called cutting off your nose to spite your face. I might have been young and foolish, but I knew neither was a true choice for me.

So we must each ask ourselves this: Can I choose to change my circumstances or are they beyond my ability to change?

If I'm unhappy with my car, I may be able to buy a new one. I can choose to change my situation. If I'm unhappy with my children, I can't trade them in. I cannot deny the genetic strands hidden in their bodies.

I realize these are extreme examples, but the principle holds: Some situations are changeable; some are not.

"But I deserve better," you say.

I deserve a better home/house.

I deserve decent neighbors.

I deserve a church that feeds me.

I deserve to be understood.

That last line was me. Didn't I deserve parents who understood me? Or at least accepted me?

When what you have and what you deserve aren't a match, your response to this less-than-perfect situation is your choice. You can be hurt and bitter. You can withdraw. You can become sharp of tongue and manner.

Or you can give up the need to get what you deserve.

Give up the need to be understood? Accepted? Just like that? I shut the book, not wanting to read his too-facile thoughts. I felt as if the depth of my hurt had been devalued. Suddenly I wasn't as upset about Clarke's silence as I'd been five minutes ago.

I managed to be mad at him a whole hour, not that he knew or even cared.

● ● ●

The third Sunday of my stint in kindergarten church I went to early service, and then I taught the kids. I'd enjoyed my morning with them in spite of the fact that today they raised wiggly to a whole new level. I was exhausted when they raced into their parents' arms and were borne away.

I lingered as long as I could afterward, straightening up already neat shelves of supplies, arranging toys in orderly rows. Still, when I walked outside, Todd was waiting for me in the parking lot. My stomach cramped at the sight of him and his I'm-so-glad-to-see-you smile.

Even before the dinner with Clarke at Aunt Betty Lou's, I'd known it was only a matter of time with Todd. Reading *It's Up to You* had confirmed what I'd already realized. Here was a circumstance I could change, *must* change in fairness to Todd. I couldn't jettison Mom and Dad for their lack of acceptance, nor did I want to, but I could release Todd. I just had to be strong enough. I shuddered.

I knew there was a good chance that Clarke would never call me, that he'd just been as caught by the magic of the evening as I, nothing more. With me, the magic lingered. With him, it seemed not. Much as I might want to, I couldn't control his choices. Common sense told me an incredible romance was not about to replace this lukewarm one with Todd.

Still, I knew what I had to do. Coward that I was, I just didn't want to do it.

Lord, I called silently as I stood in the church parking lot looking into the smiling face of this man who would be my love. *The right words? Please?*

"Hey, Kristie. How were the little devils this morning?"

"Fine."

"I envied them, spending that time with you while I had to sit alone in church. Where shall we go to eat?"

I clutched my papers and workbooks to my chest and studied the toes of my navy flats.

"Kristie?" Todd's voice became uncertain. He had sensed my hesitation. "What's wrong?"

I took a deep breath. I hated times like this! "No, Todd."

He touched my arm. I looked up and saw confusion and something else—fear?—in his face.

"No, what?" he asked. "No, you have other plans? No, we can't do anything today?"

"No to both." I forced my eyes to stay steady on his. "No, I have no other plans, and no, not today."

He looked at me silently, thoughtfully, sadly. "Tomorrow? Next weekend?"

I shook my head.

"Ever again?"

My eyes fell before the pain in his. I whispered, "No," as I leaned against my yellow car for support. I felt like an airline official telling waiting relatives there were no survivors.

"Why?" Todd asked. "What happened? What have I done?"

I shivered. This was every bit as bad as I'd feared, and my voice shook as I answered.

"You haven't done anything, Todd. You're a very nice guy. I like you a lot, but—" How could I explain something I could barely articulate to myself? I cleared my throat and tried anyway.

"I know you care for me. Or you care for who you think I could or should be, but I'm not who you want me to be. I'm just me, and I can't be anyone else. I don't want to be anyone else. And too much about me—my weaknesses and peculiarities and independent spirit—bothers you too much."

"But—" he interrupted, the lawyer in him ready to argue.

I plowed on. "It's not sensible to continue a relationship where there is such a clash of personalities. And that's the way it is with us, whether you admit it or not. I want someone who will accept me the way I am—painting, yellow car, Amish farm, and all. I want someone who doesn't get embarrassed when I burst into song. And you . . . you need someone who will cherish your guidance, not bristle under it."

I watched his eyes widen in denial and silently entreated him to understand what I was trying to say.

He studied my face intently, making me feel like a sloppy Marine at inspection.

"Jon Clarke," he finally said. "It's him, isn't it? Don't think I haven't noticed how he watches you."

He does? He watches me? My heart soared, but I forced myself not to show my elation.

"And don't think," Todd continued, "that I'm unaware that he took you to dinner at his aunt and uncle's."

Oops. Word certainly got around.

He turned and leaned against the car next to me, as if he couldn't look at me anymore. It hurt too much.

"And you know what?" He ran his hand through his curls. "I can't even get mad at him or you because I like him too. Always have, from back when he finished high school here."

He looked at me, disarranged curls sproinging, eyes sad. "It *is* Jon Clarke, isn't it?"

I blinked. "No . . . yes . . . I don't know," I stammered. "I honestly don't. But I wouldn't be thinking about him at all if I loved you the way you want me to."

"Maybe you just haven't given us enough time."

Talk about grasping at straws. I shook my

head. "No. I think two years is more than enough time."

"Kristie, please—"

"No. Because you don't really love me, Todd. At least, not the *real* me. I'm sorry." I smiled weakly, turned, and fumbled my way to my car.

Only when I began to back from my parking place did he rouse himself. He walked away slowly, shoulders drooping. I felt so guilty!

But the guilt at being a heartless heartbreaker didn't last long. By the time I reached the farm, I felt marvelous, so light and unencumbered. I truly felt bad about hurting Todd, but I was so sure I was right that I felt butterfly free.

As I changed into old jeans and pulled my mauve, lavender, and lilac sweater over my mauve shirt, I sang snatches of whatever came to mind, changing the lyrics to fit my mood. I was glad no one was home but me. I could rejoice as loudly as I pleased.

Glory, glory, hallelujah.
Glory, glory, hallelujah.
Glory, glory, hallelujah!
I'm free! I'm free! I'm free.

I took the mysterious key from my bureau and slipped it in the pocket of my jeans. Maybe today was the day I could take charge everywhere. Maybe I'd visit Mr. Geohagan and make him take the key back whether he wanted to or not.

Fat chance. I'd probably be carrying the thing around when I was an old lady and he a wizened, desiccated mummy. Still, I had more than enough to sing about as I puttered around Mary's empty kitchen making some lunch.

"I'd say you were having a good day," Jake said from his doorway. "You've been singing like a demented bird."

"Jake! You're sneaking again. And I *am* having a wonderful day! I made a momentous decision, and I'm relieved, relieved, relieved!" I threw my arms wide and spun in a circle.

"So what happened?" he asked. "You quit your job? No, you like that. You're getting married?" He shook his head. "I don't think that special someone's asked you yet. You hit it big in the lottery?" He wheeled across the room, and I poured him a Coke.

"Need a sandwich?" I asked.

"No, thanks. You sold a painting?"

"Did I tell you Clarke bought one?"

"Several times. Has another been sold?"

"Don't I wish. You'll never guess. I said farewell to my 'good friend' Todd."

Jake looked at me with a smug smile. "I knew it all along."

"Sure you did."

"Well, let's say I *hoped* it all along. I like Jon Clarke too."

I put up my hand. "No conclusion-jumping, please. Clarke and I are merely good friends."

"Hmm. And you're hard on good friends. I'd better warn him."

I put away the lunch things and tidied up the kitchen. I wouldn't want Mary to find it different than she'd left it.

"Want to go for a ride?" Jake pointed to his van in the drive. "I'm going whether you come or not, but it'd be fun to have company."

I accepted readily. "This is freedom day. We'll celebrate my release and your independence."

As we settled in the van Jake said, "I can't tell you how good it feels to drive again, to take myself somewhere instead of being taken. I'm so glad your rent payment makes payments on this possible."

His hands were steady and certain on the controls, and he hummed tunelessly as he drove. I leaned back in my seat and watched the glory of autumn in the golden oaks and brilliant sugar maples.

Jake blew his horn suddenly and waved.

"Aunt Naomi's," he explained. "That's where Mom and Father and Elam are visiting."

"You didn't want to go?"

"I feel uncomfortable when it's meeting Sunday and I know everyone's thinking that I wasn't there and should have been."

I could understand that. "Where's Ruth?"

"She and Isaiah went away for the weekend."

"Isaiah?"

"Isaiah Beiler, her boyfriend."

Away for the weekend? "Rhoda's brother?"

"A distant cousin. I think they're going to get married."

"I thought boyfriends were kept secret until the engagement was announced."

"Sometimes, and sometimes it's like Ruth and Isaiah. They've been going together for two years. How can you hide that when everybody in the group knows everybody else?"

I smiled at a tangle of goldenrod and milk-weed growing at the road's edge. "So, where did Ruth and Isaiah go?"

"To the Poconos with Dan Beiler, Isaiah's brother, and his girlfriend."

"Is Dan English so he can drive them?"

Jake smiled crookedly. "No, he's Amish. He just hasn't joined the church yet. He keeps his car in a rented garage in town."

"And Isaiah?"

"I predict he joins this fall."

"Just like Ruth and Elam?"

"You have to join to get married."

"Elam's getting married? I didn't even know he had a girl!"

"He doesn't. Just Ruth and Isaiah. Up till now

Isaiah's stayed free of church discipline. He's always intended to be Amish. He's just been enjoying his *rumspringa*, usually with my sister."

"Oh, Jake, surely not!" I was appalled at the implications of his comment.

"Oh, yes. Last fall Isaiah drove when they rented a trailer and took a long trip to New England."

"Just Isaiah and Ruth?"

"And Joe Lapp and his girl."

I was stunned. "And your parents let her go?"

"You can be certain that Mom and Father don't like these little jaunts—and the frequent overnights—but they're afraid that if they make a fuss, they'll lose her like they did Andy and Zeke and me."

Jake smiled at my consternation and confusion. "You have to remember, Kristie, that there are two types of Amishmen, religious and cultural. My parents are religious Amish. They love God and believe the church's teachings. They live by the *Ordnung* because they believe it's the avenue to eternal life, and they want eternal life."

I nodded as we drove past six barrel-chested workhorses placidly eating grass in a field.

He continued. "Ruth and Isaiah are Amish because that's the life they've been raised to live. Their families and friends live that way, so they do too. But the outer form has no inner significance. Can you understand that?"

"Sure," I said. "There are people like your parents and people like Ruth and Isaiah in my church too. Even the Bible talks about people who have the form of faith but not the substance."

Jake nodded, relieved that I understood.

"What about Elam?" I asked. I liked this intense young man.

"For a while I thought he was doing what he thought he had to do to please Father, but lately I've begun to think he's becoming a religious Amishman. He drinks some, but basically I'd say he's very moral. He seems to be looking for more than the outer trappings. I've even found him reading the Bible, something many Amish consider radical. And in English, no less! He said he wanted to understand it."

"Reading the Bible is radical and unusual?"

Jake looked at me. "Sure. Especially in English. Interesting group, my people, aren't they? Their major consistency is inconsistency."

"Well, what about you, Jake? Where do you see yourself?"

His voice turned melancholy. "I think I feel in between. I'm not Amish, but I'm not a Christian like you and Jon Clarke. I'm not sick with germs and all, but I'm not well. I'm not ignorant or dumb, but I'm not educated. I'm in between —and it's a very lonely place to be."

On this somber note, we arrived back at the farm.

"You go on in," he said. "I'm going to stay out here and feel sorry for myself for a while."

"Jake, don't—"

"See you, Kristie." It was dismissal.

As I climbed reluctantly out of the van, he turned the radio to a rock station and adjusted the volume to a level guaranteed to damage his hearing. The sound followed me into the house, muted only when I closed the door.

I told myself that the worst thing I could do for Jake was to pity him, but I found myself doing exactly that as I crossed the great room and started up the stairs. I was so lost in thought that I misjudged my step, stubbing my toe and barking my shin.

"Drat!" I said as I rubbed the painful areas.

Immediately a loud crash sounded upstairs, and Big Bird began to squawk. Simultaneously heavy footfalls slapped across the floor.

I froze in surprise and fear, memories of that night at Mr. Geohagan's crowding in. My eyes were on the door to my living space. No one was even supposed to be in the house, let alone in my rooms.

Suddenly a man I'd never seen before burst into view and stared menacingly down the stairs at me.

My stomach lurched. He was big! And he

looked so threatening with his Braves baseball cap pulled down over his forehead and his gloved fists balled.

He never hesitated. "Out of my way, girl!" he yelled and charged straight at me.

I screamed and the sound ricocheted off the walls. There was no room in the narrow stairwell for him to pass me. We were going to collide, and such a collision seemed to be his intended purpose as he raced directly at me.

I have no recollection of being pushed or falling, but given my skinny body and his considerable bulk, I must have gone flying. Suddenly I was lying in a heap at the base of the stairs as the man climbed none too gently over me. I'm sure he wasn't wearing hobnailed boots, but it certainly felt like it. I put my hands to my face and curled into a ball to protect myself. I stayed that way until I heard the front door open and the man race across the porch.

I uncurled cautiously and looked outside, and then I breathed a great sigh as I confirmed that he was truly gone. Slowly I pulled myself up and limped to the door. I must have hit my hip on the stairs as I fell; it was already stiff. Or maybe he kicked me as he passed. Sore toe, scraped shin, and bruised hip. Not bad for less than one minute of time.

I was uncertain what to do. I could call the police, but somehow the idea of the police at

Mary and John's house was unthinkable. Flashing lights and guns just didn't fit here. In fact, this peaceful Amish farm made the violence of the big man and my feelings of violation all the more intense.

I closed my eyes and tried to picture the intruder. Nothing. All I saw was a big man, a terrifying man, rushing at me. The only thing I was certain of was that he wasn't Amish, and I didn't even know why I was so sure of that fact beyond the baseball cap.

I stepped cautiously outside. No one was visible but Jake, sitting in his van with his back to the house, lost in his music. There were no cars or people on the road, and I wondered where Hawk was. There was never a biting dog around when you needed one.

I limped to the far end of the porch and peered through the wisteria vine. A bulky figure in a baseball cap was running through the corn stubble toward the Stoltzfus farm. It was my giant of an intruder, looking oddly small in the distance.

Well, at least he was gone. I limped back into the house, rubbing my sore hip.

"Quiet down, Big Bird," I called. "I'm coming."

I went upstairs one step at a time and found my room almost the way I'd left it except for my philodendron lying on the floor in a tangle of leaves, soil, and pottery shards. That must have been the loud crash I'd heard. I'd been afraid it was Big Bird and his cage. My clothing on the pegs was askew, the items on my night table slightly awry, my bureau top rearranged but nothing seemed harmed. I checked carefully, but I could find nothing missing.

It wasn't until I began cleaning up the plant that I discovered my cell phone under the mess, its casing cracked and dirt lodged in every crevice. I sighed. I wouldn't be talking to anyone on it ever again.

"In fact," I said to Jake later as I stood beside the van, "I can't think of a reason why anyone would try and rob the farm. This isn't a place where there's money, is it?"

Jake shook his head. "Father keeps all his money in the bank. He's very smart financially, and he'd never leave anything lying around. Your TV's still there?"

I nodded.

"Let me check the rest of the house to see if anything's gone. I've got several electronic things I'd hate to lose." He pushed the proper buttons and lowered his chair to the ground.

"Why would anyone risk coming here in the middle of the afternoon?" I asked as I walked to the house with him. I found I didn't want to be alone.

"Think about most Sunday afternoons, Kristie. Mom and Father visit family. You're out with Todd. No one's here but me, and I'm no great threat. Conveniently, even I went out today. If you look at it from the least chance of being caught, Sunday afternoon's it."

"But why take the risk at all?"

Jake shook his head. "We have little to steal, that's for sure. How about you? You're not keeping a stash of valuable jewels up there, are you? He was in your room."

I grinned weakly. "Only the few diamonds and rubies I've been able to buy with the overwhelming income from my paintings," I said, digging my shaking hands into my jeans pocket. I began fiddling with the key. "I've got nothing. Nothing."

14

When Mary, John, and Elam returned, I was just getting into my car to go to the hospital. I climbed out and told them about our afternoon visitor. Predictably, they were distressed, but they were relieved I hadn't called the police.

"You just be very careful, Kristie," John said. "We don't want anything happening to you," With that he and Elam went to the barn to feed the animals and milk the cows.

"Don't worry. I'll take care," I called after

him, touched by his concern. I smiled reassuringly at Mary. "I'm on my way to visit Mr. Geohagan. Tonight's his last night at the hospital. Tomorrow he gets transferred to Holiday House."

Mary nodded approval. "I know that place. My cousin Sadie Lapp, who's church Amish, had to go there when all her family died. It's nice for that kind of place. It's run by the Mennonites. They're good at taking care of people."

Too bad Mr. Geohagan couldn't talk to Mary. He didn't see his upcoming move so positively.

I had just waved goodbye to her and had my car door open when Clarke pulled into the Zooks' drive.

"Hi," I called and waved, shutting the door.

"Hi, yourself," he said as he walked over. "Are you coming or going?"

Yowzah, he's handsome! I thought, mesmerized by his smile, his eyes, his gait, his everything. I hoped I didn't look as infatuated as I felt. *Sorry, Mr. G. I think I'll just see you tomorrow.*

"She's going." Jake had rolled up silently beside me. "She's going to visit Mr. Geohagan and be Lady Bountiful, whoever she was."

"Jake!" I exclaimed.

Both men looked at me, Clarke surprised by the vehemence in my voice, Jake delighted with himself, knowing he'd gotten to me. To cover my outburst, I said quietly and reasonably, "Jake, you're sneaking again." I turned to Clarke.

"His chair doesn't make noise. I think he oils the wheels."

"I bet the hospital's noisy though, isn't it? Poor Mr. Geohagan," Jake said with mock pity. "He needs you."

I wondered what people would think of someone who beat up a wheelchair-bound man.

"You've been very faithful in visiting him, Kristie," Clarke said, watching with interest and probably understanding as I shot daggers at Jake, who was grinning like an idiot. "I hope he appreciates you."

"I think he does. I keep praying that my kindness will let him accept God's love. He's absolutely furious with God about his wife and daughter."

"It's funny." Jake was suddenly serious. "I never considered blaming God for my accident. I may not know much about the deeper things of life, but I have noticed that tragedies seem to strike both the godly and the ungodly without favoritism. I get mad at being crippled because obviously I'd rather be walking, but it's the guy who ran the stop sign that I get mad at, not God."

"The thing that fascinates me is that Mr. Geohagan blames God rather than himself or Cathleen," Clarke said. "He seems to conveniently forget that choices always have consequences."

"Yes!" I was excited that both these men saw the situation as I did. "There they all were, living without a single thought for God and in defiance of His standards. Then, when the natural consequences of their acts occurred, suddenly it's all God's fault. And believe me, Mr. Geohagan can be very brutal and caustic about it all."

"And you keep going back?" Jake asked.

"Sure. Why not?" I shrugged. "You were right. He needs me."

"But how much do you owe to a quarrelsome old man you met in the emergency room?"

"If I don't go visit, who else will? Besides, he's not quarrelsome; he's sad. And I have his key."

Immediately I realized what I'd said. *Tell no one! Promise!* I made a face and muttered under my breath.

"What's wrong?" Clarke asked.

"Nothing."

"Nothing?"

"Nothing."

"Then why do you look so guilty?"

"I do?"

"You do."

The curse of an honest face. "I just broke a promise."

"About what?" Jake asked.

Clarke looked at me closely. "About a key?"

"I'm not supposed to tell anyone I have it."

"Why not?"

"Mr. Geohagan told me not to."

"Why?"

"I have no idea."

"Let me get this straight," Clarke said. "You have Mr. Geohagan's key, you're not supposed to tell anyone you have it, and you don't know why."

"That's it."

"Why did he give it to you in the first place?" Jake asked.

"Because he might die?"

Clarke laughed, and his eyes crinkled almost shut. "Don't ask us, Kristie. We're asking you."

I grinned back at him, the tension draining away and my shoulders relaxing. It was too late to worry about saying too much now.

"Mr. Geohagan gave me a key the day we met. I think he thought he might die, and he gave it to me for safekeeping. He even wrote instructions before he had bypass surgery, leaving the key to me. I've tried to give it back to him several times, but he keeps telling me he wants me to hold it for him."

"What kind of a key is it?" Jake asked. "A house key? A car key? A safety deposit box key? A treasure chest key?"

"I don't know." I pulled it from my jeans pocket and held it out in my palm.

"Looks like a regular house key to me." Jake sounded disappointed.

"It's pretty small for that. Maybe a garage key?" I had studied the little piece of metal so many times. "All I know is that it isn't his front door key because he gave me another one when I went to his apartment."

"Too bad it wasn't a closet key," Clarke said with a wicked smile.

I made a face at him and slipped the key back in my pocket. "Now I'll have to tell him that I told you two."

"He won't mind," Clarke said.

"I hope not."

I parked my car as close to the hospital entrance as I could, which wasn't very close since the whole world seemed to be visiting this particular hospital on this particular night. I squared my shoulders, confident I'd find Mr. Geohagan in a foul mood because of tomorrow's move. Wait until he heard my confession.

"They're moving me tomorrow," he said as soon as I walked in the door. He glared at me as if it were my fault.

I smiled and nodded. "To Holiday House. It's a wonderful place." I tried to sound perky.

My good cheer made not the slightest impression on Mr. Geohagan. "What kind of name is that for a nursing home? Like it's only open on

Christmas and Thanksgiving, and the rest of the year they park the residents in the street? Or do they think that a gooey name is going to make me happy to go there? I may be sick, but that doesn't mean I can't think. Holiday House, my eye. Hopeless House is more like it. Or Humiliation House. Or Heartache House. Or Hateful House—"

"What do you do?" I asked to cut off his tirade. "Spend all your time looking for alliteration?"

He stared at me steely eyed.

Poor, lonely man.

"I must tell you something," I said hesitantly as I sat in the chair beside his bed. I forced myself to stop twisting my hands like a nervous old lady and stuffed them in my jeans pockets to keep them apart. "I told some people about your key today. I didn't mean to. It just sort of slipped out. I'm sorry."

"Who?" he asked immediately, his frown intense.

"A son of the Amish family I'm living with and a friend of his."

Mr. Geohagan relaxed visibly at that information and actually made an attempt at a smile. "Don't worry about it. I'm certain there's no harm done."

I felt great relief. "But I don't want to keep the key anymore."

"I'd feel better if you did."

I pulled my hand out of my pocket and laid the key on his night table, where it clinked quietly.

"Have you got some nasty relative who's after the fortune it unlocks or something?" I grinned at the absurd idea.

He didn't grin back.

I felt a chill. I looked at him lying there defenseless and incapacitated. I looked again at the key. Maybe I should keep it after all if it made him happy. I reached for it.

"Hey, Mr. Geohagan!"

I jumped and turned at the loud voice, key forgotten.

In walked an aide with a small tray. She smiled so broadly her gums showed. "How are you doing tonight?"

"How do you think?" Mr. Geohagan asked sourly.

She ignored his snarl. "I've got a snack for you, Mr. Geohagan." She set down the tray holding a ginger ale and two packets of saltines. She rolled the tray over to the bed. Then with a flourish she whisked a cupcake from someplace on her person and put it on the tray. "I bet you'll enjoy this. You'd better. I baked it just for you as a going away present."

"Hah!" he said with considerable force. "I haven't enjoyed one bite of food here yet, and I'm not starting now, especially if you baked it."

The aide left with a huge smile on her face.

"She drives me crazy," Mr. Geohagan said. "Everything I say or do makes her laugh."

"But it was nice of her to bring you this cupcake."

He snorted again. "She didn't do it for me. She did it for herself. She's a do-gooder."

"Like me?"

"No," he said. "You're cute."

I rolled my eyes. "And you're impossible."

I watched as he picked the cupcake to death, eating every single crumb but slowly so I wouldn't think he was enjoying it. The key lay forgotten. I didn't remember it again until I was walking across the parking lot and reached in my voluminous shoulder bag for my car key, which was hiding as usual.

I made a face. Should I go back to the room and get it? Nah. What could happen to it overnight?

Tomorrow. I'll get it tomorrow.

I grabbed one strap of my shoulder bag with my left hand and pulled it open with my right, peering hopefully into the dark interior, willing my car keys to walk to the surface of the collection within.

So quickly that I didn't have time to react, a man's hand grabbed my bag, pulling on it with a force that threw me off balance. At the same time his other hand shoved me hard in the middle of my back, sending me reeling.

Attacked twice in one day! Not fair!

As I went down, some instinct kept my hands clamped to my purse rather than reaching out to break my fall. Nobody was going to get my things, not if I had anything to say about it! I had no idea of half the stuff that was in my bag, but I knew I didn't want some stranger pawing through any of it.

Don't let him get it, Lord!

I twisted slightly midair so that I landed on my side rather than my face, and my twisting broke the thief's hold. It was either let go or fall with me. I hit the ground in a bone-crunching thud, bounced a time or two, and through the daze of pain rolled protectively onto my stomach, my purse beneath me.

I took a deep breath and tried to scream, but only a gurgle emerged.

I sensed more than heard that my attacker was gone, and I slowly, painfully began pulling myself to my feet by using my car door handle. Soon a small crowd converged on me, and as I tried to get to my knees, gentle hands helped me the rest of the way up. I looked gratefully at a security guard, an orderly, and two other men I presumed had been visiting the hospital.

"Are you all right?"

"Did he get your purse?"

"Uh-oh. Look at your elbow. Your sweater's torn, and you're bleeding."

"How's your head? Can you tell me your name? Should you be standing?" The last was from the orderly.

I was grateful for the strong arms supporting me because once again my own knees weren't up to the job.

"He's gone, isn't he?" I managed to ask.

"Yeah," said the security guard. "He had a car waiting over there." He pointed to the edge of the lot. "Let's get you inside so they can check you over."

"I'm fine," I insisted. "Really, I'm fine." Fortunately, none of my rescuers listened.

They shepherded me into the ER, the two strangers making a seat for me with clasped hands. The orderly walked beside us, reaching over to take my pulse. The security guard scurried ahead to open the door with great dramatic flare, an unnecessary act since the door was automatic, but it seemed to make him feel better.

I clutched at the man on my left to keep from sliding off my perch as the men slewed sideways to fit through the door without missing a step. My purse, still slung over my shoulder, bumped rhythmically against the one man's side as the orderly led us through the waiting room into the treatment area.

An hour later I was finally alone. I ached and knew that tomorrow I'd be black and blue all down my right side. I'd landed on the same spot on my hip as when I'd tumbled down the steps this afternoon. My shoulder was stiff and tender, but an X-ray showed nothing was broken. My right hand, arm, and leg were painted bright red where I had brush burns, and there was a good-sized lump above my right temple where my head had bounced on the macadam.

A policeman had patiently taken my tale, but both he and I knew that nothing would come of the report. I'd seen no one, and I didn't even know why I felt so certain it was a man who had pushed me. The one positive thing was that when I took inventory of my bag, nothing was missing. I even found my car keys.

Now I sat on a bench and waited for Clarke to come and get me. The doctor had insisted that I not drive home because of the lump on my head.

"You have a slight concussion," he said. "You mustn't risk getting dizzy while driving."

Just last week—just yesterday—I would have called Todd. In all honesty and from sheer habit, he still would have been easiest to call even now, but it wouldn't be fair to him. I had removed him from the place in my life where he was that special person to call on in trouble. I had to leave it that way, even if calling Clarke felt like imposing.

Drained, I closed my eyes to rest. I opened them some time later to find Clarke sitting beside me.

"He didn't mind," I said.

"I beg your pardon?"

"Mr. Geohagan. He didn't mind that I told you and Jake about the key."

"Hang Mr. Geohagan," Clarke said with feeling. "How are you?"

"Fine." I smiled, feeling weepy at his concern. "They just won't let me drive."

He smiled back and pushed my bangs aside. "From the looks of you, they were right. I'm glad you called."

"Poor Clarke. You probably won't believe this, but I'm not accident prone."

He slid his arm around my waist and led me to his car. Unfortunately, it was parked right outside the emergency room doors. I would have preferred a longer walk to enjoy his solicitude.

The evening was warm and velvety, the light soft. I leaned against the headrest and relaxed as he drove out of town, heading for the farm.

"There are a lot of buggies out tonight," I said as we waited for a break in traffic to pass one.

"Families returning from social visits and young people going to sings." Clarke passed one buggy only to find himself behind another. "Do you feel well enough to take a little drive?"

"I think so." *As long as it's with you.* "Where to?"

"Over 23 to Morgantown and down 10 toward Honey Brook."

"As long as I don't have to move, it sounds fine."

He turned at Smoketown to take the back roads to 23. "Poor Kristie. Beaten up by dogs and thieves. Did he get anything?"

"No. When I fell, I rolled on my bag and started screaming." I smiled when I recalled the thin stream of sound that had pushed its way passed my closed throat. "At least I tried to scream. He didn't have time to get anything. My heroes chased him away."

I realized that as I talked I had picked up my purse from the floor, put it on my lap, and wrapped my arms around it. I returned it to the floor.

"Not that he'd have gotten much. I'm sort of a magpie when it comes to my purse. Tissues, empty Lifesaver wrappers, deposit slips, a couple of Magic Markers, and a small sketchbook. Stuff like that. Still, I'd have hated to replace the credit cards, my driver's license, and my Social Security card. Then there's the coin collection littering the bottom of the bag and weighing it down, a great financial reversal if lost."

I was pleased that he grinned.

We were silent for a while, and then I asked, "Have you ever been robbed?"

"Not personally, like having my pocket picked, but we were robbed when I was about thirteen. We came home from vacation to find the house ransacked. I lost an extensive coin collection my grandfather had given me shortly before he died. It was underinsured, but it wasn't the monetary loss that hurt. They took something very special to me, and I remember how bad I felt. It was like Grandpop being taken twice. Thieves are cruel in a way they probably don't even consider."

I nodded and immediately wished I hadn't. My head swam. I closed my eyes and lay my head on the headrest again until we turned south onto 10.

Soon Clarke said, "Look."

Directly ahead of us was a line of buggies, the line broken here and there by cars slowly weaving their way through the pack. Clarke began the passing and waiting game too.

"I've never seen so many," I said, sitting up. "There must be fifty to sixty of them."

All the buggies were open two-seaters. In some two young men rode, in some couples sat shoulder to shoulder. But what delighted me most were the double dating couples. One boy and girl sat conventionally, but the second couple sat on their laps, the boy on the boy and the girl on the girl. The topmost boy handled the reins.

All the girls were prim and correct with their shawls draped over their shoulders against the growing chill of the evening and dark bonnets over their organdy *kapps*. The young men, black felt hats firm on their Dutch boy haircuts, proudly drove their best horses. Couples called from buggy to buggy, laughing and joking together. The long line crested a hill, and I watched as buggy after buggy turned into one farm lane.

"I've heard of buggy jams before, especially around Intercourse on a Saturday night, but I've never seen a procession like this before." I couldn't stop smiling. "And I love the double dates!"

"I thought you would."

As I watched the buggies, I tried to reconcile the otherworld appearance of innocence with what I knew to be reality. These Amish kids were like any other group of kids. Some came from fine families, some from hypocritical families, some from strong families, some from fearful families. And appearances to the contrary, they were being touched more and more by modern technology. Many had iPods and laptops, and some even belonged to spas and pumped iron. *Rumspringa*.

"You know," I said, "while I don't agree with the Amish way of life, I hate the thought that it might pass away. It's so fascinating!"

Clarke grinned. "You sound like a sociologist. Just never forget that Christ died to release us from bondage to the law, whether it's the Mosaic law or the *Ordnung*."

Suddenly I realized we were approaching the

twin hills south of Honey Brook, the place where Jake had had his accident. I sat up straight and watched as Clarke's headlights picked out the intersection where someone had run a stop sign and changed a young man's life forever.

"This is the spot," I said. Clarke nodded. He slowed as if in respect for Jake.

"Look!" I grabbed his arm and pointed.

There beside the road, just visible in the dusk, was a little white cross, the kind people sometimes put to mark a place where someone has been killed. I stared at the little marker on which hung a small wreath decorated with a gold bow and gold flowers.

"Someone else was in an accident here," I whispered. "And whoever it was must have died."

I felt Clarke glance at me, and I tried to smile reassuringly. He reached out and softly touched my cheek.

"Why don't you take tomorrow off to recuperate?" he suggested when we arrived back at the farm. He helped me out of the car and we walked slowly toward the steps. "Uncle Bud and I will see to it that your car is back by tomorrow evening. Okay?"

"Thanks," I said. Even though I was feeling pretty much back to normal—if I didn't turn my head too quickly or try to raise my arm above my shoulder or put all my weight on my right hip and leg—I knew school would be more than I could handle. "You're a good doctor, Dr. Griffin."

I reached out impulsively and hugged him. I was more than pleased when he returned the embrace with enthusiasm.

15

One evening I carried my art portfolio downstairs after the dinner dishes had been cleared away and went to the kitchen table. I needed to select a new picture to take to The Country Shop to replace the one Clarke had bought, and I might as well see what reaction I got from Mary as I did so. My feeling was that she'd come running.

I placed the paintings on the table and began shuffling through them. In a short time I had two piles—possible and not possible.

"What are you doing?" Ruth asked as she wandered over. "Oh, look! It's our barn!"

She picked up the watercolor and held it for everyone to see. John and Elam glanced up and nodded, and then they went back to their reading. Mary put her darning aside, rose, and came over for a closer look. She'd managed to resist longer than I'd expected.

"Why the two piles?" she asked.

"I think these might be good to mat and frame for possible sale, and these I don't think are all that good."

"They all look good to me," Ruth said.

Mary spotted one of a salt marsh I'd painted on a visit to New England last summer. "Where is that from?"

"It's what the tidal marshes look like near the ocean in Connecticut." I doubted she'd ever been to the shore. "Lots of birds live there as well as other animals."

Mary reached out and touched the paper with a tentative finger. "I love the soft effect that watercolors can give, but how did you get the effect of the little blurred circles? I saw it before in a book at the library, but it didn't say how it was done."

"While the paint is still wet, you sprinkle a little sea salt on it. The salt absorbs the paint, leaving lighter, star-shaped areas the size of the salt crystals."

"Sea salt?" Mary was fascinated. "Does the salt melt?"

"No, it dries on the picture and you have to brush it off."

She pulled out another picture, this one of the night sky. "That's not just white paper for the moon. What did you do?"

"That's called wax resist. I drew the moon on

the paper with a soft yellow candle before I painted. The paint doesn't stick to the wax, and you have an interesting textural detail."

She looked carefully at all the paintings in both piles, asking questions as she looked. Finally she turned to John, her face vivid with some emotion I couldn't quite read. Worry? Despair?

"John?" she said.

Pleading, I realized. She was begging him for something.

He looked up and studied her quietly, thoughtfully. His eyes moved to me and then back to Mary. She stood with her eyes closed and hands clasped as if she were praying, waiting.

"Okay," he said, ever taciturn, and went back to his magazine.

Mary's face shone, lit from within by some great joy. "I'll be right back."

She ran from the room. I looked at John and saw him follow her with his eyes. Something in his expression let me know he had just made a great concession for her. I realized that John loved his wife, and that pleased me. In typical Amish fashion they didn't show much affection in public, but there was deep emotion behind the stoic German facade.

Mary hurried back with an art tablet hugged to her chest.

"They're not like yours," she said shyly and held the tablet out to me.

I knew I was holding something very precious, and I opened it carefully. On the first page was a watercolor of a table, this table if the cover was any indication, with a basket of apples sitting on it, a trio of the fruit caught rolling across the surface. She pointed to the patch of white on one of the apples, the reflection of light.

"I read that you don't paint white. You let the paper be your white. Is that right?"

I nodded as I turned the page. A horse grazing. A fat ewe with a lamb frolicking beside her. A bouquet of dahlias. A weeping wisteria.

"Mary, these are very good." I wasn't being polite. They *were* good. The technique, though elementary, was sound and the composition excellent.

"Oh, look!" Ruth pointed. "It's the barn again."

I studied Mary's painting of the barn. It was more realistic than mine, very detailed, but nicely done. Ruth pulled mine free from my pile and laid it beside her mother's.

"This is early morning." She put a finger on Mary's painting and then mine. "And this is in the afternoon."

"I love to capture light and shadow," Mary said.

"The sign of a true artist." I smiled at her and she beamed in reply.

Next came a collection of quilt paintings—a Star of Bethlehem hanging on a line, a Log Cabin draped over a chair, a Wedding Ring lying

over a bench. I thought of the Susie Riehl postcards I'd seen. "Mary, let me show you something," I said, grateful for this perfect opening.

I ran up to my room for the Susie Riehl postcards and, on my return out of breath from my
dash, I put Susie's postcards in Mary's hands.
"I bought these in a quilt store."

Mary nodded, not getting my point.

I turned the card over for her so she could
read Susie's brief bio. "She's Old Order," I
said.

Mary blinked. "And she sells her paintings?"

I nodded. "Just like other women sell their
quilts or the carpenters their woodwork."

By now Elam and Jake were also gathered
around the table looking at the postcards and
Mary's art. The air hummed with excitement and
possibilities.

I indicated Mary's paintings, some of the
subjects similar to Susie's but in Mary's unique
style. "Would you ever sell any of these?"

Mary looked at John, who had been pretending
to read while listening carefully. At the word
"sell" he looked up. He didn't say anything, but
maybe his silence was a good sign. If he didn't
want her to sell because it was against the
Ordnung, surely he'd have said something immediately. And it wasn't the selling that was the
issue. Not really. It was the painting itself, the
creating of something that wasn't practical like a

quilt, that didn't actively turn people's hearts to God like writing, that had no intrinsic value except beauty.

"Income, John," Mary said softly, her voice almost lost in the hissing of the lantern. But John heard her.

I knew that in many ways income was the least of it for Mary. It was the pictures, the painting. But if income in a financially strained family legitimized the painting, it was all right with her. She fairly glowed.

I also knew that putting the word "Amish" in front of the word "artist" would make Mary's paintings a collector's dream.

John nodded. "I have to think."

"Let her sell them, Father," Jake said, not a surprise.

Elam nodded. "I agree." And that was a surprise.

John looked at his son, the person to whom the financial health of the farm mattered immensely. *"Ja?"*

Elam nodded again.

John looked at Mary. "I'll think. We'll talk." With that he went back to the latest issue of *Amish Life*.

I set my easel so I had a fine view of the brook that ran through the patch of woods on the acreage down the road from the house. I'd already done a charcoal value study of the scene and knew what

I wanted to do. As I prepared to paint, filling my water bottle from the brook, taping my nubby paper in place, preparing my palette, I despaired of catching the mystery, the life of the moving water.

In the small brook there was a pool no more than five by five feet, and capturing it and the tiny cascade that fed it meant painting negatively or painting shadows. I wet the paper and then added a wash of manganese except on the rapids and on the bright spot where the sun cut through the trees. Using cobalt and a little burnt sienna, I dry brushed the blue-gray very lightly over the white areas so the tint rested only on the nubs of the paper, creating subtle shadows.

I knew any reflections of the trees and grasses that lined the brook would be more ambiguous than the real object and, though duller, more interesting. I painted the actual forms realistically, the reflections more vaguely, working quickly because of the moving light. To suggest the leaves floating on the pond, I used a bit of cadmium orange-red and cadmium orange, and then I added rice. The pigment concentrated under the rice, creating strong splotches of color.

I finished by making marks or little lines to suggest thick tufts of grass and the reaching tree limbs.

As always I was lost in my work, and it wasn't until I was finishing up that I heard the snap of a twig. A deer? A smaller animal? How long had I been painting? I rubbed the back of my neck and looked toward the road and the sound.

A man stood watching me. Often people stopped to watch when I did plein air painting. Many times I had stopped to watch another artist at work. Why did my spine prickle so over this man? He looked harmless in khaki cords and a navy sweater, but somehow I felt threatened.

"Nice picture," he said as he walked toward me.

I nodded, watching warily. I knew that he couldn't begin to see the painting from his angle and distance.

"I saw you painting when I drove by and I had to stop. I've always wanted to know how a person painted." When I was noncommittal, he moved closer. "What's the first step? Do you start from the top and work down or what?"

"The background comes first with water-colors," I said hesitantly even as a shout cut across my comment.

"Come on, Kristie! It's time to go!"

Thank You, Lord!

"That's Jake" I announced. "He's come for me. I have to go."

I got up quickly from my camp stool. I knew my relief must be obvious, but uncharacteristically I didn't care. I gathered my supplies, hurrying to get away from this man who so inexplicably bothered me. I dumped my water, stuffed the used paper towels in a plastic bag, threw the paint tubes into their box. I collapsed my easel, telescoping its legs and stashing it in my canvas bag.

As I threw the bag over my shoulder and held my painting carefully flat in front of me, I glanced at the stranger.

But he wasn't there. I looked around in surprise. Sure enough, the woods were empty. With an eerie, unsettled feeling, I hurried to Jake's van.

"Who was that?" Jake asked, pointing to a car disappearing over the crest of the hill.

"I don't know. He said he saw me working and stopped because he wanted to know how I painted."

"He saw you painting?"

"That's what he said."

"From the road?"

I nodded.

Jake shook his head. "You can't see the brook from the road. The underbrush is too thick. Even I couldn't see you, and I knew you were there. That's why I yelled."

I looked back the way I'd just come. My spine prickled again as I saw Jake was right. No casual driver could ever have seen me. The man had known I was there and had sought me out.

"Did you see what he looked like?" I asked.

He shrugged. "Just a man in a Braves cap."

I stared, mouth suddenly dry. "A Braves cap?

He wasn't wearing one when he talked to me."

"He slapped it on as he hurried toward his car."

"That's what that other man wore," I managed to whisper.

Jake looked at me, concern all over his face. "The one who pushed you down the stairs?"

I nodded.

To distract myself, I reached to adjust my watercolor as it lay on the floor behind me. The brook pleased me, as did the little waterfall that fed it. "I'm not sure about the reflections," I said. "Are the colors strong enough?"

Jake looked behind him. "They look great to me, but I'm no expert. I only—"

"—know what I like," I finished for him.

He laughed. "You've got me pegged."

As we started down the road, my mind glommed on to the man in the Braves cap. Jake glanced at me.

"Kristie, it's okay. Don't worry about him." I felt comforted until he continued, "Though I'm glad we'd made plans for me to pick you up."

During the drive to White Horse and the farm auction, I forced myself to relax. I was here in the van and the man wasn't. I was safe. Besides, I couldn't do anything about him anyway because I couldn't swear he was the man I'd seen in the house that Sunday. The man today hadn't touched me, hadn't been anything but polite. You can't turn a man in to the authorities because he makes you feel creepy.

By the time Jake became embroiled in the minor traffic jam of cars, buggies, and horse-drawn wagons lining the road or jockeying for position in the barnyard in White Horse, I no longer felt threatened. I was too fascinated by everything around me.

Jake managed to get a parking place near the drive and next to a wagon loaded with a refrigerator, a treadle sewing machine, a double bedstead, a kitchen table, and five mismatched chairs. I watched in fascination as a red-bearded Amishman and his young son maneuvered a bureau and a rocking chair onto the already overloaded wagon and lashed everything into place.

Jake watched them with a cocked eyebrow. "Red Daniel is buying furniture. I wonder which of his girls is getting married? Poor man has six daughters and only Little Daniel."

"What's so bad about six daughters?" I challenged.

"A lot in a culture that looks on unmarried women as not fulfilled. A spinster aunt is always treated nicely, and sometimes she even has a little home of her own. She might get a job as a housekeeper or work in a shop or teach and support herself. But unmarried women depend on their fathers. Red Daniel doesn't want that."

"Why not?" I asked, grimacing as Red Daniel gave a mighty tug on his rope, shifting the load and almost burying Little Daniel under the bureau.

"You don't know his girls!" Jake said, laughing.

When Red Daniel and Little Daniel finally departed, we located Elam and Big Nate Stoltzfus. We found the two examining a flatbed wagon.

The old man nodded frostily in our direction. "Chake," he said, pronouncing Jake's name with the Dutch *ch*. He nodded briefly to me, eyed my jeans, scarlet shirt, and wildly patterned sweater with a jaundiced eye and then left immediately, his old back straight and proud.

"About one quarter of the Amish are named Stoltzfus," Jake said as he watched the old man go. "It means 'proud foot.' My father says it means the Stoltzfuses have their feet planted firmly and proudly on the faith. I don't know. It seems too kind an explanation for some people."

Elam grinned at his brother. "Nasty, nasty, Chake. You know what Mom'd say if she heard you."

The brothers looked at each other and began chanting in unison, "Let no corrupt communication proceed out of your mouth, but that which is good for the use of edifying, that it may minister grace unto the hearers." Only they said it in High German, not King James.

After Elam translated for me, Jake said,

"Whenever we got mad at each other and started yelling like kids do, Mom ran that by us."

"And," Elam said, "if we ever said anything against another in the community, we had to repeat the verse and ask for forgiveness from God."

"Mom ran a tough shop," Jake said with admiration. "Great lady."

Elam shrugged, uncomfortable with the compliment. "She was just doing what was right. Now where'd you hide the van? I got the tools Father wanted and for less than he felt was an acceptable price."

"Good going," Jake said. "He'll like that. No man appreciates a bargain more than Father."

Wondering how two such different men could come from the same home and training, I watched the brothers put what looked like a collection of rusty antiques in the back of the van.

"What will you do with them?" I asked.

"Make our own repairs on bridles and other equipment," Elam said. "We have a little blacksmith shop set up in the shed beside the barn. It's hard to get things repaired these days, especially the hardware on the buggies. It's a dying art, so we do as much of our own repair work as possible."

"What about the guys who make the buggies originally? Won't they do the repairs for you? Sort of like a car dealership?"

Elam shook his head. "There are too few of

them, not nearly enough to meet the demand. We ordered a new buggy months ago. I doubt we'll get it before winter."

Elam turned to Jake. "By the way, Big Nate told me that he's noticed a car hanging around our farm recently."

"How in the world did he notice a car around our farm?" Then Jake grinned broadly as a thought popped into his mind. "Binoculars? He spies on us? Isn't there a law against that somewhere in the *Ordnung*? There must be!"

Elam smiled and shook his head hopelessly at his brother's glee. "I didn't ask how he knew. I just thanked him for the information. He said the car often parks on the wagon road that cuts between our two farms, and it always faces us. Father and I have been working on the other side of the farm baling hay, so I haven't seen it."

"Neither have I," Jake said as he looked thoughtfully at me. "But I'll certainly be watching from now on."

I was willing to bet that the driver wore a Braves cap.

When we arrived home, I carried my painting and supplies inside, stopping to show Mary.

She studied it carefully. "Sometimes I look at scenes like this and think that I'll paint them later. Then I get home, and I can't remember the details."

"You can make them up, you know. Painting doesn't have to be an exact representation."

Mary looked a little uncomfortable with that thought. Maybe she thought painting as you wished the scene looked instead of as it actually was equal to a form of lying.

"A painting is your vision of something or some place. That's the primary way it differs from photography, which is an exact reproduction."

"But the barn is the barn. When you painted it, you made it look like the barn. I made it look like the barn."

"Only because I wanted to. And because it's accurate, I could call the picture The Zook Barn. If I'd played with the image, I would just call it Amish Barn."

She looked thoughtful. "As is," she finally said.

"Then you need pictures. Maybe a little digital camera?"

She grimaced. "No, no. No cameras. It's bad enough I paint."

In other words, you could only push the church authorities so far. I wondered if any of her friends were aware of her art.

"Maybe I could take the pictures for you? Would that be all right?" I knew that's what Susie Riehl's English friend Shirley did for Susie. They drove around, and when Susie saw a scene she liked, Shirley photographed it and gave prints to Susie, who then painted from them.

To me that idea sounded a lot like the rule that you couldn't drive cars but you could ride in them. But every district had its own particular take on the *Ordnung* and what was okay in one district often wasn't in another.

But Mary liked my idea. I could tell by the light in her eye. "Let me ask John what he thinks," she said. "I'll let you know."

Poor John. He had a lot to think about.

I was smiling as I went upstairs to get ready for a date with Clarke. I had been so pleased when he actually called and asked me to save the evening for him that I'd positively sputtered. I'm sure I did.

At one point in my preparations I glanced at myself in the mirror and was surprised by my sparkling eyes and high color. "What am I going to do with you, woman?" I grinned at myself, and then I stared in disbelief at my cheek.

Where Hawk had gotten me with his fang, I now had a little scar that made a perfect dimple! I smiled again to make certain, and voilà! There was that dimple again.

I'd always wanted a dimple. When I was growing up, I had a friend named Marly who was a beautiful blonde with naturally curly hair. She floated when she walked and wore soft yellows and creams and baby blue. And she had a dimple in each cheek. All the boys swarmed to her, and when she favored them with a smile, the dimples knocked them mute.

And now I had a dimple too! I no longer wanted to be a powder blue blonde—too anemic —but I loved my new dimple. When Clarke showed up, I was careful to smile as broadly as I could. I did not knock him mute.

"How'd you like to see Adam Hurlbert in action?" he asked as we walked to his car.

"You're taking me to a thousand-dollar-a-plate dinner! How nice! I'm so glad I'm wearing my best jeans and red jacket."

Clarke had the most gorgeous smile, which he flashed my way. "He's speaking at a rally at Park City Mall at six. We could listen to him and then go get dinner."

"Happy days are here again," I sang. "Sounds good to me."

We found a large crowd gathered at one end of the parking lot at Park City and joined them.

"Shall we push our way to the front?" Clarke asked.

I looked at the wall of backs we'd have to work our way through and said, "I think I like it right here."

A raised platform waited for Adam and Irene, its folding chairs, podium, and red, white, and blue bunting looking jaunty.

It wasn't too long before a helicopter appeared overhead and lowered itself to the ground amid a great rush of wind and gravel. Obviously, Adam and his campaign people had a handle on the effect of that cornerstone of good theater, the entrance.

"Only fifteen minutes late," Clarke said. "Not bad."

"Whetting our appetites."

The door of the helicopter opened and Adam and Irene stepped out, flanked by advisors and security and followed by the detestable Nelson waving as though he was the candidate.

The lead people cut a path through the crowd, much as Moses split the Red Sea. People fell back willingly, standing on tiptoe to catch a glimpse of the celebrities. Cheers of "Yea, Adam!" and "Hurlbert for president!" rang above the high school band that played "God Bless America."

"Hurlbert for president?" I said.

"A partisan who plans ahead," Clarke replied.

He reached out to rest a hand on my shoulder just as a very round, very enthusiastic lady pushed between us and stopped there. I looked over her head at Clarke, who shrugged helplessly.

The woman held a handmade sign painted on a yellow pillowcase, waving it vigorously over her head. I had to duck to avoid getting it flung into the side of my head. *Hurlbert today to save the USA* it read.

Suddenly she planted herself firmly about two inches from my shoulder, put her fingers between her teeth and gave the loudest, shrillest whistle I'd ever heard. Everyone nearby looked dazed at the sound coming from this rotund woman. I was certain I was permanently deafened.

I couldn't help laugh as I watched Clarke, glassy eyed, give an abrupt head shake to clear his unexpected case of tinnitus. The din in my own head gradually lessened, just in time for the next verbal onslaught.

"Come here, Barney!" the woman screamed at a decibel level OSHA would declare required ear protection for anyone within miles. She reached through the crowd to a little old man wearing a scowl of heroic proportions and a parka three sizes too big. I got the distinct impression that he wished he were anywhere but here, especially when she plucked him bodily to stand beside her, separating me farther from Clarke.

"Hold this, Barney," she ordered, thrusting one corner of the pillowcase into his hand. "Now wave it!" She lifted her hand high and began vigorously fluttering the pillowcase. "I want him to see us. I want to be on TV with him. I want the news people to talk with us so we can tell everyone how wonderful he is. Now wave! And do it like you mean it!"

The little man dutifully raised his arm and

began to move it back and forth, back and forth, but not like he meant it. The end result of their partnership was that the lady turned red from the exertion, the man kept dropping his end of the pillowcase as her vigor pulled it out of his hand, and the message was totally unreadable.

I was trying to stifle an impolite laugh—not that she'd have noticed—when I was abruptly pushed from behind. I shot forward, literally lifted off my feet, but I could do nothing to save myself because of the press of the crowd. I let out a long "Ohhhh!" as I collided violently with the chubby whistler/sign waver. We fell to the ground in a great and unladylike tangle of arms and legs.

"I'm sorry! I'm sorry!" I kept repeating as totally unsuitable giggles escaped. I had a vision of what we looked like as we thrashed about, and every time I saw it in my mind, fresh giggles slipped out.

Kind hands reached out and pulled the two of us to our feet. Clarke grabbed me and held me up with a strong arm about my waist.

"Are you okay?" he asked.

I looked at him and giggled. I slapped my hand over my mouth. When I thought I could talk without embarrassing myself further, I said, "I think so."

I had a hole in my jeans and a skinned knee. My sore hip had taken another shot, but otherwise I was fine. I giggled anew at the sight of *Adam today to save the USA* draped over Barney's thin shoulders.

"Oh, Bitsy! Oh, Bitsy!" He was genuinely distressed. "Oh, Bitsy, are you all right?"

My unwilling human cushion had a bloody nose and badly scraped hands. As soon as I saw the blood streaming down her front, I sobered abruptly.

"I'm sorry," I said again, this time with great sincerity. "I was pushed and I lost my bal—"

I stopped and looked frantically around, already knowing what had happened.

"My purse! Clarke! My purse has been stolen!"

"What?"

I groaned. "My purse! My credit cards. My driver's license. My checkbook. My new phone! This time it's really gone!"

Clarke looked around as though he expected the thief to be standing next to us waiting to be spotted.

"Did you see a man in a Braves cap?" I asked him.

"A baseball cap?"

"A *Braves* cap," I repeated. "Did anyone see a man in a Braves cap?" I looked around the circle of people who had collected about us. Of course no one had.

A policewoman arrived about then to check out the disturbance. She escorted Clarke and me and Bitsy and Barney to an area inside the mall that was obviously the control center for the political appearance. Bitsy mumbled through the yellow pillowcase pressed to her nose that she was Mrs. Bitsy Snodgrass and the little man was her husband, Barney Snodgrass.

"We just love Adam Hurlbert," she said as she pulled the pillowcase away to check if blood was still flowing. It was. She reapplied it.

As a nurse attended to Bitsy Snodgrass, the policewoman talked with me.

"I'm sorry, Miss Matthews," she said. "Unfortunately, such petty crimes are commonplace at large gatherings like rallies and concerts."

"It's the second time it's happened," I said forlornly, my mind still on all the things I'd need to replace.

"The second time?"

"Well, not quite the second time. Someone tried to get my purse the other night, but he wasn't successful." I felt very tired.

"Are you having trouble with someone specific bothering you?" the policewoman asked with great interest.

I thought of the Braves cap, but I didn't know that he had anything to do with this evening or with the attempt at the hospital. Besides "Look for a man in a Braves cap" wouldn't be very helpful. "It must be coincidence," I said simply.

She nodded and finished filling out the police report.

"We'll contact you if we recover your property," she assured me.

Just then Adam and Irene Hurlbert were ushered into the room. Adam was deep in conversation with a tall, bony, anorexic young man while Irene, oozing charm and graciousness, was talking to a woman who was obviously a reporter. I watched, interested in seeing these two up close and in action. Irene was beautiful, no doubt about it, and Adam was every bit as handsome as I'd thought that day in the hospital corridor. And he definitely treated his hair.

Another man walked up to Adam and his companion and talked quietly for a couple of minutes. As he talked, the politician looked at me and Bitsy. I smiled, flashing my new dimple, and Bitsy simpered in spite of the cotton now packing her right nostril.

Shaking his head as if greatly distressed, Adam walked over to us.

"My dear lady!" He took Bitsy's hand in his, patted it gently, and kept it. "To have been injured at a rally sponsored by my people! Please accept my sincerest apologies and make sure we receive any medical bills that might result from this monstrous occurrence. We must make this terrible thing right and restore your confidence in Lancaster County and Pennsylvania."

I doubted her confidence in either had been much shaken. If anything, she was one happy cookie that she'd been the second-degree victim of a crime. How else would she have gotten to meet Adam Hurlbert?

I glanced at Clarke to see his response to this gushing performance and watched one of those fascinating dark eyebrows arch in skepticism.

"And you, young lady," he said, adopting a brisk, businesslike tone with me. He took my hand, pressed it briefly, and then dropped it. "I understand you had the misfortune of being robbed this evening. Please accept my apologies that such a thing happened at one of our rallies. Let my office expedite the replacement of your driver's license and any other items within our purview."

"Thank you for your concern and for your help. I appreciate them both," I said politely. My mom would have been proud.

"It's the least we can do," he said, reaching to shake Clarke's hand too. "And you, sir, take good care of her." The handshake Adam gave Clarke was firm, quick, and manly. I was willing to bet he and his team discussed how much was acceptable flesh-pressing time for different types of voters. If so, he'd learned the lessons well.

As Adam Hurlbert smiled charmingly at me one more time, I had to admit it: The guy was really, really good. I just hoped I hadn't looked as delighted as I felt when he'd taken my hand in his and given it that quick, warm squeeze. At least I hadn't drooled like Bitsy.

A tug on my arm turned my attention from the smooth politician. Standing before me was Nelson, curiosity bristling from every inch of his lumpy little body. I had forgotten all about him.

"What happened, Miss Matthews?" He was all agog as he took in my torn jeans and bleeding knee and Bitsy's wounds and bloody pillowcase.

"She was robbed, son," Adam said pontifically. "Isn't that terrible?"

"Yeah?" Nelson's eyes nearly popped out of his head. "Wow! I didn't know people robbed teachers. Wait till the guys at school hear!"

I hoped my lip wasn't curled in a snarl when I said, "Thanks for the sympathy, Nelson."

The kid was in his glory. Not only a helicopter ride, but crime and blood and guts as well.

"What happened to the fat lady?" He pointed indelicately at Bitsy.

"I bumped into her."

Nelson laughed happily. "Hey, Mom!" he screamed across the room. "My art teacher beat up on this fat lady!"

Irene's flawless eyebrows arched delicately as she looked at me. "Really?"

"Shh, Nelson." Adam grabbed for the boy's shoulder and missed as Nelson artfully dodged.

"We must let these kind people go. They've had a very tiring night."

Nelson, however, stepped closer, planting himself in front of Clarke.

"Are you Miss Matthews' boyfriend?" he asked in a typical display of tact.

Clarke nodded. "And may you be so lucky when you grow up."

Nelson looked at me, clearly seeing me in a whole new light. "Wow!" he said.

My thought exactly.

16

A great surge of activity was taking place around the farm. Jake was suddenly engrossed in painting the porch and the fence that lined the yard. Elam was on a ladder painting windows. Ruth had taken time from her pretzel factory again, and every time I saw her, she was in the kitchen with her mother, busy about the stove. Mary had stopped going to the farmers' market and was seeing that all the preserves, apple butter, and chips were stored in the basement. One day I came home from school to find the entire family cleaning and whitewashing the cellar, which had already been scrupulously clean.

The reason for all this activity became obvious the last Sunday in October, two weeks after Elam and Ruth knelt to take the vows of their church. It was a messy, cold, rainy day, the nasty kind of autumn day that made me wonder if Todd hadn't been right about my freezing this winter. My little ceramic heater was chugging away close to Big Bird's cage, and heat rose through a grate in the hall by the stairs, but it wasn't central heating. I needed to remind Jake about that baseboard heating before I froze.

I wrapped myself in several layers of clothes as quickly as I could and hurried downstairs to enjoy the radiant warmth coming from the great wood stove. I planned to sit beside it and warm my outsides while I drank a huge cup of tea to warm my insides.

"Ruth!" I stopped and stared at the girl sitting in the rocker by the window, reading. I had never seen her read before. But the bigger cause for surprise was that I had heard the Zooks leave for church hours ago. I distinctly remembered thinking how uncomfortable a buggy must be on a day like this and how thankful I was for the heater in my yellow car.

"What are you doing here?" I asked. "Don't you feel well?"

Ruth grinned. "I feel great! In fact, I've rarely felt better."

There was an undercurrent of excitement

crackling about the girl. Her gray eyes sparkled, her color was high, and she seemed more like the ever-active Elam than her usual quiet self.

"What's going on?" I asked.

From the doorway of his apartment, Jake said, "She and Isaiah are being published today. That means the minister is announcing their engagement."

"Oh, Ruth, I'm so happy for you!" I said with a hug. "Now all I need to do is meet your Isaiah."

"You will," Ruth said. "And very soon. He'll be living here from now until the wedding."

"Here? Really? And when is the wedding?"

"A week from Thursday."

"You're getting married next Thursday? As in—" I counted quickly—"eleven days from now?"

Ruth nodded happily. "It was the first Thursday in November, the first good date we could pick."

"There'll be weddings every Tuesday and Thursday in November and into December," Jake explained. "Sometimes there'll be more than one a day. Harvesting's done and it's time to relax before preparing everything for next year. It's the one time all year that weddings won't interfere with farming."

"But how will you ever get everything ready so fast?" I asked. I felt overwhelmed, and it wasn't even my wedding.

"Oh, most things are ready now. We—or I should say, Isaiah—has to ask the people we want to help with the wedding meal and the couples we'd like to be in the wedding, but much of the other preparation's done. Why do you think we've been painting and cleaning like crazy? And why do you think Mom and I have been baking and storing so much food?"

"Then you've quit your pretzel job for good?"

She nodded. "There's no need for me to work anymore. Besides, there isn't time. There's still a lot to do to get ready. And then afterward we'll be visiting relatives for a while."

"Where will you live when you've finished visiting?" I asked, thinking that I'd like a more private honeymoon when it was my turn.

"Besides their family farm, Isaiah's father has a small farm in Honey Brook, not too far from where my sister Sarah and Abner live. We'll live there."

"How very nice for you," I said, meaning every word. "With land being so scarce, you're lucky to have your own place."

"I don't think Isaiah could be happy if he wasn't farming," Ruth said. "He loves it. And I'm going to love being his wife." She smiled at me with the delightful smugness of someone who's getting exactly what she wants.

I thought about Ruth's impending marriage as I drove to church. I found it fascinating to think about how settled the girl was, how secure she felt in her thinking, how lacking in curiosity she was about life beyond Isaiah and the Amish community. Even her *rumspringa* had been gentle, and she gladly joined the church, accepting the restrictions as normal and right.

She would marry, have children, and live and die in the same pattern as generations of Amish women before her. She wouldn't be moved to go back to school at forty-five, as my aunt had been. In fact, should such a thought enter her mind, she would squelch it. Education made you proud and interfered with the development of that much-desired quality, humility.

Did Ruth feel shortchanged by her life? I didn't think so. In a culture that gave few choices, she appeared satisfied with what I saw as limited horizons.

Even her quiet rebellion had not been so much against Amish legalisms as against biblical standards. When she and Isaiah went off on their jaunts, they were still readily identifiable as Amish. *Kapp*, straight pins, and black stockings; black brimmed hat, broadfall trousers, and suspenders—all were in place. It was not the *Ordnung* that got short shrift in Ruth's life; it was the Word of God.

Not that Ruth's life was bad by any means. Just the opposite. She was part of a close, loving, encouraging family and community. Many

English people would give all they had to belong like that. Ruth knew Isaiah wouldn't leave her. She knew she'd always have a home, always have someone to look after her, always know exactly what was expected of her.

Such well-ordered rigidity was not for me. The exhilarating freedom of being a Christian woman with a future limited only by the will of God was something I'd never change for temporal security. I liked asking questions, trying new things, exploring my options. I was a modern Christian, not one caught in a pleasant, restrictive, and loving time warp. God and I—together we would make the many choices in my life.

It wasn't until after church that it dawned on me that the Zooks should be allowed to celebrate Ruth's engagement without an interloper hanging over their shoulders. But what would I do if I didn't go home? Clarke was away today, speaking at a friend's church, and doing anything with Todd was out of the question. I thought for a minute and decided to drive over to Honey Brook where Ruth and Isaiah would be living. Not that I expected to find their farm, but I could see the area.

I took Route 23 east to Route 10 and went south. When I got close to Honey Brook, I began taking side roads. I thought once again how beautiful this whole area was, whether back in Lancaster County or just across the line into

Chester County, where I now was. I loved the patchwork-quilt farms and rolling vistas, the wandering streams, and the rich black soil. Even with the end of the color and richness of the growing season, the countryside filled my artist's eye with light and shadow, harmony and contrast.

Everywhere I drove, I saw signs of the growing cottage industries among the Amish—greenhouses, woodworking shops, and signs announcing the selling of quilts, preserves and baked goods, picnic benches, puppies, and rabbits. All the signs also read Closed Sundays. These businesses were the practical way the Amish dealt with the twin concerns of dwindling farmland and increasing population. I was struck again with what a marvelous mixture of accommodation and isolation the Amish were.

Eventually I came to the steep hills south of Honey Brook where Jake had had his accident. I looked again at the side of the road for the cross marking that intersection as a death spot. I wanted to stop and examine the cross, to see if there was a name written on it, to wonder what had happened to this person. The line of traffic behind me precluded that.

Instead I drove through the intersection and came almost immediately to a business drive on the left. I pulled in and turned, stopping just before I drove back onto the road. I looked the area over carefully, and my eye was drawn to the house nearest the intersection. Maybe those people knew something about the accident the cross commemorated. Maybe they knew something about Jake's accident too.

I noted the name on the mailbox as I pulled up to the house: Martin. A good Lancaster County name relocated here in Chester County.

I rang the bell and a woman about my mother's age answered. I introduced myself.

"I'm interested in information about the cross at the intersection. Do you know anything about it?"

"I should say I do," the woman said. "My daughter Rose put it up and takes care of it. Come on in and you can talk to her."

Mrs. Martin led me to her living room and left me in a navy overstuffed chair with a Wedgwood blue-and-rose afghan lying over its back. She was back in the briefest of moments with a young woman with curly brown hair and glasses worn over brown eyes. She wore jeans and a red sweater over a white turtleneck.

"I'm Rose," she said, extending her hand. "Mom says you want to know about the cross."

I nodded. "I have a friend who was hurt at this intersection too, so I was wondering what the story is."

Rose walked to the bow window and looked out across the lawn to the cross.

"I'm a nurse," she said. "I should have been able to help save him."

Her voice and face were full of pain.

"When did it happen?" I asked.

"Last October. October twenty, to be exact. The worst day of my life. My fiancé and I had a horrible fight. I broke up with him and he got furious, even nasty. I'd never seen him like that before. 'Who's the other man? You'd better just tell me because I'm going to find out and kill him!' "

She was still having trouble with the memory a whole year later.

"When I handed him his ring," she continued, "he rushed outside into the rain, ran across the yard, and threw the ring into the field across the street. 'If you won't wear this, no one wears it!' "

"He threw away a diamond ring?"

"A bit melodramatic, wouldn't you say?" Rose put her hand to her forehead and rubbed.

"A bit idiotic, I'd say," Mrs. Martin chimed in.

"Mom." Rose made it a gentle warning.

Mrs. Martin ignored Rose and turned to me. "We never did like him, her father and I," she said. "We thought he was two-faced, a hypocrite. But Rose couldn't see it."

"I couldn't," Rose agreed.

"We thank God every day that she broke up with him."

"Are you sure he didn't just fake throwing the ring to make you feel worse?" I asked.

"I've thought of that, especially since Mom and I have searched for the thing over and over all year with no luck." She shrugged. "I really don't care."

"I do," Mrs. Martin said. "I want to get some value out of the mess he made!"

Rose shook her head. "Mom, not now. Kristie doesn't want to hear your opinion of Ben."

"She already did." Mrs. Martin put her hand up quickly to silence Rose, who was becoming quite agitated. "But I know I've said too much already." She got to her feet. "I'll try to redeem myself by leaving you two alone."

Rose watched her mother leave the room. "She's still mad at him for all that he put me through," she explained.

"Moms are like that," I said knowingly.

Rose went on with her story. "After he threw the ring and yelled a few other lovely things at me, Ben got into his car and roared out of the drive. I had turned to go back inside the house, trying to decide whether I was relieved or devastated. That's when I heard a screech of metal and saw sparks sliding along the road. I heard a thud and a terrible scream. There are no street lights out here, and the night was dark because of the clouds. I ran to see what had happened, and there was a man pinned under a motorcycle."

"A man pinned under a motorcycle?" *Wait a minute!*

She nodded and shivered. "I knelt beside him and felt for his pulse. He was still alive. I had to leave him to rush back and call for the ambulance. Then I went back and sat with him until the ambulance and EMTs came. They finally ended up medevacing him. They put the helicopter down in the field over there." She pointed directly across the road from her house.

In my mind I could see the flashing lights, hear the crackle of static from car radios, feel the cold wash of the rain, smell the leaking gasoline and fear. And I could see Rose sitting by the road, holding the hand of the injured man, talking, talking to help fight shock, both his and hers.

"I sat in the rain with him for twenty minutes or more," she said. "He was in and out of consciousness, but he didn't seem to be in pain, which worried me a lot. As the medics worked on him, I saw them look at each other and I could tell their thoughts. No hope. No hope. That's how I knew he was going to die. 'Hold on,' I yelled at him as they carried him to the helicopter. But he was unconscious. Then suddenly the helicopter was gone, and so were the emergency vehicles. It was just us Martins again, and we never heard another word about anything. But I made him the cross."

"Oh, Rose!" I was so excited I was bouncing.

"He didn't die. I think that was my friend Jake."

"What?" She looked at me as though she was afraid to believe me.

"It was Jake! It had to be Jake. How many motorcycle accidents can you have out here? He's a paraplegic, but he's very much alive!"

Her hands clutched each other in her lap and her face was tense. "How can I find out if it's really him?"

"I know Jake's accident was last October, but I don't remember the date. I do know that it was at this intersection. I'll talk to him and then call you."

"Could you call him now?"

"I think this deserves a face-to-face conversation because the accident is such a painful subject for him," I said. "But I'll talk to him as soon as I can and let you know what he says."

Rose stared at me, tears in her eyes. "I've always thought the accident happened because Ben ran the stop sign when he left here in such a temper. I don't *know* that because I didn't see it, but he lives in that direction. I've always blamed myself. If it weren't for me, Ben wouldn't have been mad. If it weren't for me, he wouldn't have run that sign. If it weren't for me, that man wouldn't have died. It would be such a relief if he wasn't dead after all!"

I bet it would, after living with all that guilt for a year.

And of course he wasn't dead. He was alive and grumpy right up in Bird-in-Hand. Rose cried when I called her and told her that her cross could be taken down. No one had died that evening at that intersection, though I wasn't convinced Jake was completely living yet, either. But time and God could deal with that.

"You ought to meet her, Jake," I said to him one evening. "She's a very nice person and cute too. I think she'd feel so much better seeing you."

"Did she suggest this meeting?" he asked in an icy voice.

"No. It's my idea. It would set her mind at rest."

"Absolutely not!" he said, surprising me. "I do not want to meet this woman."

"She sat with you in the rain," I said, trying to shame him into it. "She made a cross in your honor."

"Kristie, don't push me. I do not want to meet her! Let me have some dignity, would you?" With that he stormed off to his rooms.

I sat in the front room and tried to understand why he was so angry with what I still thought was a great idea. The closest I could figure was that he was embarrassed that Rose had seen him as he'd been that night, injured, diminished, and in a situation beyond his control.

That was when I realized that Jake, for all his

passivity, was a control freak. In fact, I now understood, his passivity was his control mechanism for a life that was largely beyond him right now.

The first Sunday in November, the week after Ruth and Isaiah's banns were published, proved to be another rainy, cold day. As I drove to church, I hoped Thursday would be better for the wedding. After all the cleaning around the farm, it would be a shame if the mud and mess of a rainy day dimmed the gleam and shine of everyone's hard work. And where would they put well over a hundred people if some couldn't stand around talking outside while others sat eating inside? The barn?

I spent the morning in kindergarten church due to an emergency call last night from the November teacher who had a sick child. I was more than willing to help her out. There were fewer kids present than usual, probably due to the weather.

My paper bag pumpkins were a big success, though some of the drawn-on faces required loving, parental imagination to discern the features. But the kids were proud of their work, and that was what counted.

I waved goodbye to my last charge and gathered my supplies, hoping I'd see Clarke and we could go get something to eat. I could tell him Rose's story. Maybe we could talk about Ruth's wedding. With his knowledge of the Plain culture, he could probably tell me what to expect with the actual wedding ceremony itself.

I smiled to myself. One topic was as good as another. It was the man across the table who was important.

I hadn't seen Clarke since the Hurlbert rally, and I missed him. I couldn't deny it. I didn't even know him that well yet, and already I felt closer to him than I ever had to Todd. When we were together, it seemed he felt the same way, but he hadn't called.

I was belting my raincoat, humming to myself about being in love with a wonderful guy, when I glanced out the window. There was Clarke hurrying to his car. Without waiting to see me. And he wasn't alone!

He had his arm around the waist of a slim young woman who was trying to hold her umbrella over the two of them with somewhat limited success. Clarke was laughing as the rain slid off the umbrella and down his collar.

I was both surprised and appalled at the ferocity of my thoughts. For all I knew, Clarke was merely helping someone to her car. He was, after all, a nice guy and a gentleman.

Yeah, right. I watched with a sinking heart and thought of the times he had put his arm around my waist.

When Clarke and the girl reached his car, he opened the passenger door for her and assisted her in. He and she laughed together as she attempted to get the umbrella down and in without getting all wet.

Cute, I thought sourly. *So cute.*

Clarke climbed in his side of the car, and the girl turned to him. She threw her arms around him and kissed him happily on the cheek. Then she reached out and rubbed the side of his face, probably removing lipstick. He reached over and ruffled her hair. They drove away without a backward glance.

Waves of depression washed over me. I had thought—as recently as five minutes ago—that I was in the beginning stages of a most promising romance. Apparently I was the only one who thought so. I had leaped to a conclusion because the man looked at me kindly a few times and indicated to Nelson that he was my boyfriend— though now that I thought about it, he had never actually said those words. Nelson had. Clarke'd just been too polite to embarrass me in front of an obnoxious child.

I obviously was misinterpreting his intentions to fit my wishes rather than reality. A dinner with his aunt and uncle, two hospital taxi runs, a purse snatching, and a ride on a railroad do not make a deathless romance. In reality they didn't even make a good friendship.

I walked slowly to my car, strangely satisfied that the skies were crying with me. I couldn't help wondering if Ruth's ordered life allowed for romantic misjudgments like mine. Had she and Isaiah ever had a misunderstanding of any significance?

Or was I just experiencing the "freedom" I'd been so superior about just a couple of hours earlier?

I began to sing "Greensleeves."

Alas, my love, you do me wrong
To cast me off discourteously . . .

17

Once I had finally dragged myself to my car, I just sat behind the wheel, staring at the empty parking lot without seeing it. I was more than a little surprised at the intensity of the despair that twisted my heart. I'd known I cared a lot for Clarke, but the aching emptiness inside left no doubt that I had fallen a lot harder than I realized.

I watched rivulets of water slide down the windshield and thought melodramatically that I was watching my life slide away too, quietly, colorlessly, inevitably, disappearing into the gloom.

I remembered his hand cupping my cheek, his arm about my shoulders, his "May you be so lucky" to the lumpy Nelson. He had even bought one of my paintings. I sighed and wearily turned the key. When the engine of my sunshine yellow car turned over like always, I was strangely angered and offended.

"Don't you realize that we're broken here?" I whispered. My voice caught on the word "broken."

The car's mechanical heart didn't understand, and the purring continued. I drove to a burger drive-through, where I ordered a cheeseburger and a Coke. When they handed me the food, the smell made me nauseous. I handed it back to the disbelieving boy and drove away without even asking for my money back.

Somehow I made it to Holiday House where, still enveloped in melancholy, I made my way to Mr. Geohagan's room. I paused just inside his door, blinking against tears.

It took me a minute to realize that Mr. Geohagan was every bit as preoccupied as I was, but where I was drained, weary, and hurt, he was alert, all but sitting at attention as he listened intently to the man standing beside his bed. The man spoke to Mr. Geohagan in clipped, forceful sentences, and I was struck by the visual contrast between the frail old man in the bed and the tall, extremely thin man beside it.

"I'm sure you understand our concern," the man said.

Mr. Geohagan nodded. "I understand the problem quite clearly, but as far as I'm concerned, you needn't worry. Remember that something like this can affect me every bit as much as the rest of you."

"That's what I keep telling everyone, and I almost believe myself. Almost." The man rubbed his fingers back and forth across his forehead as if it hurt. "You're as involved as the rest of us; more, if the truth be known. You wouldn't do anything to upset things for us. You couldn't. But you understand why I have to ask."

"Sure," Mr. Geohagan said. "And I repeat: Don't worry about me."

The men's eyes locked with unusual intensity, and I felt waves of hidden meaning roll over the room like hurricane surf.

"If you say I needn't worry, Ev, I won't," the visitor said, but I heard reserve and uncertainty in his tone. "Your word has always been trustworthy."

"And it still is."

"There's a lot at stake here."

"I know exactly what's at stake," Mr. Geohagan said, his voice every bit as clipped and urgent as his visitor's. "And as you said, I have every bit as much riding on this whole thing as you do. You can trust me, Bill."

The man looked out the window, sighed, and turned back to Mr. Geohagan. "Quite honestly, Ev, they're worried about you."

Mr. Geohagan smiled sourly. "They are so thoughtful to be concerned about my health and the staggering costs of my care."

"Costs? That's not—" the man began, and then he stopped abruptly. "Costs?"

"Insurance only goes so far."

The man's jaw tightened. He gave a brief nod, turned, and strode from the room, his face angry and uncertain. He was no more aware of me than Mr. Geohagan was.

That's okay, guys. You don't need to acknowledge me. I feel pretty invisible anyway. Unnoticed. Unappreciated. Unwanted. Unloved.

My mother, strong lady that she was, always became angry at me when the melancholy part of my personality kicked in.

"I don't care if artists are sensitive and emotional," she'd say, finger waving in a most choleric way under my nose. "That's no excuse for letting your feelings run away with you. You always assume the worst. You always know it's the end of your world." She'd make an unpleasant noise in the back of her throat. "Kristina, for heaven's sake, get some backbone!"

Well, Mom, maybe tomorrow. Maybe it won't hurt as much then.

But I suspected it would. Tomorrow and tomorrow and tomorrow.

When the tall man left the room, Mr. Geohagan had fallen back on his pillows, completely spent, his eyes closed, his breathing raspy and strained. He scared me enough to pull me out of my morose and myopic self-absorption. Suddenly my pain wasn't the most important thing.

"Mr. Geohagan, are you all right? What can I get for you?" I asked, hurrying forward.

His eyes flew open and I saw fear there, desperation. "My oxygen," he whispered.

I pushed the buzzer beside his bed and held his hand as we waited for the nurse to come. Holiday House had, so far, been more than I had expected, and the care had been excellent.

"You mustn't allow that man to upset you so," I said. "It looked to me like he was trying to bully you."

"Don't worry . . . about it," he rasped, pausing to breathe after every two or three words. "I upset him . . . more than . . . he upsets me." His lips twisted in what was supposed to be a sly smile. "And . . . I love it."

"Why, Mr. Geohagan! I'm surprised at you!" I said it lightly, as though he had made a joke.

"I can be . . . a pretty tough . . . old bird . . . if I need to . . . be."

His thin hand went to his chest, and his whole body heaved as he struggled to draw in the air to sustain himself. I found myself taking great gulps, as though that might help him. I felt as I had that day in the emergency room, when I was certain he would die before Harriet returned. This time he was going to die before the nurse came. I pressed the emergency button several more times.

"Kristie, will you . . . do me a favor?" His hand grasped mine with unexpected strength in spite of the barely audible voice.

"Shh, don't get agitated." I patted his shoulder. "Of course I will." I tried to imagine the terror of gasping, of having lungs so impaired that they no longer could expand and contract enough to provide the necessary oxygen to the body.

"I need . . . some things from . . . storage."

"What do you need and where is it stored?"

"A garage. The key." He gestured toward the bedside table. "In the top drawer."

I opened the drawer and took out the familiar key, its mystery now solved. A storage garage, of all things.

A nurse suddenly appeared and I backed out of the way. In a few seconds the oxygen cannula was in place under Mr. Geohagan's nose, and in a few minutes he was breathing much more easily. While he rested for a bit, I sat and read the *Sunday News*—or tried to. My powers of concentration weren't working very well.

"Much better now," he said after about ten

minutes, and then he returned immediately to the subject on his mind. "Now this garage. I rented it so I'd have some place to keep the things Doris and I had. When I sold our house, I just couldn't bring myself to throw my whole life away. I felt dead enough as it was. So I stored it all."

He paused for a minute to think.

"Bring me everything on the desk," he whispered. "And everything in the left-hand file drawer." I listened carefully as he described the garage's location.

We both fell silent, he to rest, I to feign reading. When I looked up some time later, I found him studying me.

"What's the matter with you?" he asked. His voice, though far from strong, was much firmer.

"Nothing."

"Ha! Don't give me that. Hasn't anyone ever told you that you're a bad liar?"

"As a matter of fact, yes."

He nodded. "So what's his name?"

"What?"

"What's his name? A hound dog face like yours usually means some man's been doing some dirty work."

"How'd you get to be so smart?" I asked.

"Cathleen," he said. "I learned a lot of painful lessons from her there near the end."

I nodded. I just bet he did. I was silent a

minute, thinking of her extreme response to a failed romance. I knew that no matter how much I hurt, I would always consider her way out no way.

"I don't know that anyone's actually been unkind to me," I finally said. "It just seems that all the castles were as insubstantial as the air they were built on and all the happily-ever-afters were only in my imagination."

He blinked at me.

"In other words, I read more into things than was there." I shrugged, hoping my nonchalance hid the heartbreak. "It happens all the time, though not usually to me."

"Well, any man who'd let you get away must be crazy."

He was such a *nice* man. "You are very gallant, sir. And while I agree with your assessment of things, I'm still stuck with having to resort to a stiff upper lip and lots of prayer."

He flicked his hand like he was brushing away something of no value. "I doubt either will do you any good. What you need is another object for your affections."

Right. At the snap of my fingers another man not only worthy of my time but also interested in me would appear. "I can tell you haven't tried to date recently. Nice guys are scarcer than hen's teeth."

"No nice guys at work? Or where you live?"

"All the men I work with are already spoken for, and I live on an Amish farm, remember? I don't think I'd be happy married to an Amishman, no matter how nice he was. Culture and stuff."

"They're religious like you."

"They're religious, but not like me. Not like me at all. It's works versus grace."

"Whatever. Where'd you meet your last beau?"

I laughed. "Beau? Nobody's used that word since the days of Scarlett O'Hara. And I met him at the farm. He's the one whose car I bled all over the day I got bitten."

"And you don't want to resort to another physical ploy to get a new man? If it worked once . . ."

"This face can only take so many risks." I felt my dimple/scar. "There has to be a better way."

"Don't you have a favorite bar where some decent guys hang out?"

"I'm afraid I'm more a church mouse than a barmaid."

"Did this man go to church?"

I nodded. "It was one of the many things I liked about him."

"You can't trust men who go to church, Kristie."

"What?"

"I mean it. They're too honestly stupid."

I missed his strange logic.

Mr. Geohagan looked exasperated at my lack of understanding. "They don't lie on their income taxes. They don't cheat on their wives."

"This is bad?"

"They don't speed. No, cut that one. In fact, some of them drive like they've got God sitting in the seat beside them. But they don't take money out of the collection plate. I bet they don't even take office supplies for personal use. And they don't know right from wrong."

I laughed. "Don't you think you're being a bit inconsistent? It sounds to me like you've listed some very desirable traits except for the last one."

He shrugged.

"Okay, I'll bite. Why don't men who go to church know right from wrong?"

"Because they're too dumb to know what a wonderful woman you are. That's why!"

I luxuriated in his kind words. "Doris is a lucky woman."

He smiled, self-satisfied. "That she is. But I'll tell you one thing. She never met me at church. Never took me there, either, except the day we got married." There was a strange pride in his voice.

"And I say that's your loss." I kept my voice light.

"My loss?" His voice was suddenly harsh. "Just tell me one thing, Kristie. What's God ever done for me? And what's He doing for your broken heart? Don't you hurt, even though He's supposed to be loving you?"

I leaned forward and took his hand again. "God never promised to keep us from the problems and pains that everyone in the world has. All He promised to do was see us through the hurt, bear it with us, and reassure us that we aren't alone. That seems like a lot to me."

He sniffed. "You suffer from low expectations."

"Mr. Geohagan!"

"You'll never convince me that God cares. Never."

"Even though He gave His Son to die for you?"

"Rumor. Tradition. Lies."

"Truth."

He looked at me with pity. "I thought you were too intelligent to get taken in by religion."

"Are you bored in here?" I asked.

"What?" He seemed thrown off balance by my change of topic.

"Bored as in you don't have enough to do."

He frowned, unable to see where I was going. "Of course I'm bored."

"Then I've got a good project to fill some of your time. Read the Bible and check out God's claims and promises."

He looked less than excited with my idea. Boredom was obviously preferable. "I haven't got a Bible."

"Sure you do." I reached into his bedside table and pulled out a Gideon Bible. "I challenge you to read the Gospel of John. I'm going to get your papers for you. You read John for me."

He looked at me as though I had suddenly developed a bad odor.

"It's better for you than your daily diet of soaps," I said.

If possible, his lip curled further in disgust. "No wonder that guy dumped you," he said nastily. "You're too dictatorial."

I decided that maybe Doris wasn't so lucky after all.

18

There were pockets of time when I thought I'd die from the sharp pain that pierced my heart whenever I thought of Clarke. My breath would catch in my throat and my eyes would fill.

Maybe I'm overreacting, I'd tell myself as I struggled for control. Maybe I'm jumping to conclusions. Maybe there's nothing for me to be upset about. Maybe being kissed by a beautiful girl in the church parking lot doesn't mean a thing. After all, it could be a most trivial matter.

Then again, maybe it did mean something.

Maybe it meant a lot. Clarke wasn't the type to go around kissing girls lightly. After all, he was a responsible Christian leader, a counselor and teacher. Maybe the problem was my conclusion-jumping, but not in reference to him and her. In reference to him and me. I saw romance where there was none, affection where there was mere consideration and appreciation. After all, when Nelson blasted him with that question, what could he say?

"May you be so lucky when you grow up."

All that statement proved was that Clarke was too polite to embarrass me in public. If he really cared, he'd call or come see me.

And he did neither.

I sighed. Was this the pain and distress Todd was feeling? If so, it served me right to reap what I had sown.

Surprisingly, the arrival of Isaiah at the farm was a great help to me. He turned out to be one of the most pleasant people I'd ever been around. He had an indefatigably positive outlook on life, and he shared his good spirits through an unending stream of admittedly adolescent practical jokes.

John had the dubious pleasure of having the saltshaker lid and all the salt fall into his morning oatmeal as Ruth giggled in delight at the cleverness of her betrothed.

Mary lifted the lid on one of her pots and

screamed when she found four severed chicken heads where there should have been gently stewing bodies.

I bit into an egg salad sandwich only to notice a strange taste. When I lifted the top slice of bread to see what was wrong, I found one of Hawk's Milk Bones sitting soggily amid the eggs.

All this had happened within twenty-four hours of Isaiah's arrival.

On another front, Mary told me, "I think John will say yes to selling my paintings." As she spoke, she looked over her shoulder to see where Isaiah was. "But we won't do anything until after the wedding."

That made sense to me. "I'll do some scouting for places willing to carry your paintings while you wait." I knew that most of the area stores and galleries would jump at the chance to be part of the rare phenomenon of an Amish artist. We just had to find the situation best for Mary.

Ruth was giddy and Mary glowed with a quiet satisfaction. I tried not to be the little black cloud that dripped on everyone else's happy parade.

Living with the gentle paranoia Ruth's intended induced not only held up John's decision; it also helped me keep thoughts of Clarke at bay. Still, I thought it was a bit much the Monday evening before the wedding when I pulled out a chair and sat down at the kitchen table to talk to Mary and sat on Hawk's metal brush, bristles up.

"Ruth thinks he's wonderful," said a sympathetic Mary, trying not to laugh as I rubbed my punctured anatomy. "They've driven me wild with worry on many occasions, but I'm hard pressed not to like him."

"Ruth will never be bored," I said, placing the offending brush in plain view lest someone else get similarly perforated.

Mary sat across from me. "At least they're staying Plain. You probably don't understand how important that is to us, and I don't think I can begin to explain how thankful we are."

"I know how my parents would react if I turned my back on the Lord," I said, honored by Mary's openness.

She nodded. "Lately I've been so pleased to watch Elam develop a real faith. I hope that in time Ruth and Isaiah will learn not just the *Ordnung* but the living faith beneath it."

I rested my elbows on the table after checking carefully for any other booby traps. "How do you define faith, Mary?"

She frowned in thought. "Well, there's Jesus and there's the church. You believe in Jesus and keep the rules of the church, and you hope for the best. Of course, it's very important to be separate from the world so you don't become worldly and proud."

"You believe not being worldly is important to salvation?"

"Oh, yes. Don't you? 'Be not conformed to this world.' You have to be obedient to the *Ordnung* to be redeemed."

"Then living your life properly is as important as believing in Jesus?"

"Living in harmony with the church is necessary," she said, not really answering my question.

"Which is why I can't become a Christian," Jake said as he rolled into the room. "As you both have undoubtedly noticed, the church and I aren't exactly in tune."

Pain shot across Mary's face at her son's remark.

He smiled amiably, either oblivious to his mother's distress or ignoring it. "Do we have root beer, Mom?"

"There's some in the refrigerator. Let me get it for you." She pushed herself up from the table and went to the refrigerator. She pulled out a bottle and brought it to him. Then, with tears in her eyes, she went upstairs.

I turned on Jake. "How long were you eavesdropping?"

"Long enough. And don't scowl at me like that. I don't make a habit of skulking around with my ear to the wall. I happened to be coming in and hesitated a minute to hear what you two had to say." He shrugged. "Discussions about religion interest me. I keep hoping I'll learn something that allows a little bit of leeway for a black sheep like me."

"Don't do that, Jake," I said softly.

"Don't do what?"

"Don't hide behind the traditions of your family."

He watched me warily. "What do you mean?"

"You keep using your family's Amish-ness as an excuse for not becoming a Christian."

"What do you know about Amish-ness?" His voice was hard. "Do you think a couple of months on an Amish farm makes you an expert? You don't know anything about the pressure, the sermons, the rules."

"You're right; I don't. But you're missing my point. Being a Christian has nothing to do with traditions of any kind, no matter how much you love them or hate them. It has to do with a personal faith in Jesus as the Christ. Either you choose to believe in Him or you don't."

"That's not what they say."

"See what I mean?"

"What?"

"You're hiding behind them."

"I am not," he defended himself angrily. "I'm just stating what they say."

"The issue is what *you* say, Jake, not what they say," I said. "You can't spend your whole life saying it's everyone else's fault that you don't believe."

"Do you have any idea how tired I am of everybody telling me what I should do, what I should believe? Like I'm not smart enough to reach any conclusions of my own! 'Jake, do this.' 'Jake, do that.' 'Jake, go to school.' 'Jake, believe in Jesus.' You'd think I lost my mind, not my legs! Even you get on me, and not just about religion!"

"Me?"

"You want me to meet this Rose person. I have enough trouble just getting through every day without meeting the person who saw me at my worst!"

I refused to sympathize. "See? You're doing it again. Everybody's picking on you, so it's everybody's fault, not yours. It's even Rose's fault that you won't meet her because she happened to be indiscreet enough to be at the accident scene. I think you're hiding behind 'everybody' to avoid making choices of your own."

"No wonder you and Jon Clarke make such a good couple," said Jake stiffly. "I'm surprised he's not here by your side to help you reel me into the kingdom."

The phone in his apartment rang, and we both looked in its direction, distracted. I forced myself back to the subject at hand.

"Clarke has nothing to do with this conversation. And another thing! You sure are quick to change subjects when you don't want to talk!"

"It sure beats leaving the room," he called after me as I ran upstairs. "Lecture, lecture, lecture, run. Shouldn't you be getting me on my knees? After you heal my legs, of course?"

What an awful person he can be! I threw myself across my bed. *Terrible. Nasty. Ugly. Why should I waste my time worrying about him when I could worry about me instead?*

How proud the Lord must be of that mature, Christian attitude.

Tuesday was a bad day at school. I don't know whether the kids picked up on my distress and reacted to it, or whether they would have been terrible even if I'd been singing "I'm a Happy, Happy Christian" all day.

One of the first grade boys lost his lunch all over my desk, ruining my plan book and perfuming the room.

Two girls got in a hair-pulling, clothes-tearing fight over whose artwork was the best, and I was kicked and elbowed when I broke them up.

A troubled student took umbrage at an uncomplimentary comment from his neighbor about his most unique, all-black painting, and I got there just in time to prevent his braining the neighbor with a chair.

The mother of one of the girls in the fight came

after school and harangued me for allowing her daughter to be attacked. I refrained, but barely, from giving her my opinion of her "darling girl."

When I finally arrived at Ripley's Storage Garages, I was in as snarly a state of mind as I'd ever been. It was already four forty-five and getting dark fast. Eastern Standard Time had returned with the first weekend in November, and the earlier dusk was evident between the rows of garages that made up the Ripley complex. As I drove through the gateway in the chain-link fence, I was glad for the lights at regular intervals along the rows.

An older gentleman in the office gave me directions to Mr. Geohagan's unit, and I found it at the end of a long row of beige garages. I decided Mr. G must have a thing for corner properties.

I parked my car in front of the unit, and in the illumination from a light on the wall three garages down I fitted the key into the lock and lifted the lightweight fiberglass door.

By feeling along the wall inside the door, I found a switch. As light flooded the little room, a jumble of furniture, boxes, and miscellany sprang into view. I was looking at the putting away of a life, the ending of what had once been vibrant and alive and was now only a collection of dust-covered memories.

Lord, I don't know what You have in mind for me, but if it's possible, please don't let it be a hospital bed and a storage garage and nothing else. Please.

Along the left wall was a small work area containing a gray metal desk with a gooseneck desk lamp, a padded, ergonomically sound chair, two dinged and dreary gray file cabinets, and a very handsome, very out-of-place navy leather easy chair.

The desk was awash with papers left by a man obviously planning to return. But he hadn't, and probably he never would.

Why did he work here in the discomfort of this garage instead of in the relative comfort of his apartment? Certainly the apartment wasn't cheery, but it was better than this. And that leather chair—why keep it here instead of at home where he could kick back and read Louis L'Amour?

I glanced over my shoulder at the gaping door as I began gathering up the papers. How dark it now looked out there. I felt uncomfortable, vulnerable, alone, sort of itchy all over. Maybe I should close the door. But then I'd have to open it, and my imagination would conjure up all kinds of things just waiting for me on the other side.

"If I'm ever widowed," I once told my mother, "the first two things I'm going to buy are an electric garage door opener and an electric blanket."

Mom had only laughed. "Let's get you married before we worry about your being widowed."

But my comment was heartfelt, especially about the garage door opener. I had hated going out at night at my old apartment when I had to lift my garage door on unseen darkness. Who knew what would be lurking there, waiting to pounce on me? I hated just as much coming home, getting out to lift the door, pulling into the garage, and getting out again to lower the door. At least at the farm I parked out in the open, where it felt safer somehow.

I shivered as I turned back to Mr. Geohagan's desk, and not from the cold. I stuffed all the papers in a large accordion folder they had obviously been in before. I was just reaching to open the left file drawer in the desk when the hair on the back of my neck began prickling. I made myself turn around.

Two men stood in the doorway, silently watching me.

"What do you want?" I asked, my voice a mere whisper.

I looked from one to the other. They appeared ordinary. One had on a down vest and jeans and a Braves baseball cap. The other had a neat haircut, glasses, and his rugby shirt could be seen beneath a fleecy anorak that looked straight out of L.L.Bean.

"If you'll just get in your car and leave and

make believe you've never been here today, we won't bother you at all," the one in the anorak said. "We have no quarrel with you."

"What?" It wasn't one of my better moments.

"Go. Get out. Leave now and you won't get hurt."

"Just beat it out of here, lady." It was the man in the baseball cap.

He moved quickly toward me, and I had a flashback of this very man rushing down the steps at me. I backed away instinctively, bumping into the low arm of the easy chair. It caught me just behind my knees, and I fell backward into the soft, enveloping cushions.

Before I could extricate myself, he was beside me, grabbing me, pulling me upright, and pushing me toward the door. I stared in fascination at his hand on my arm. It was covered with a light-weight plastic glove.

"Hi," said an unexpected voice.

We three spun toward the door.

The old gentleman from the office walked up to the garage. He smiled brightly at me. "I just wanted to be certain you were all right back here before I went home for the day."

"She's fine," said Anorak Man. "We got here just a few minutes ago to help her move some of these things."

"Funny," the office man said. "I didn't see you drive in."

"You were busy," Anorak Man said reasonably. "We just drove on back. Don't worry about Kristie. We'll take care of her."

Somehow those words weren't comforting.

I smiled weakly at the office man, unable to open my mouth because of the paralyzing effect of a small, round object rammed into my back. Braves Cap Guy was actually holding a gun on me, and I'd heard a small click as he released its safety!

Suddenly hospital beds and storage garages and elderly ending of days looked very attractive.

The garage man waved cheerily and walked back into the night. As he disappeared from my view, I felt I was losing my dearest friend.

"Good girl," Braves Cap Guy said as he lowered the gun. He reached out to flick off the light in the garage. The darkness wrapped around me, scaring me, making me jumpier than I already was.

"Too bright," he said. "Now get in your car and disappear. And don't bother to send the police or draw pictures for them or anything. We know exactly where to find you, all cozy at that Amish place. And you'll regret it if we have to find you, believe me."

I believed him.

"Go!"

I started for the door, knowing that one or both of these men must be Mr. Stoltzfus' watchers.

But why in the world would anyone want to watch me?

But, of course, it wasn't me. It was Mr. Geohagan's papers. I was important only because I led them to the documents. As were my room and my purse important as they might provide some clue—or key—to the same thing.

Mr. Geohagan worked here rather than in his apartment to protect a secret. I looked at the desk and the papers resting there. Why were they so valuable?

Anorak Man saw my look and gave a low, wicked chuckle. I had last heard that laugh on the other side of a closet door.

I looked away quickly. If he thought I recognized him, he might not let me drive away so easily. I concentrated on Braves Cap Guy as he bent to pick up some papers that had fallen on the floor. As he bent, the beak of his cap hit the edge of the desk, and the cap fell to the floor.

Another non-surprise. Even though the light was faint, seeping into the garage from the lot lights, I easily recognized the man who had approached me in the woods. The cap, pulled down tight, had changed the lay of his ears to his head and covered his bald forehead. It had also made him look a little dim.

"Stupid," said Anorak Man. "Look at her face. She recognizes you. She can identify you."

Braves Cap Guy shrugged. "So what? She's not going to." He smiled at me, and all I could think of were night prowlers and beasts of prey, fangs dripping saliva in the moonlight.

"We can't let her go," Anorak Man was adamant. " She'll draw your picture for the cops, maybe not this week or next, but eventually. And then she'll draw mine. She's like that, honest and all. They'll have you in no time. And then me."

They stared at me, obviously trying to decide what to do. I wanted to yell that I'd keep quiet forever if they'd just let me go. But I knew they were right. I *would* draw their pictures or identify them from those huge books of mug shots everyone always studied on cop shows. I was like that.

"They said no rough stuff." Braves Cap Guy looked uncertain.

"So what?" Anorak Man said. "I'm in charge here, and I say we don't have a choice. We have to protect ourselves."

We were all quiet for a few minutes. I was too frightened to be thinking about much of anything, but I was as sure as I could be that they were considering ways to dispose of me.

"Gimme the gun!" Anorak Man said to Braves Cap Guy. His voice was so abrupt I jumped. He sneered at my fear as he held out his hand.

Braves Cap Guy hesitated.

"Give me the gun!" Anorak Man repeated through clenched teeth.

I'd have given him my gun if I had one. There was something incredibly commanding in a nasty, evil way about this man.

"But it's mine," Braves Cap Guy whined.

Anorak Man just stared, one eyebrow slightly raised above his glasses. If I could learn his trick of domination, I could teach senior high, even junior high, any day.

Reluctantly Braves Cap Guy held out the gun.

Anorak Man took it casually and held it, safety still off, at his side. "Now back our car to the door so we can empty this stuff fast," he ordered. "Then we'll take care of her."

As I stood with heart pounding and knees knocking, Braves Cap Guy, hat back in position, turned their car and opened the trunk. Casually he pulled out a tire iron, walked down three garages to the light and broke the bulb.

"Better get the next one too," Anorak Man said.

In the disorienting darkness I heard another bulb shatter, and I hugged myself as if I could hold onto what little courage I still had. Violent, irrational men were much more terrifying in person than in any book or movie.

"No one can see us now. And don't you try going anywhere." He grabbed my arm. "The gun is still pointed at you."

I couldn't see it, but I believed him.

Braves Cap Guy laid down the tire iron, and in the faint illumination of the trunk light began emptying the desk and file cabinets. He lugged load after load as Anorak Man and I stood in the deep shadows and watched.

"Get every piece," Anorak Man ordered. "Every single scrap of paper."

"You could at least help," Braves Cap Guy complained.

"And leave her alone?"

"Then she can help."

Anorak Man shook his head, though I doubt the Braves Cap Guy saw. "I like knowing exactly what she's doing. Just cut your grousing and move it." He sighed as if he bore a great weight. "I can't wait to get away from you and your whining!"

"I do not whine!" Braves Cap Guy spun and looked furiously at Anorak Man. As he did so, he lost his grip on the armload of papers he was carrying, and they slithered to the ground in a pulpy waterfall. An errant breeze caught some, and they fanned out across the drive.

"Stupid!" Anorak Man reached to catch a few sheets that fluttered in his direction.

As he reached, I pulled free and pushed. He fought for balance. I caught him in the rump with my foot, and he toppled over on his face. His gun went flying as he put his hands out to protect himself. It struck the ground and discharged. I could hear pings as the bullet ricocheted.

Braves Cap Guy screamed, but I couldn't tell whether in pain or anger. And I didn't wait to find out. I tore out the door and around the corner at the end of the line of garages into total blackness. My heart hammered in my throat as I put my hands out in front of me and ran sightlessly. Any risk was better than standing around docilely, waiting to be shot. My back itched and I hunched my shoulders as I anticipated the smash of a bullet into my body.

I flew around a second corner and felt true terror as I ran headlong into the grip of a third man.

19

My heart stopped as a hand clasped firmly over my mouth.

"Don't make a sound," a voice whispered in my ear.

I couldn't have spoken if my life depended on it.

"Run!" it whispered.

Like I needed to be told to do that.

I fled willingly behind the sprinting figure. We rounded one corner, then another, zigzagging through the rows of garages. Now that I was back in the main part of the complex, the little lights on the garages showed us the way. Of course, they would also show the bad guys the way.

Shouts and shots followed us as Anorak Man and Braves Cap Guy gave chase, but we always managed to be at least a corner ahead. Even so, my back twitched and I imagined the staggering impact of a bullet tearing through sinew and spine, piercing the heart, *my* heart.

We stopped to catch our breath in the shadows of a rented moving van parked before a storage unit. It was in that moment that I realized my rescuer was Clarke. He held out his arms, and I buried my face in his chest and clung. My legs were like spaghetti, and my breath rasped. I'd never been so terrified and so happy in my life.

"What are you doing here?" I panted.

"Are you all right?" he said into my hair. His arms were a steel vise clamping us together. All the worries and conjectures of the few days fell away.

A shout from Anorak Man sounded just around the corner, and Clarke and I broke apart. I made a strange little hiccupy noise as I swallowed a scream.

He grabbed my hand and we dived to the ground

together, rolling under the moving van. We lay huddled in the middle, arms wrapped around each other. Any other time it would have been my current version of heaven to be so entwined, but now all I could think was, *Lord, don't let any of our feet be hanging out, okay?*

"You check down this aisle," yelled Anorak Man. He was mere yards away, so close my skin retracted in aversion. "I'll go to the gate to make sure she doesn't get out there. We can't let her escape!"

Footsteps thundered toward us and came to a stop beside the truck. I stared at a pair of black-and-white sneakers just inches from my face, as mesmerized by them as a cobra is by the charmer's music. The heels were toward me, and I could see that Braves Cap Guy ran the left one down pretty badly. Bad hip? Who cared?

I was afraid to breathe, though Braves Cap Guy was puffing so hard he probably wouldn't have heard me if I had a major sneezing fit.

The sneakers turned to face the truck. The toes were scuffed and one lace was undone. Maybe he'd trip the next time he ran, we should be so lucky. Of course, that might mean that we were also running, having been discovered down here.

"Okay," yelled Braves Cap Guy. "Come out of there!"

I flinched as if he'd hit me, and I felt Clarke

go rigid beside me. How had he known? A reasoned guess? Maybe I'd underestimated him. Or maybe it was just luck? Or was something hanging out after all? A foot? A jacket?

Oh, Lord, please, no!

The black-and-white sneakers walked right up to my nose, and I squeezed my eyes shut on the if-I-can't-see-him-he-can't-see-me premise.

"Out!" he ordered. And he yanked the door of the truck cab open.

Clarke and I sagged with relief.

Braves Cap Guy swore as he slammed the door shut. In frustration he swung his tire iron viciously into the side of the truck just inches from me, not once but twice. The clanging of metal on metal at such close quarters reverberated inside my head.

Braves Cap Guy stood quietly beside the moving van, listening. Then he turned away and rounded a corner.

Relief made my ears buzz. In the warm flush of temporary safety I thought I would be happy just lying here all night beside Clarke. Surely the men would decide to leave with the revealing light of morning, and then everything would return to normal, whatever that was.

Clarke tightened his arm around me and pulled me close.

"We're going up," he whispered in my ear. "It's too dangerous here!"

Up? Up? To what? And how?

He rolled out from under the truck, and I followed. He quickly climbed onto the vehicle's hood, reached down, and pulled me up after him. When he said up, he meant it quite literally.

I cringed at the pop and crack of the metal underfoot. Surely Braves Cap Guy would hear, would come flying around the corner and catch us midclimb. The thought of his tire iron across my shins or knees made me shiver uncontrollably.

"Hurry!" I whispered, as if Clarke needed my encouragement.

He clambered up the windshield to the roof of the cab and then onto the roof of the truck body, and I climbed right after him. In a quick surge of movement he was on the garage roof. He turned to give me a hand, but I was already crouched on the roof beside him.

Suddenly Anorak Man raced down the passage below us, and we fell flat. A small cloud of dust rose about us as years of accumulated roof dirt was disturbed. I fought the urge to sneeze by rubbing my nose like mad.

"Did you hear that?" Anorak Man hissed.

Braves Cap Guy limped behind him, winded and unhappy. "What?" he gasped. "I didn't hear nothing."

Anorak Man snorted. "Of course you didn't. How could you? You're panting too hard to hear anything. I can't stand it! Why do they keep making me work with you? You drive me crazy!"

"Don't push me, Marty," Braves Cap Guy snarled.

"Put that tire iron down, you idiot." Marty's voice dripped condescension. "I don't have time for your macho nonsense. We've got to find that girl. Besides—" There was a lengthy pause, and I could just picture them, each trying to stare the other down. "Don't forget that I have the gun."

There was a moment of tense silence, and then Braves Cap Guy must have blinked. I heard Marty snort derisively.

He said, "You go that way. I'm going this."

Clarke and I stayed still until both men were some distance away. Then, bending low, we moved cautiously along the flat, shadowy roof away from our erstwhile ladder. At the far end of the building, we lay huddled in a darkness deepened by the entrance lights below. I listened in heart-stopping tension as Marty and Braves Cap Guy ran up and down the rows below us.

Dear Lord, don't let them think to look up! Please! They're not in the mood to be kind.

When the men stopped immediately beneath us, I squeezed my eyes shut and ducked my head. Clarke's arm tightened around me. Once again we were afraid to breathe.

"Maybe she . . . got out after . . . all." Braves Cap Guy was gasping, speaking only two or three words at a time, sounding as bad as Mr. Geohagan. The man needed an exercise program desperately.

"She didn't get out." Fury filled Marty's voice. "I would have seen her. And she didn't scale the fence, not with that barbed wire around the top of it. No, she's here somewhere. There are a couple of stored RVs in the back. Look in them."

"I already did. She's not there."

"Well, let's look under them."

And they were off.

I leaned close to Clarke's ear. What a nice ear. And he smelled good too. "You sure called that one right," I whispered. "If we'd stayed under that truck, they'd have found us in time."

I felt him smile. "I have to tell you," he whispered in my ear. "When I heard those lights break and then that shot, my heart stopped." His voice shook at the memory. "Try not to do that to me again, okay?"

Then he kissed me, and I melted against him. Most appropriately, bells and whistles sounded, accompanying the fireworks exploding in my head.

No, not bells and whistles. It sounded more like sirens.

I pulled back. "Sirens?"

"The cops," he said.

"Where'd they come from?"

"We called them."

"We did?"

"Not you-and-me we but Mary Ann-and-me we. And the attendant." He leaned over to kiss me again.

I put a hand to his chest. "Mary Ann?" A chill went down my spine. "Mary Ann?" I just bet she was blonde and cute and had an umbrella.

Below we heard shouting, running, cursing, and brilliant searchlights blazed. A shot, then two, tore the night.

Braves Cap Guy yelled, "Don't shoot! Don't shoot! I'll talk! I didn't do nothing!"

"Shut up," Marty bellowed at him. "We'll be out by morning!" He must have turned to the cops because his next words were, "I demand a lawyer."

"Sure, sure," said a new voice. "You have the right to remain silent . . ."

The confusion below was nothing compared to the confusion I felt. My knight had come to my rescue, but he had brought along the fair Mary Ann.

That wasn't the way it was supposed to work!

I started to get up. No more coziness on the roof for me.

"Get down here!" Clarke grabbed me none too gently and pulled me back.

I lost my balance and fell on him. Accidentally my elbow caught him in the gut. I tried to feel badly as he wheezed, "Dangerous. Bullets."

There hadn't been any bullets for several moments.

I rested my head on Clarke's chest and listened to his two-timing heart beat. "How did you know to come here?" I asked in what I hoped was a cool, detached manner.

"I went to the Zooks," he said, "and Mary told us you might be here. We arrived just as the attendant was leaving. He told us you and your two friends were in the garage at the end of the third line. As soon as he said 'friends,' I was worried. You've had too many strange things happening to you recently. 'Is one of them wearing a baseball cap?' I asked. 'Yeah, now that you mention it,' the attendant said. 'A Braves cap.' And then the lights were broken. We heard them shatter. I told Mary Ann and the attendant to call the cops, and I took off to see if you were all right. When the shot was fired, I . . ."

"I was doing okay," I said with a distinct lack of appreciation for his emotional turmoil and his gracious rescue effort.

"That you were," he agreed magnanimously, kissing me on the top of my head.

Suddenly we noticed that it was quiet below.

A woman's voice rang out. "Clarke! Jon Clarke! Where are you?"

"Mary Ann," he told me needlessly.

"Oh, goody," I said. "I'm so glad."

He didn't even hear my sarcasm.

We got to our feet and leaned over the roof. We watched as people in blue scurried up and down the rows, looking strangely out of perspective. Red and blue lights flashed, and a pair of men in handcuffs were being put in a police car. The attendant and a blonde stood off to the side, looking worried. She was wringing her lovely hands while the attendant patted her on the back to comfort her.

"Up here!" Clarke yelled. "Up here!"

I was vaguely aware of a ladder being placed against the building, vaguely aware of climbing down it. All I could see was the little curly-haired blonde whose face lit up when she saw Clarke in one piece. She pointed and jumped up and down and clapped her hands, and I hated myself for my jealousy.

"I was so worried about you!" she shouted as she rushed forward. She threw her arms around Clarke as soon as his feet hit the ground. She kissed him with obvious affection, looking far more lovely than worried.

I didn't even want to think about what I looked like, rolling around on the ground under trucks, lying on dirty roofs. Some comparisons are too painful.

"Mary Ann, I want you to meet Kristie." Clarke smiled from one of us to the other.

Mary Ann smiled charmingly at me. "I'm so glad to meet you!"

I tried to smile back. I wondered if I looked as pickled as I felt.

"Excuse me, Miss Matthews, but we need to speak with you a few minutes." It was one of the policemen, saving me before I thoroughly disgraced myself by saying what I was thinking or by bursting into tears. He took my arm and led me gently but firmly to his car.

I looked back over my shoulder at Clarke and shrugged. I hoped I looked what-can-you-do? In reality I felt so relieved to be out of a situation I wasn't certain I could handle that I wanted to hug the cop.

"Just sit right down and tell me what happened here tonight," he said briskly. Brisk was good. I could deal with brisk. It was kindness and sympathy I didn't think I could handle.

Another officer began talking to Clarke and Mary Ann and the attendant. Then I heard Mary Ann say, "But if we don't leave now, Clarke, we'll miss our plane." She turned to the officer they had been talking to. "I haven't be n home in over a year, and I can't wait for us to get there!"

Us. How delightful.

"Kristie," Clarke called as Mary Ann pulled on his arm.

I smiled sweetly at him and turned my back, giving my full attention to my interview. It was preferable to murdering him and/or Mary Ann in full view of the authorities.

20

I drove to Holiday House on my way home from school the next day, Wednesday. I walked up the front walk past the great copper beech with its masses of golden leaves gracefully bending to touch the ground. Clusters of lavender, crimson, and bronze chrysanthemums brightened the front porch and sat in brass pots in the lobby. Heavy brass chandeliers hung from the ceiling, casting a warm glow over the green-and-wine upholstered furniture and oriental rugs.

Holiday House was a beautiful place. When the time came for me to go to a care facility, I sure wouldn't mind coming here. If I could ever afford it. I couldn't begin to imagine how expensive it was, especially for someone with a private room like Mr. Geohagan.

I found him sitting in bed surrounded by reams of paper.

"Kristie!" he said as soon as he saw me. "Are you all right? They didn't hurt you, did they? And the police treated you with respect? The press didn't bother you?"

"I'm fine," I assured him. Not happy. Not excited about life. Not ever planning to laugh again. But also not physically harmed. Fine.

"The police told me what happened when they brought me my material this morning." He laid a protective hand on the stack of innocent-looking papers resting on his stomach.

I stared somewhat resentfully at the papers. What was in them that made those unknown men take such extreme action? And what could possibly be worth putting me in such jeopardy not just last night but several times?

Mr. Geohagan saw me staring at them and misunderstood. "These aren't the originals," he said. "They're copies. The police need the originals for evidence against those guys. They said you made a great ruckus until they promised to deliver copies to me." He grinned at me. "I'm proud of you. I just wish I'd seen you in action."

It was a good thing he hadn't seen me last night. I had behaved quite badly. I'd been upset about Clarke—massive understatement—and I focused all that distress on the poor policeman who had to deal with me. I think I even cried a bit over how important it was to get those papers to the poor and dying man to whom they belonged.

"He was counting on me," I had said with exaggerated histrionics. "Please don't let it look like I've disappointed him. I couldn't stand that! He has no one else in the whole world!"

In retrospect it was enough to make me gag.

Mr. Geohagan took my hand in his thin, dry

one. He patted me gently. "I spent the last couple of days worrying about you," he said. "First there was that louse, What's-his-name, and then those terrible men last night!"

"I'll be fine," I said. I tried to smile reassuringly, but I gave up the effort. "Eventually, anyway. I'm sad right now, but I'm strong, you know. I certainly don't plan to do anything like Cathleen, either on purpose or accidentally, if that concerns you. I plan to depend on God to help me get through it all."

Some of Mr. Geohagan's solicitude faded.

"Don't go getting mad at the mere mention of God," I said. "You look like a thundercloud trying to find the energy to crack the skies open."

"That bad?"

I nodded. "Worse. Almost as bad as me."

We sat in companionable silence for a few moments.

Finally I said, "Well, I got your papers for you. Did you read the Gospel of John for me?"

"Believe it or not, I did. It was kind of interesting."

I think I hid my surprise. "How was it interesting?"

He cleared his throat self-consciously. "I wasn't aware that Jesus was so outspoken about Himself. 'I'm the Bread of Life.' 'I'm the Lamb of God.' 'I'm the only way to God.' I thought men had made all those things up because they wanted them to be true. Of course, maybe they still did. After all, Jesus didn't write the book of John. John could say anything he wanted."

I nodded. "Sure, John or others could have made those things up, but would they then die for things they knew were lies?"

"Maybe they didn't lie. Maybe they told the truth as they knew it. Maybe Jesus lied," the old man said. "Maybe He's no more God than the nut on the corner."

"Could be," I agreed. "But would people die for someone who was a liar or nut? Or live for one, either?"

"People are notoriously gullible. There's always some group following some demented guru somewhere."

"True. But those cults always die out, sometimes by their own hand. We're talking about millions of people over a period of two thousand years when we talk about all those who have followed Jesus."

He looked at me. "You obviously think He was telling the truth."

"I do."

He pulled a piece of paper off one of the piles on his bed and turned his attention ostentatiously to it. "I'm not so sure myself. Maybe I'm just not as trusting as you." He grabbed a second sheet of paper. "I need to think about it some more."

I recognized the finality in his tone. There would be no more talk about God today. That was all right. I would allow him to set the pace. It wasn't my job to change his heart, just to help him consider. I reached in my new handbag for a paperback and settled back to read as though I still had the ability to concentrate. Hah! All I saw when I looked at the page was a beautiful blonde with her arms wrapped around Clarke's neck.

Oh, Lord! How did this happen? How did I get so emotionally involved so quickly?

I turned a page so Mr. Geohagan would think I really was reading.

How had I misunderstood Clarke so? Was I really that stupid? That gullible? My father should be thanking his lucky stars that I hadn't gone into the law. Someone as foolish as I was would have made a rotten attorney.

There was a knock on the door, and a young man with the strangest shape I'd ever seen entered. His legs seemed to begin under his arm pits, and he looked as though he had no chest. I studied him, wondering where he kept his heart and lungs and other thoracic items, happy to think about something besides my own misery.

He nodded politely at me but turned his attention to Mr. Geohagan. "I think you wanted to see me?"

"Ah. Yes, yes, yes. Come in. Come in." Such

enthusiasm made me study the unusual man even more.

Looking hopeful, the strangely shaped man oozed to the side of the bed without seeming to move, an impressive accomplishment considering that he was all legs.

"Kristie, I don't mean to be impolite, but I must talk to this young man for a while," Mr. Geohagan said, smiling apologetically.

"I understand." I got quickly to my feet and waved a friendly farewell. "I'll see you later."

I left Holiday House and drove home, back into all the chaos and excitement of Ruth's wedding. Just what I needed. I sighed as I climbed out of my car.

What ironic timing, Lord. My world's falling apart while Ruth is building hers. I'm glad for her. I really am. I want her and Isaiah to be as happy as any couple ever was. But does everything have to be so hard for me right now? It hardly seems fair.

I went upstairs and lay on my crimson-and-blue quilt, where I stared miserably at the ceiling. When a stray tear began rolling across my temple into my hair, I turned on my side and let it be absorbed by the quilt. I shivered, and then I twitched and turned until the quilt was covering me. I curled on my side again, trying to get warm.

I shall stay here forever, Lord, curled in this tight little ball of pain. You don't mind, do You?

Even if the Lord didn't mind, which I suspected He did, I knew that eventually Mr. Edgars would. He had this thing about his teachers coming to work each morning. At least I had arranged to take tomorrow off for the wedding. I sighed deeply, a melancholy and self-pitying habit I had recently acquired.

I'll break it, Mom. I promise. Someday. When I'm happy again. If I ever am. Just don't wave that finger in my face. This isn't buck-up-my-girl time.

I sighed again. Between thoughts of Mom and Mr. Edgars, my wallowing had lost its flavor. I might as well get up and go eat dinner—if I could swallow. I pulled myself upright and went downstairs to see who was here now.

Friends and relatives I had never seen before had been visiting all week, helping with preparations and offering good wishes, and the festive air had intensified as the wedding day grew ever closer. A new Amish family was about to be established, and the whole society recognized the significance and importance of this fact. The Lancaster County Amish community was healthy and growing. The retention rate after *rumspringa* was impressively high. And Ruth and Isaiah were another patch in the quilt of the People's lives.

With tomorrow the big day, the shed off the kitchen bulged with food, provisions had been made to stable all the horses expected, and the big downstairs room had been emptied of all of its everyday furniture.

"How long will this wedding last?" I asked Jake. "The actual ceremony, I mean."

He sat in the doorway to his apartment, and I sat on the bottom step leading to my rooms. We were a little pocket of calm in the whirlwind that had been sweeping the house since daybreak.

The men had been killing and cleaning chickens, ducks, and turkeys; the women had been baking pies, making dressing to stuff the fowl, and peeling enough potatoes to feed my entire school. The men also cleaned the celery, emptied the garbage, and built temporary tables for the wedding feast. These tables now lined the entire downstairs room. The house was redolent with the scent of onions, celery, and spices.

"The service will take three to four hours," Jake said stiffly. He was still slightly angry with me over my accusation two nights ago that he hid behind others. Or maybe it was from the suggestion that he meet Rose. I didn't have the emotional energy to figure it out right now. Maybe later.

"It takes four hours?" I stared at him with no enthusiasm. "I'm used to sitting still for thirty-five to forty-five minutes for a sermon at most. Four hours is a bit long, isn't it?"

"And wait until Old Amos gives his sermon,"

Jake said with a harsh laugh. "He says the same thing every time. The same thing. Not that you'll understand." He looked at me. "It'll all be in High German."

Four hours of High German. Maybe I should just go to school after all and show up in time for the feast.

Ruth gave a sudden peal of laughter at something Isaiah said, and as I watched them, I knew I wouldn't miss this wedding for anything. Not only was I curious, but I liked Ruth and her practical joker very much.

"What will this Old Amos say that I won't understand?"

"He always talks about Noah," Jake said. "He used to do Sarah and Abraham until finally someone told him that he always said the same thing. So he switched, and now he always says the same thing about Noah."

"What does he say?"

"He talks about how corrupt Noah's world was and how Noah and his family followed God and how God kept them safe through the flood. So everyone should be certain they raise up a family that follows God, and He'll keep them safe through the floods of life."

"That doesn't sound too bad," I said.

Jake shrugged, forgetting to be angry for the first time since our fight. "It takes him at least a half hour to say it."

I laughed. "How about your father? Does he speak at weddings?"

"Always, but he tries to tailor his comments to the couple, and he works hard to be short and to the point."

"That's not surprising," I said as Jake's phone sounded in the distance. "Your father's a very fine man."

Jake stiffened suddenly, looked at me as if he'd never seen me, and then wheeled into his rooms without a word. He shut his door firmly behind him.

I sat, confused, thinking back over what I'd just said. How could I have upset him by saying his father was a fine man?

I went back upstairs feeling as dynamic as melted ice cream.

I didn't feel much better the next morning as I dressed for the wedding, but the excitement was contagious as soon as I came downstairs. Ruth and Isaiah and their two attending couples had already left for the Stoltzfus farm where the ceremony was to take place, but the Zook farm was bustling with last-minute activity. I was surprised to learn that John and Mary probably wouldn't go to the wedding. They would be too busy with the duties of preparation and hosting.

My mother would die before she missed my wedding—if and when I ever had one. And Dad had big plans to give his baby away, even though he always teased about holding the ladder so my groom and I could elope. It seemed very sad that John wouldn't get to preach at his own daughter's wedding.

"Won't Ruth and Isaiah feel bad if your parents aren't there?" I asked Jake as he drove me to the Stoltzfus farm. He offered no explanation for his abrupt leaving last night, but his stiffness had returned.

"Parents often don't go to the wedding," he simply said. "They're too busy with last-minute preparations for the feasting. Everybody understands."

I shrugged mentally. If everyone understood, then it wasn't an issue. Cultural differences were such fascinating things.

I took a seat on the back bench in the women's section and watched the festival of Amish life swirl around me. Several of the women whom I had previously met nodded shyly to me and smiled. I was relieved to see I wasn't the only English guest, but we were a definite minority. I saw Andy and Zeke slip into seats beside Jake. It was warming to see the brothers shake hands with obvious affection. The rest of the English family, including daughters-in-law and grandchildren, sat near me in the back. Though they were relatives, this was a community day, and none of us were part of the community.

Ruth and Isaiah sat on the front row with their

attending couples. One by one the district ministers rose and gave their sermons on the responsibilities and privileges of marriage. Just as Jake had warned, Old Amos rambled on and on. By contrast, the others spoke briefly and forcefully. I had no idea what any of them said, but everyone listened carefully and nodded their heads.

I thought of the last wedding I had attended, that of my college roommate. There had been flowers and music, and Mandie had worn yards of lace. The groomsmen had worn morning coats, and the bridesmaids, including me, had been resplendent in a gorgeous shade of teal and carried nosegays of pink and crimson roses with trailing ivy. We had purposely and forcefully called attention to ourselves, dressing extravagantly for the special occasion.

By contrast Ruth and Isaiah were dressed much as they were any other day except that everything they wore was new. Ruth had told me that she would take the fresh white cape and apron she was wearing and pack them away, not wearing them again until her burial, but Isaiah's shirt and pants and hat would join his wardrobe as Sunday clothes.

My back hurt before the service was half over, but I tried not to squirm, especially since the children around me were sitting so quietly. One mother near me touched her fidgeting three-year-old, and he immediately stilled. A small piece of whoopie pie was his reward.

Suddenly, all I wanted in this world was a whoopie pie.

When the service finally ended, everyone headed for the Zook farm. Jake and I arrived first, and he pulled as far out of the way as he could. The rest of the family parked off the farm and walked over.

Soon buggy after buggy turned into the drive. The horses were quickly released from the shafts and led to the makeshift barn, where they were tethered, fed, and watered. Buggies filled the drive, a sea of gray enclosures and black wheels, the shafts pointing to the sky.

The men gathered in groups to talk and tell stories, their black felt hats firmly in place. The teenagers eyed each other in the manner of teens of any culture, and the little children played tag and kicked an old soccer ball, working off some of their contained energy. The women, chattering and laughing, gravitated to the kitchen and the final preparation for serving the food.

As I watched the press of people, I felt very much apart from them. I wanted only to be alone. I *needed* to be alone. All the camaraderie and love was more than I could deal with at the moment.

I slipped upstairs and traded my heels for a pair of flats. I hoped Ruth didn't see me leave, but I doubted it would even register if she did. The scores of people milling around gossiping, storytelling, and eating made it impossible to know who was doing what or going where.

I walked slowly down the road to Aunt Betty Lou's and Uncle Bud's, where I'd parked my car. It was a crisp November day, sunny and bright. The branches were largely bare, the flowers dead, shriveled by the sharp snap of frost last week. It was the beginning of the stark season.

I drove my yellow car aimlessly for a while, and then I found myself pulling up in front of Holiday House.

Well, why not? I parked and went up to Mr. Geohagan's room.

When I walked in, he was busy talking to the guy with no chest, the one who had visited him yesterday. They were examining some of the papers Mr. Geohagan had spread all over the bed.

They stopped talking as soon as I walked in the room, looking at me and then at each other as though I'd caught them spiking the punch at the high school dance. Mr. Geohagan frowned and the strange man stared as though he couldn't believe I had been so tactless as to enter.

I suddenly felt thirteen, the awkward, inept intruder who wanted to be part of the gang but would never be accepted. I blinked in surprise. What was happening here? The strange man was the one who didn't belong, not me. I'd literally risked my life for this old man. I was the true and loyal friend. Wasn't I?

Mr. Geohagan waved his hand dismissively at me. "Another time, Kristie," he said abruptly.

"Sure," I said and left.

I told myself all the way down the hall that the tears stinging my eyes were foolish, that Mr. Geohagan hadn't meant to hurt my feelings, that I was just super sensitive right now. And while I knew I was right, I still had to blink like crazy to keep tears from spilling over and streaming down my cheeks.

If I didn't count stray tears, which I didn't, I hadn't cried about Clarke yet. I knew that when I did, it wouldn't be a pretty sight. My skin gets blotchy and my nose turns red. My face scrunches up in a pathetic mask. If and when I cried, I'd better be alone.

In the lobby I picked up the last copy of the morning's *Intelligencer Journal*. I looked at the front page as much to protect my wobbling self-control as to see what was going on in the world. A supremely confident Adam Hurlbert, the perfect candidate, smiled at me from under an astonishing headline that read:

ACCUSATIONS HURLED AT HURLBERT
Would-Be Senator Cited for Tax Evasion

21

I read the article with the byline of Barnum Hadley in disbelief.

Adam Hurlbert, Pennsylvania's front-running candidate for the United States Senate, has been accused of tax-evasion. The *Intelligencer Journal* has turned over to police evidence uncovered by this reporter that documents these charges.
Included in the evidence is a record of Hurlbert's personal expenses for the years 1990–2006. The record clearly shows Hurlbert spending money far in excess of his declared income for these same years. Receipts for many extravagant purchases, such as vacation villas, furniture, and jewelry, even a yacht— "the tip of the iceberg," says an unidentified source—are included as proof of the charges.
Also included in the evidence turned over to the police is a detailed financial statement purporting to show that when Hurlbert Construction contracted or sub-contracted with firms, Adam Hurlbert,

CEO and sole owner of Hurlbert Construction, inevitably made large personal investments in the stock markets or large deposits in banks outside the country. The timing of these financial transactions is at best suspect.

Authorities will investigate the possibility of illegal kickbacks.

Hurlbert's local campaign headquarters refuses to comment on the story, saying only that the candidate and his wife, Irene Parsons Carmody Hurlbert, daughter of former Pennsylvania governor Benjamin Parsons, are in western Pennsylvania soliciting last-minute support for Tuesday's election.

I looked up in shock. "He's a crook? I can't believe it!"

I must have spoken aloud because a man walking by said, "I know. I can't believe it, either. And I was going to vote for the guy!"

"Me too," I said, holding out the paper. "Do you think it's all true?"

"Do you think they'd print it if it weren't? The evidence must be pretty solid, or they'd never risk the legal consequences."

Still shaking his head, the man shuffled off to his unknown business, and I walked slowly to my car.

Poor Irene! What must it be like to wake up one morning and find you're married to a criminal? I couldn't imagine.

I cocked an eyebrow. If she hadn't already known.

I actually felt sorry for Nelson, the poor little twit. It was going to be bad enough for him without having the kids rag on him about his stepfather. How the mighty are fallen.

Friday morning's *Intell* story took my breath away.

HURLBERT CAUSES GIRL'S DEATH
He Deserted Young Lover for Irene

In front of me was a picture of Adam Hurlbert and a lovely young woman identified as Cathleen Geohagan. I stared at the photo. She was gorgeous, truly beautiful with her radiant smile. No wonder her father had said I didn't look like her.

The *Intelligencer Journal* has learned that Pennsylvania's home and family candidate for the United States Senate, Adam Hurlbert, 52, was involved in a sexual relationship as recently as last year with Cathleen Geohagan, then 21. When he left her without warning for Irene

Parsons Carmody, the widowed daughter of Pennsylvania governor Benjamin Parsons, Geohagan collapsed. A short time later she took her life by mixing alcohol and prescription drugs.

Not only did Hurlbert's marriage to Irene Carmody allegedly lead to the death of Cathleen Geohagan, but shortly thereafter Geohagan's mother, Doris Geohagan, 62, suffered a massive stroke. Mrs. Geohagan lives today comatose in a nursing home with no hope for recovery.

The girl's bereaved father, Everett Geohagan, 64, now childless and a virtual widower, shared with this reporter from his nursing home bed his great and continuing sorrow that a man capable of such cruel and immoral behavior seeks to be elected to one of the highest offices in our land. "Dare we trust a man who behaved as Adam Hurlbert did?" Everett Geohagan asks. "His opportunistic transfer of affections killed my daughter as surely as if he'd pulled the trigger of a gun he was pointing at her. And for what? So he could be senator?"

Another article on the front page, a follow-up

to yesterday's tax evasion story, was an account of Hurlbert's arrest. He had surrendered to authorities at his home upon his return from Pittsburgh the previous evening. Accompanying the story were pictures of the police at the door of the Hurlbert home and another of Hurlbert in the backseat of a police car, looking drawn but defiant. There was even a picture of Irene looking brave and loyal with poor, bewildered Nelson by her side.

When I finished reading as I waited for my first students of the day to arrive, I crumpled the *Intell* and stared ahead blankly.

So Mr. Geohagan—for he had to be the source of all this information about Cathleen—had gotten his revenge for the wrongs he felt Hurlbert had done him and his family.

But at what a price!

He had smeared his daughter's reputation.

He had paraded his ill and defenseless wife.

He had endangered my life not once but repeatedly—all for his own ends.

Everything he'd done since I'd met him was meant first to protect, then retrieve those precious papers so he could give them to—I uncrumpled the paper and searched for the byline on the articles—Barnum Hadley. The man with no chest.

The night in the closet, the attempted and actual purse snatchings, the watchers at the farm, the man on the stairs, the man in the woods, the flight for my life at the storage garage, all were because of Mr. Geohagan.

I looked at the paper again and studied the picture of Irene. Standing behind her and Nelson was a tall, anorexic man identified as William Bozner, Adam Hurlbert's campaign manager. He was the man with Adam the night of the rally and robbery at Park City. He was also, I realized now, the man I had seen visiting Mr. Geohagan, the man to whom Mr. Geohagan had pledged his trust.

"You can trust me, Bill," Mr. Geohagan had said.

Hah!

Somewhere along the line the Hurlbert forces had found cause to distrust Mr. Geohagan and sent Bozner to talk with him. Why? What had happened to rouse their suspicions? How had he attracted their attention?

Were the men who threatened to kill me Adam's men hired to foil the threat? Of course they were. It made sense.

First they searched Mr. G's apartment, as I knew only too well, but all they found was me. Their concern intensified with their failure to find information, as did their need for said information. Since Mr. Geohagan was confined because of illness, they began following the one with ready access to him, the one who ran his errands, mailed his letters, and sat with him by the hour. Me.

And did Mr. Geohagan warn me? No. Just the opposite. He knowingly allowed me to remain in ever greater danger. I had poured hours of care and prayer into this man, and all I got was a knockout punch in my emotional nose.

And I'd felt so guilty when I let the presence of the key slip to Jake and Clarke. How he must have laughed.

Lord, how could he do this to me? It's not fair!

I sighed deeply but couldn't enjoy my mope because twenty-five second graders came piling into the room. Putting Mr. Geohagan firmly from my mind, and forcing him from my thoughts the many times he returned through the long, hard day, I took care of my kids. Finally, when school was over, I drove slowly to Holiday House.

One hard question kept racing through my mind. As I pondered it, I drove automatically. I think I stopped at the proper stop signs and red lights. I think I obeyed the speed limit. I think I stayed in my lane and ran over no errant pedestrians. At least, no officer pulled me over for a violation.

Am I sorry I gave so much time and care to Mr. Geohagan?

What had compelled me to return again and again to visit him? Why was I willing to mail his letters and run his errands, to hold his hand

and talk about my private life, to encourage him and let him encourage me?

The answer was very important because it would show me a lot about myself. Did I do these things out of pity or sympathy for a lonely, old man? Did I do them to show everybody what a nice person I was? Did I do them so people would *tell* me what a nice person I was? Did I do them because he needed somebody, and I was willing to be that somebody? Did I do it because I wanted to model God's love to him?

All the above, I had to admit. A mixture of motives at best. The trouble was that I now realized the object of my sympathy wasn't worth it. I understood that being nice, at least in this case, was just a synonym for being dumb, for being taken advantage of, for being manipulated and being too naive to realize it.

But he did need you, that soft voice whispered into my anger and bitterness. *He still does. You did the right thing. Being taken advantage of is not the worst thing in the world.*

Hah! I yelled silently as I shut my ears to the breath of God and elbowed my way self-righteously through the TV crews and newsprint reporters clogging the front lawn of Holiday House. *Hah!*

And just how long would it be before these media people wrote about Kristie Matthews, the dumb and gullible enabler that Mr. Geohagan deployed to accomplish his plans, even from his hospital bed? I could hardly wait for the embarrassment and invasion of privacy.

Only by waving down a passing nurse who had seen me here several times before was I able to talk my way past the new security guard at the front door.

"You need a list of regular visitors," I said tartly, just before I let the door slip shut in the man's face. "Some of us are important around here."

He pushed the door open and called politely after me as I stalked across the oriental carpets, "A list is being drawn up now, miss." He smiled sweetly as he withdrew his head.

I ground my teeth. I hated being one-upped on any day. Today it made me crazy.

I burst into Mr. Geohagan's room full of rationalized and justified feelings of betrayal. Did I have a speech planned for him! It'd burn his ears, flay his skin, pull out his emotional fingernails.

I stopped short at the sight of the wizened old man lying in the bed, eyes closed, oxygen cannula at his nose. Somehow, in the time since I'd realized what he'd done, in my mind he'd grown two heads and begun to breathe fire. He was an unrepentant Darth Vader, an evil Ming the Merciless, a gluttonous Hannibal Lecter.

But he wasn't a monster. He was a sick old

man who looked worse than ever. And he needed me more than ever whether he realized it or not.

He must have sensed my presence for he opened his eyes, saw me, and smiled.

"I was afraid you'd never come back," he whispered.

"I came to yell at you," I said as I walked to the bed. "I don't think I've ever been so upset."

"Not even over What's-his-name?"

"Different ballgame. Today you hurt me more than he has, and that's no small accomplishment."

"I had to tell, you know," he said earnestly. "It wouldn't be fair to people to let them elect Adam. You understand that, don't you?"

"No, I don't," I said firmly. "And please, Mr. Geohagan, don't condescend to me by making false claims of altruism. If you were really concerned about justice and fairness for the people and all those other ethical issues, you'd have gone to the police quietly ages ago. You've obviously been collecting this information for a long, long time. You waited until now to release it because now is when it will hurt and humiliate Adam most."

"I knew you wouldn't understand." He began pleating his sheet in agitation, just as he had the first time we talked about Cathleen.

"You're right. I don't understand. I guess I can

345

accept that you could use me to help accomplish your schemes, even endangering my life—"

"I never meant that!" he said quickly, but I kept on.

"—but I just can't understand what you did to Cathleen and Doris. Explain to me how you could tarnish Cathleen's memory before the world, how you could parade your defenseless wife in public."

He looked at me, his eyes suddenly cold, his lips pinched together with anger. "You don't have any acquaintance with hate, do you?"

He was right. I didn't.

"Remember the day Bill Bozner came to visit you?" I said.

Mr. Geohagan nodded.

"You lied to him. You said he could trust you."

"No lie." His voice was full of virtue. "He could trust me to do exactly what I did."

He had truly convinced himself that he was guiltless.

"Why did Bozner even think at that point that maybe he should distrust you?"

The old man grinned. "They had never once suspected that for years I'd been saving every evidence of Adam's financial indiscretions and wrong-doings I could get my hands on."

"Right," I said dryly. "You're the King of Duplicity. But how did you ever have access to that information in the first place?"

"I was comptroller for Hurlbert Construction from its beginning, Kristie. Didn't you know?"

I stared at him. "Comptroller?" I thought of the apartment and the garage. They certainly didn't indicate a man with a position of that importance or the salary that went with it. I wondered about the house he had sold, the one he had shared with Doris and Cathleen, the one I had never seen. "All I knew was that you worked for him. I assumed in construction itself."

"Not me," he said. "I'm a CPA, a Wharton School MBA. I've been on the inside of Hurlbert Construction from the get-go. I've always known exactly where the company stood financially, where *he* stood financially. I never cared that Adam was taking kickbacks or evading his tax payments. Everyone does that. But if he ever got caught, I was vulnerable as the company's CFO. I was just making certain I wasn't going to be his scapegoat or get taken down with him."

"Even back then?"

"Always. Or at least from the beginning of his dishonesty, anyway. He was straight at first. The greed kicked in later."

"But how'd they know to be distrustful of you *now*, after all those years?"

"You sent them letters." He looked at me with great satisfaction. "You sent them letters."

"I sent them letters?"

347

"Think you're innocent, huh? You're not!" He was gleeful. "You sent them the letters! The first said *I know all about you!* and the second said *Think no one knows about your financial secrets? Just wait!*"

I stared at him as I remembered the letters. They'd been in his shirt pocket that day in the emergency room. He'd given me one to mail the first time I'd visited, and I mailed the second on my way to spend the night in his closet. And I'd teased him about contributions!

"Did you always hate Adam so?"

"No. I used to like him," he admitted. "But I've distrusted him for years. That's why I began keeping my private set of books. He's a charming man. Funny. Clever. And I never expected to use my information. I didn't want to hurt him, just protect myself if the need ever arose. Turn state's witness. Plea bargain. That kind of thing. And that's the way it probably would have remained if he hadn't killed Cathleen."

"Mr. Geohagan! *She* made that choice."

"*He* did! And he crippled Doris and ruined my life!" His voice shook with the intensity of his emotion. "He took away everything I've ever valued. Well, I just managed to do the same to him."

The implacability of the obsessed, I thought as I watched him struggle to breathe. I patted his hand to calm him. "Easy. Take it easy."

He attempted to draw a deep breath. He couldn't, not really, but I waited for a bit while he seemed to let some of his anger go.

"Why wasn't I supposed to tell anyone I had your key?" I finally asked. I couldn't see how that mattered at all.

"Because I didn't want one of those strange coincidences that can stalk life to ruin my plan. What if you had by some chance known Adam? A lot of people do. You might have unintentionally messed things up."

"You really had it planned, didn't you?" I said. "Considered all contingencies."

Mr. Geohagan looked at me with narrowed eyes. "Don't judge me, Kristie. You're not the issue here. Neither's Cathleen or Doris. Adam is, and he deserves everything that's going to happen to him. Look what he did to Cathleen, to Doris, to *me*. He ruined my life!"

By the time he finished his tirade, he was gasping.

I leaned forward. "Shh! Calm down. It's not good to get so upset."

He snorted. "You think I care? I've got nothing left."

"I care." I was surprised to find I meant it. "I want you to get better. I want you to let go of your hate and bitterness. It's making you sicker than your physical problems. God can help you forgive and recover."

"No! I don't want to forgive and recover! No! Not God! Not Adam!"

I felt unbearable sorrow as I finally understood that he had chosen revenge and hatred over God.

"Shh," I said around the choking knot of emotion in my throat. I took his clenched fist in mine and rubbed my thumb back and forth over his hand in what I hoped was a soothing manner. Slowly his short, jerky breaths began to ease.

The door banged wildly against the wall, making us both jump, and in flew a fury named Irene Parsons Carmody Hurlbert. Her hair was unkempt, and her face without its usual masterful makeup was blotched and pasty. Her jaw jutted forward and her eyes flashed fire.

She strode to the bed and stood across from me, staring down at Everett Geohagan. Her face was ugly with loathing.

"How did you get in here?" I asked. "What do you want?"

She ignored me. All her energy was focused on Mr. Geohagan, and I didn't even exist.

"You cruel old man! You foul, filthy beast! How dare you!" Venom dripped from each carefully enunciated word.

Mr. Geohagan shrank into his pillow, his face losing what little color it still had.

"Stop that!" I reached across the bed and grabbed awkwardly at Irene's wrist. "Let him alone!"

She shook me off and grabbed Mr. Geohagan's

shoulders, digging long, perfectly manicured talons into his frail body.

"How long have you been planning this, you evil creature? Ever since Adam left your sniveling daughter? Well, don't think we'll let you rip us apart without tearing you open too!" She shook his shoulders. "We'll take you down with us, I promise!"

"Let him go!" I grabbed Irene's hands, trying to pry them from Mr. Geohagan. She was so consumed by her hatred that I had all the impact of a fly.

"We'll make sure the world knows Cathleen was nothing more than a common whore," Irene spat. "And you're no better, keeping your information for years and then selling it for a tidy profit!"

I jerked with surprise, finally drawing Irene's attention and scorn.

"You didn't actually believe his sanctimonious lies about protecting the people, did you?"

"Well, no," I said weakly. "But money?" I looked at him in dismay and he stared stonily back. While I hadn't been naive enough to believe his stated rationale, I'd never imagined he'd been paid for his betrayal.

Irene laughed, sounding like the evil queen in *Snow White*. "Not the *Intell*. *People* magazine. They called us for a statement to include in the story he sold."

National shame and humiliation.

She turned back to Mr. Geohagan. "I'll get you, old man. You can depend on it." She reached for him again, grabbing a wrist and squeezing, squeezing. "You'll know the taste of gall, and you'll hurt like you didn't know you could hurt." She leaned over and hissed in his face like Cleopatra's asp. "You're a dead man."

"Stop it!" I yelled, running around the bed. "You're going to kill him!"

"Yes!" she yelled. "Yes!"

I wrapped my arms around her waist, pulling her, dragging her back from the bed. "Help!" I screamed. "Help!"

It took all my strength to pull the woman away, so great was her fury. We stood locked together, my face buried in her back, while she fought to get free. Then slowly she calmed; slowly she began to breathe more evenly.

"I'm okay," she finally spit. "Let go."

I had just released her when a nurse and an aide arrived in belated response to my screams. The nurse gasped at what she saw.

Irene and I looked with her at the bed. Irene smiled. Then she turned and calmly walked through the door.

"Out!" the nurse screamed at me as I stood frozen. She leaped astride Mr. Geohagan and began the first movement of the Resuscitation Ballet. "Crash cart!" she yelled at the aide, who was already running.

I stood alone in the hall and watched the personnel and machines pour into Mr. Geohagan's room. I watched alone as the same people walked defeated from the room, wheeling the machinery before them. I cried alone as the nurse walked up to me and said, "I'm sorry."

22

I found myself in the woods, sitting beside the little pond I had painted not too long ago. The brilliant leaves were now gone from its surface, and the surrounding oaks, poplars, and maples were drained of color, the few clinging leaves brown and shriveled. But the burble of the tumbling water was somehow comforting, its gurgling music soothing.

I watched a bubble detach itself from the froth of the little waterfall and float in circles on the pool's surface. Suddenly it burst, gone forever, never to be seen again.

Like Mr. Geohagan.

I'd slept little last night, his voice with its various shadings and emotions running through my mind like a loop of audio tape.

"Did I ever tell you that you remind me of my daughter, Cathleen?"

"You can't trust men who go to church, Kristie. They're too dumb to know what a wonderful woman you are."

"I spent the last couple of days worrying about you. First there was that louse, What's-his-name, and then those men last night. Are you really all right?"

"You don't have any acquaintance with hate, do you."

I lay my face on my knees and let a fresh wash of tears wet my jeans. I hadn't cried over Clarke, maybe because the hurt went so deep, but the absolute finality of Mr. Geohagan's rejection of God and the unalterable reality of his death undid what little emotional restraint I had left.

The Zooks had been so kind to me, so solicitous. Mary had hugged me and John had prayed with me—in High German—asking God to ease my heart's hurt. If I hadn't understood the words, I'd understood the tone, felt the concern.

And Jake. Early this morning he'd been in the great room as I tried to force myself to eat, and he'd taken my hand in his.

"I'm sorry, Kristie," he said. "I know how much the old man meant to you. I'm sorry he died and—" he swallowed hard, "—And I'm sorry for everything else too. I hope you'll forgive me." He smiled awkwardly and turned bright red. "Uh, I'm going to my first GED class Monday."

I smiled weakly. "Good," I whispered. "I'm glad."

Then I went outside and walked and walked, trying to come to terms with Mr. Geohagan as the complex and all too human man that he had been. Encourager and destroyer. Kindly friend and implacable enemy. Lover of family and hater of any who harmed them. My cheerleader and my manipulator.

I finally came to the patch of woods with the pool and sank onto my rock. So much had happened in so little time. My head and heart swam.

Monday I had had the discussion with Jake about hiding behind his family's faith. Judging by his kindness this morning, he had finally forgiven me.

Tuesday Clarke had come to my rescue—and then left to fly home with Mary Ann.

Wednesday Barnum Hadley had showed up.

Thursday Ruth got married and Adam's perfidy was revealed.

Friday Cathleen's involvement with Adam became common knowledge, Mr. Geohagan made the absolute choice to hate instead of to know God, and Irene got her supreme revenge.

No wonder I was weary beyond concentration.

Oh, God, at least You're always there and always dependable.

I don't know how long I sat staring at the bubbling water as it leaped fearlessly over the edge of its falls, joyously seeking what came next, singing as it went. I decided that I most certainly wasn't up to leaping and singing, not up to being joyous. I wouldn't be for a long time. But I knew I wanted—I needed—to move on with God.

Whatever waits ahead, God, I want to go through it with You. I choose You. I choose Your way.

Both the silence of the woods and the babbling of the brook seemed confirmation from God that we had a pact. We sat quietly together, He and I.

I thought that sometimes this choice would put me at odds with my parents. I wanted their approval and encouragement, but what if I never got it?

I'd been willing to forgive Mr. Geohagan for putting me in danger. Surely I could find the strength to forgive my parents for trying to force me into their mold. I thought of the young Clarke forgiving his parents for going to Brazil.

"I've learned to be content whatever the circumstances."

"Lord, give me the grace to let go of the need to be understood. Help me—"

I broke off as the woods came alive with the sound of someone charging ahead, twigs snapping, leaves crackling. I jumped to my feet, back in the unpleasant and fearful memories of the man who had accosted me here before.

"Kristie!" called the man thrashing his way in my direction. My heart began to pound. I turned and managed to take a step or two before he reached me, but that was it. He grabbed me with an intensity and ferocity that undid me.

"Shh." Clarke pulled me close. "Don't cry. It'll be all right. I'm never leaving you again. Oh, Kristie, I'm so sorry I wasn't here with you when you needed me!"

Then I really cried, soaking the front of Clarke's jacket.

"He never believed," I sobbed. "He chose to hate."

"Some people do," he said, stroking my hair. "God doesn't force us to trust in Him. Jesus may have died for the world, but all the world doesn't believe. For His own reasons, God allows that."

"But it's so sad! It's bad enough to have him die, but to have him die in unbelief breaks my heart."

He held me as I snuffled some more. Finally I pulled back and we both stared at the huge wet spot on the front of his jacket.

"It's supposed to be waterproof," he said in a disillusioned voice.

"You should never believe advertising claims," I hiccupped, running a shaky hand over my eyes, wiping away my tears. At least I hadn't put on mascara, so I didn't look like a raccoon. Just very red rimmed. And blotchy. Oh, well. He might as well find out how the real me looked now. It'd save him the shock later.

"Now tell me, guy," I said, trying to sound at least a tad self-possessed. "What are you doing here? Where did you come from?"

"From home, of course," he said.

"I thought you were gone for good, off with the fair Mary Ann."

He looked at me quizzically. "We just went home to visit Mom and Dad. Mary Ann's been on the road for a year, so this was a family reunion of sorts. My only regret was that I couldn't take you along too."

Mom and Dad? Family reunion? I looked at him through narrowed eyes. "Just who is Mary Ann?"

"She's my younger and only sister. Why?" Then he understood and began to laugh, having a wonderful time at my expense. "You thought . . ." He couldn't finish the sentence for his laughter.

I stood as straight as I could and stared haughtily at him, no small trick when you look as much like a sick chicken as I did. "If you'll think back, you never told me who she was. All I know is that she kissed you in the church parking lot last Sunday and that you and she flew off together Tuesday night. And you never contacted me after she appeared. Not once." My voice wavered.

"Poor baby," he said, cupping my cheek.

I pushed his hand away. "Not that you contacted me much before she appeared, either. If I hadn't been beaten up so many times, I'd probably never have seen you."

He looked at me, his smile wide. "I've just been waiting to see if Todd was truly a thing of the past," he said. "Do you know, I fell for you the first time I saw you, holding your cheek, your beautiful face all white and scared. Then you looked at me as we waited in the hospital and said in a haughty, don't-mess-with-me voice, 'I was just trying to make decent conversation.'"

"I did not!"

"You did, sweetheart. I recognized you as a woman of spunk even then."

"Spunk! You like me because I've got spunk?" I was appalled. Where was the romance? The appreciation of all my finer qualities?

"No," he said. "I don't like you because you have spunk. I love you because you have spunk. And a kind heart. And a godly spirit. And the cutest red nose." He bent and kissed it, and then he hugged me again.

"I . . . I love you too," I whispered into his shoulder. "I died a little each day when I thought you were gone forever." My arms tightened around him. "Don't leave me again, okay?"

Clarke tilted my chin. "Never," he said. "I promise." And he kissed me.

Then we sat together on my rock, his arm around my shoulders, my arms wrapped around his waist.

"About my sister," he said as his hand played with my hair, my very messed up hair. "Mary Ann showed up unexpectedly Sunday morning. She sings with a Christian contemporary group, and they were driving from southern New Jersey, where they had sung Saturday night, to Harrisburg for afternoon and evening concerts. They dropped her off on the way through, and I was to drive her to Harrisburg. I didn't even know she was due in the area or I'd have made sure I took you to hear her sing. She has a wonderful voice. I looked for you Sunday morning to take you to Harrisburg with us, but I didn't see you."

"I was in kindergarten church. I got an emergency call Saturday night and covered for a woman with a sick child."

He made a face. "All I knew was that I couldn't find you before or after the service, and Mary Ann kept saying that we had to go because she couldn't be late. Then she had this past week off, and she stayed with Aunt Betty Lou and Uncle Bud until Tuesday evening when we went home. I wanted you two to get to know each other, so I called Monday evening as soon as I got home from work, but Jake said you weren't there. He said he'd give you my message."

"You called Monday night?" I felt like the

guys in that ad about missed calls of consequence because of no bars, only mine was no phone. But he'd called!

"I also called Tuesday as soon as I thought you'd be home from school. When I said I had to leave town and absolutely must see you before I left, Jake said he didn't know where you were. Finally, when we left for the airport, we stopped at the Zooks'. Mary told me you were at the storage garages."

"You called Tuesday?"

"And Wednesday and Thursday and Friday. Several times."

"And Wednesday and Thursday and Friday? Several times?"

Clarke took me by the shoulders and gently shook me. "Do you always repeat what people say? You've got to get your own phone again, you know."

Clarke had called! He had tried to reach me!

"I didn't know you called," I said. "Jake never told me. He was mad at me."

Clarke nodded. "I know. Really mad. That's why he didn't mention the first couple of calls. Then he was too embarrassed to tell. But when you came home last night and told him about Mr. Geohagan, he knew he had to contact me and confess."

"He called you? That's why you're here? Why didn't he tell me?"

"He's afraid you're going to beat him up."

"Not a bad idea. The last few days have been horrible!"

Funny how strong arms can make horrible memories less haunting.

"Anyway," Clarke said, "Jake called me. I've been on the phone, at the airport, in the air, and on the road for hours."

I noticed for the first time how weary he looked. "All for me?"

"All for you."

Now that was romantic.

Discussion Questions

1. People find the Amish culture fascinating. What about it attracts you? What bothers you? What did you learn in the course of reading A Stranger's Wish that you didn't know before?

2. Mary tells Clarke that people should be able to read the Bible and apply it without help from people like him. Is she right? Why or why not? Read Romans 15:15 and 2 Corinthians 3:5. What is the balance here?

3. Did Kristie fail with Mr. Geohagan? Or waste her time? What does God ask of us in terms of our relationships with others?

4. Kristie feels misunderstood by her family. Is this an unusual feeling? Have you ever felt it? Over what issues? Read Exodus 20:12 and Ephesians 6:2. What do these verses ask of us?

5. Mr. Geohagan blames God for Cathleen's death. What do you think? Read Galatians 6:7. What is the principle that Mr. Geohagan forgot?

6. Jake is a very complex person. He doesn't blame God for his paralysis, but he blames

the culture in which he was raised for keeping him from God. Your thoughts?

7. Statistics say that by far the majority of Amish young adults choose to be baptized and join the church. Why do you think this is?

8. If keeping the *Ordnung* is so very important to salvation as the Amish say, what about the millions who aren't Amish and don't even know the *Ordnung* exists?

9. There is no denying that law brings structure. We would not want to be without civil law or we'd have anarchy. But law (like the *Ordnung*) that governs one's spiritual life can also bring rigidity and an obsession with keeping every little detail, as well as the idea of earning one's way to heaven. Such legality is stifling and demeaning. Read 1 Corinthians 6:12 and 1 Corinthians 10:23. What is the balance you find here?

10. Disagreeing does not mean disrespecting. Kristie disagreed with the Zooks, with Todd, with her parents, with Jake, with Mr. Geohagan. How does she still show respect to these various people?

11. What is your favorite Kristie characteristic? Is it a quality you'd like to develop in your life? How about Clarke? Jake?

About the Author

GAYLE ROPER is an award-winning author of more than forty books and has been a Christy finalist three times.

Gayle enjoys speaking at women's events across the nation and loves sharing the powerful truths of Scripture with humor and practicality. She lives with her husband in southeastern Pennsylvania where Gayle enjoys reading, gardening, her family, and eating out as often as she can talk Chuck into it.

Center Point Publishing

600 Brooks Road ● PO Box 1
Thorndike ME 04986-0001 USA

(207) 568-3717

US & Canada:
1 800 929-9108
www.centerpointlargeprint.com